Lifted Masks and Other Works

Lifted Masks and Other Works

Susan Glaspell

Edited by Eric S. Rabkin

Ann Arbor Paperbacks

THE UNIVERSITY OF MICHIGAN PRESS

First edition as an Ann Arbor Paperback 1993

Published in the United States of America by
The University of Michigan Press
Manufactured in the United States of America
♾ Printed on acid-free paper

2003 2002 2001 2000 5 4 3 2

A CIP catalogue record for this book is available from the British Library.

Library of Congress Cataloging-in-Publication Data

Glaspell, Susan, 1882–1948.
Lifted masks and other works / Susan Glaspell ; edited by Eric S. Rabkin.
p. cm. — (Ann Arbor paperbacks)
ISBN 0-472-09509-9 (alk. paper). — ISBN 0-472-06509-2 (pbk. : alk. paper)
I. Rabkin, Eric S. II. Title.
PR3513.L35L54 1992
813'.52—dc20 92-42425
CIP

Contents

Introduction

Eric S. Rabkin

Susan Glaspell (1876–1948) has been little studied, yet she was a crucial figure in American letters. Her indispensable contribution to the legendary Provincetown Players, which put an indelible mark on the American theater, is often undervalued in comparison with that of her charismatic husband, the Provincetown's founder and director, George Cram Cook (1873–1924). As a dramatist, Glaspell won the Pulitzer Prize for the last of her fourteen plays, *Alison's House* (1930), based on the life of Emily Dickinson, yet today her best-known dramas are two widely performed one-act plays: *Suppressed Desires* (1914), her first play, a satire of Freudian analysis cowritten with Cook; and *Trifles* (1916), a quietly forceful examination of the differing approaches of men and women to the discovery of other people's motives and to the assignment of guilt. She published nine novels, many quite popular, yet today her best-known narrative is "A Jury of Her Peers" (1917), the short-story version of *Trifles.* Although she ultimately published forty-three short stories, her one fiction anthology, *Lifted Masks* (1912), has been out of print for eighty years. Fortunately, the current interest in feminist writing is leading to a reappraisal of Glaspell's work. The republication of *Lifted Masks* with three other key pieces is designed to help make possible a fuller rediscovery of this neglected talent.

Although most biographical sources list Glaspell's

birthdate as 1 July 1882, Arthur Waterman, her first biographer, has been able to establish from records at Drake University (Glaspell's alma mater) that she was actually born 1 July 1876. Her grandparents had helped pioneer the white settlement of the Mississippi River town of Davenport, Iowa, in 1835. Her father was a none-too-successful merchant and her mother a housewife. Glaspell attended Davenport public schools while growing up in the small city but spent summers on her aunt's outlying farm. The Midwestern experience, and its values, informs all her writing.

She began selling stories of college life to *Youth's Companion* magazine while still a college student herself. After receiving her Ph.B. from Drake (1899), she remained in Iowa's capital to work as a legislative and political reporter for the Des Moines *Daily News.* In addition to printing the facts of bills and votes, Glaspell stalked the halls of government and soon wrote a column, "The News Girl," in which she offered her personal views. The News Girl developed the persona of a naive young woman who progressed from wide-eyed observations of government life to commentary on farm life, then city life, and, finally, simply, life. At the same time, Glaspell continued to sell short stories. Her successes led to her 1901 decision to return to Davenport and commit herself full-time to the writing of fiction, which she pursued even during a 1903 stint at graduate work in English at the University of Chicago. Glaspell finally earned substantial royalties from the publication of her first novel, *The Glory of the Conquered* (1909), the story of a scientist who goes blind and, just as he is about to make an important discovery, dies.

While working at the *Daily News,* Glaspell had become friends with fellow reporter Lucy Huffaker. Huffaker later went on to become a prominent journalist in Chicago and an important contributor to the development of New York City's Washington Square Players. Glaspell used the money from her first novel to spend a year in Europe with Huffaker. They remained life-long friends.

Glaspell had met the flamboyant, bohemian Cook, then divorced from his first wife, in Davenport in 1907. While she was successfully pursuing her writing, he failed at a number of enterprises, including farming and a second marriage. After her European travels, Glaspell settled in New York. Cook followed her there and, after his second divorce, the two were married in Weehawken, New Jersey, on 14 April 1913. They went to Provincetown, Massachusetts, for their honeymoon and continued thereafter to spend their summers in Provincetown and their winters in New York.

By this time, the European "little theater movement," which had begun with the Théâtre Libre established by Antoine in France in 1887, had spread with the establishment of the Freie Bühne in Berlin in 1889; the Independent Theatre in London, 1891; the Moscow Art Theater, 1898; the Irish Literary Theatre, 1899; and Dublin's Abbey Theatre, 1904. In America, some attempts had already been made to offer an alternative to Broadway's formula musicals and melodramas, most notably Maurice Browne's Chicago Little Theatre, 1911; the New York Stage Society, 1912; the Liberal Club of New York, which in 1913 staged some plays employing a number of people who soon would become part of the Provincetown Players; and the Washington Square Players, 1915.

In 1911 Cook was impressed with Browne's production of Euripides' *The Trojan Women* but even more impressed with the touring Irish Players. This group, unlike the American little theater groups, had a distinctly nationalistic aim that appealed to Cook. In 1915 he offered *Suppressed Desires* to the Washington Square Players, but, although he had helped mount their first production, they rejected his and Glaspell's play as too unusual in subject matter. Undaunted, Cook decided to present the play himself. That summer, borrowing the Provincetown wharf dwelling of a friend, he and Glaspell inadvertently launched the Provincetown Players by offering their play for friends at no admission charge.

Although only Cook and one other officer ever took even a small salary, the Provincetown always struggled financially because Cook was an abysmal businessman. But his idealism and charisma inspired many to new achievements, and the Provincetown lived up to its goal of establishing an indigenous American theater. It was the first theater to restrict its offerings to the works of American playwrights, and it further required that all plays be directed by their authors. Some, like Glaspell, even acted in their own works. Despite its meager foundation, this revolutionary theater managed to support the development of astonishing talent, including in more or less intimate ways Djuna Barnes, Cook, Theodore Dreiser, Max Eastman, Edna Ferber, Glaspell, Edna St. Vincent Millay, Eugene O'Neill, John Reed, and Wallace Stevens. Of these, only O'Neill, who joined Glaspell as the group's other leading playwright, had any formal theater training.

To keep the group functioning, both in its remodeled Wharf Theater and in its additional Provincetown Theater in Greenwich Village in New York City, Glaspell continued to write plays, including *Trifles* and the powerful *Inheritors* (1921), about the clash of pioneer ideals with modern life on a Midwestern college campus; short stories, including "'Finality' in Freeport" (1916); and novels, including *Fidelity* (1915), about a young woman who elopes with a married man, and her most radically feminist work, *The Verge* (1921), about a heroine who is unfaithful to her husband, rejects her daughter, and even destroys her own plant breeding experiments when they fall back into the ordinary from the verge of taking the next evolutionary step.

Cook, Glaspell, and company were conscious iconoclasts and progressive idealists. For example, they flouted the Broadway custom of using white actors in blackface and instead cast a black actor, Charles Gilpin, in the title role of O'Neill's *The Emperor Jones* (1920)—and nonetheless sold out the theater. Unfortunately, the failure of the plants in *The Verge* to generate a new breed foreshadowed the fate of the Provincetown. With its growing success, its plays would fulfill only their contractual two-week runs in Greenwich Village before uptown producers would lure them to larger and more lucrative Broadway theaters. Cook saw the Provincetown coming apart, a victim of its own achievements. In 1922 he decided to leave for Greece, and Glaspell went with him.

In Greece Cook again urged nativism, this time speaking classic Greek to twentieth-century peasants, teaching them their ancient ritual dances, and reviving rural culture. When he died at Delphi in 1924, the Greek government bestowed upon him a unique honor in recognition of his contributions to Greek national life and his generosity of spirit: a stone was taken from the Parthenon to mark his grave. Glaspell remained in Europe and wrote Cook's biography, *The Road to the Temple* (1927).

In Europe Glaspell had met Norman Matson and in 1925 they married. They even collaborated on a play, *The Comic Artist* (1928), which was produced in London. However, the marriage was unhappy and was dissolved in 1931. Glaspell never married again.

Although she gave up short story writing after 1922, Glaspell continued to write novels. After her return to the United States, she published *Brook Evans* (1928), *Fugitive's Return* (1929), *Ambrose Holt and Family* (1931), *The Morning Is Near Us* (1939), *Cherished and Shared of Old* (1940), *Norma Ashe* (1942), and *Judd Rankin's Daughter* (1945). During the New Deal, she served as Midwest director of the Federal Theater Project (1934–35). She died in Provincetown of viral pneumonia on 27 July 1948.

Glaspell's only volume of short stories was *Lifted Masks*. This collection ranges from the sentimental to the genuinely moving, always revealing a hopefulness and commitment to community values. While Glaspell's collection is by no means as great as *Dubliners* (1914), like James Joyce, Glaspell sought the illuminating epiphany, the recognition, in her case usually by the retelling of some past event, that changes forever the meaning of the narrative present. But while Joyce's recognitions were typically tragic, like those of ancient Greek drama, Glaspell's are typically tragicomic, sad but somehow uplifting. The volume's epigraph, "Loftier than the world suspects," is from a poem by Robert Browning called "A Grammarian's Funeral" (1845). Browning's grammarian, like many of the characters in Glaspell's stories, is carried in death to a symbolic mountaintop. In life this man of language and learning had said "'What's time? Leave Now for dogs and apes! / Man has Forever.'" In death his narrator/bearer ends the poem thus: "Loftily lying, / Leave him—still loftier than the world suspects, / Living and dying." In Glaspell, the past and idealism struggle often, and sometimes lose in practical terms, against the present and realism, but as one character says, "'There is good and there is bad in every human heart, and it is the struggle of life to conquer the bad with the good.'" In Glaspell's world, this conquest usually occurs, but at a cost.

At her best, Glaspell captures this moral duality with the most homely details. The heroine of "From A to Z," who had gone to the city glowing with visions of a glamorous life in publishing, is forced to accept a dusty and tedious job compiling a new dictionary from older ones. She "seated herself and her buried hopes in this chair which did not whirl round, and leaned her arms upon a table which did not even dream of mahogany." Glaspell's empathy, one suspects, is supported by the heartland traditions of her youth. Subtle biblical references abound in these stories, including pointed generational shifts of forty years. But always, across the generations, the social classes, and the ironies of fate, there is in her world a common humanity, if only we can see beneath the masks.

The notion of masking is crucial to virtually all the stories. A mask, of course, conceals, and in stories like the deceptively simple "One of Those Impossible Americans," when someone finally lifts the mask, the real self shines through. However, while masks conceal, they also reveal. Glaspell is as careful to show us how and why people choose which mask to wear as how and why they remove their masks. The concept of "personality" has always been tied up with masks and drama, for the very word *person* comes from the Latin word *persona,* the mask worn by ancient actors in order to make their characters visible to the audience. Glaspell's masks too project personalities in both her drama and in her short stories. To make visible the connections between her work in these two genres, we have also reprinted here her twin works, *Trifles* and "A Jury of Her Peers."

To assess Glaspell's full range, however, one needs to go beyond these materials. In 1893 Octave Thanet (pseudonym for Alice French) published the very popular *Stories of a Western Town* set in "Freeport," which was Thanet's name for Davenport. Glaspell subsequently set twenty-six of her own stories in Freeport, and perhaps the best of these is "'Finality' in Freeport," a sharp yet tolerant satire of society, religion, and learning that was first published, surprisingly, in *Pictorial Review,* a dressmaking journal. The story makes reference to George Sand, the fine French author notorious for her unconventional life, and to Ludwig Lewisohn, the first critic to give Glaspell's Provincetown dramas extended, serious criticism while they were in original production. To the best of my knowledge, this story, which is also reprinted here, has never before been available since its first publication.

A comprehensive study of Glaspell's writing, would, of course, include her full-length plays and novels, but as an excellent way to approach her work, in both its ordinary and its extraordinary faces, we can begin with *Lifted Masks.*

For their generous encouragement and assistance, I wish to express my gratitude to Thomas C. Burnett and Tatiana P. Falk of the University of Michigan Graduate Library, Andrew H. Lee of the New York Public Library, Gail Cohen of Vineyard Haven, Massachusetts, and Mary C. Erwin and Robin A. Moir of the University of Michigan Press.

Ann Arbor, Michigan
July 3, 1992

LIFTED MASKS

STORIES BY

SUSAN GLASPELL

"LOFTIER THAN THE WORLD SUSPECTS."
—*Robert Browning*

To

THE MEMORY OF MY FRIEND
JENNIE PRESTON

CONTENTS

I

"ONE OF THOSE IMPOSSIBLE AMERICANS"

"N'AVEZ-VOUS PAS —" she was bravely demanding of the clerk when she saw that the bulky American who was standing there helplessly dangling two flaming red silk stockings which a copiously coiffured young woman assured him were *bien chic* was edging nearer her. She was never so conscious of the truly American quality of her French as when a countryman was at hand. The French themselves had an air of "How marvellously you speak!" but fellow Americans listened superciliously in an "I can do better than that myself" manner which quite untied the Gallic twist in one's tongue. And so, feeling her French was being compared, not with mere French itself, but with an arrogant new American brand thereof, she moved a little around the corner of the counter and began again in lower voice: "*Mais, n'avez* —"

"Say, Young Lady," a voice which adequately represented the figure broke in, "*you* aren't French, are you?"

She looked up with what was designed for a haughty stare. But what is a haughty stare to do in the face of a broad grin? And because it was such a long time since a grin like that had been grinned at her it happened that the stare gave way to a dimple, and the dimple to a laughing: "Is it so bad as that?"

"Oh, not your French," he assured her. "You talk it just like the rest of them. In fact, I should say, if anything — a little more so. But do you know," — confidentially — "I can just spot an American girl every time!"

"How?" she could not resist asking, and the modest black hose she was thinking of purchasing dangled against his gorgeous red ones in friendliest fashion.

"Well, Sir — I don't know. I don't think it can be the *clothes*,"— judicially surveying her.

"The clothes," murmured Virginia, "were bought in Paris."

"Well, you've got *me*. Maybe it's the way you wear 'em. Maybe it's 'cause you look as if you used to play tag with your brother. Something — anyhow — gives a fellow that 'By jove there's an American girl!' feeling when he sees you coming round the corner."

"But why — ?"

"Lord — don't begin on *why*. You can say *why* to anything. Why don't the French talk English? Why didn't they lay Paris out at right angles? Now look here, Young Lady, for that matter *why* can't you help me buy some presents for my wife? There'd be nothing wrong about it," he hastened to assure her, "because my wife's a mighty fine woman."

The very small American looked at the very large one. Now Virginia was a well brought up young woman. Her conversations with strange men had been confined to such things as, "Will you please tell me the nearest way to —?" but preposterously enough — she could not for the life of her have told why — frowning upon this huge American — fat was the literal word — who stood there with puckered-up face swinging the flaming hose would seem in the same shameful class with snubbing the little boy who confidently asked her what kind of ribbon to buy for his mother.

"Was it for your wife you were thinking of buying these red stockings?" she ventured.

"Sure. What do you think of 'em? Look as if they came from Paris all right, don't they?"

"Oh, they look as though they came from Paris, all right," Virginia repeated, a bit grimly. "But do you know"— this quite as to that little boy who might be buying the ribbon —"American women don't always care for *all* the things that look as if they came from Paris. Is your wife — does she care especially for red stockings?"

"Don't believe she ever had a pair in her life. That's why I thought it might please her."

Virginia looked down and away. There were times when dimples made things hard for one.

Then she said, with gentle gravity: "There are quite a number of women in America who don't care much for red stockings. It would seem too bad, wouldn't it, if after you got these clear home your wife should turn out to be one of those people? Now, I think these grey stockings are lovely. I'm sure any woman would love them. She could wear them with grey suede slippers and they would be so soft and pretty."

"Um — not very lively looking, are they? You see I want something to cheer her up. She — well she's not been very well lately and I thought something — oh something with a lot of *dash* in it, you know, would just fill the bill. But look here. We'll take both. Sure — that's the way out of it. If she don't like the red, she'll like the grey, and if she don't like the — You like the grey ones, don't you? Then here" — picking up two pairs of the handsomely embroidered grey stockings and handing them to the clerk —"One," holding up his thumb to denote one —" me," — a vigorous pounding of the chest signifying me. "One" — holding up his forefinger and pointing to the girl —" mademoiselle."

"Oh no — no — no!" cried Virginia, her face instantly the colour of the condemned stockings. Then, standing straight: "Certainly *not*."

"No? Just as you say," he replied good humouredly. " Like to have you have 'em. Seems as if strangers in a strange land oughtn't to stand on ceremony."

The clerk was bending forward holding up the stockings alluringly. " *Pour mademoiselle, n'est-ce-pas?* "

" *Mais — non!* " pronounced Virginia, with emphasis.

There followed an untranslatable gesture. " How droll! " shoulder and outstretched hands were saying. " If the kind gentleman *wishes* to give mademoiselle the *joli bas —!* "

His face had puckered up again. Then suddenly it unpuckered. " Tell you what you might do," he solved it. " Just take 'em along and send them to your mother. Now your mother might be real glad to have 'em."

Virginia stared. And then an awful thing happened. What she was thinking about was the letter she could send with the stockings. " Mother dear," she would write, " as I stood at the counter buying myself some stockings to-day along came a nice man — a stranger to me, but very kind and jolly — and gave me —"

There it was that the awful thing happened. Her dimple was showing — and at thought of its showing she could not keep it from showing! And how could she explain why it was showing without its going on showing? And how —?

But at that moment her gaze fell upon the clerk, who had taken the dimple as signal to begin putting the stockings in a box. The Frenchwoman's eyebrows soon put that dimple in its proper place. "And so the *petite Americaine* was not too — oh, not *too* —" those French eyebrows were saying.

All in an instant Virginia was something quite different from a little girl with a dimple. "You are very kind," she was saying, and her mother herself could have done it no better, "but I am sure our little joke had gone quite far enough. I bid you good-morning." And with that she walked regally over to the glove counter, leaving red and grey and black hosiery to their own destinies.

"I loathe them when their eyebrows go up," she fumed. "Now *his* weren't going up — not even in his mind."

She could not keep from worrying about him. "They'll just 'do' him," she was sure. "And then laugh at him in the bargain. A man like that has no *business* to be let loose in a store all by himself."

And sure enough, a half hour later she came upon him up in the dress department. Three of them had gathered round to "do" him. They were making rapid headway, their smiling deference scantily concealing their amused contempt. The spectacle infuriated Virginia. "They just think they can *work* us!" she stormed. "They think we're *easy*.

I suppose they think he's a *fool.* I just wish they could get him in a business deal! I just wish—!"

"I can assure you, sir," the English-speaking manager of the department was saying, "that this garment is a wonderful value. We are able to let you have it at so absurdly low a figure because—"

Virginia did not catch why it was they were able to let him have it at so absurdly low a figure, but she did see him wipe his brow and look helplessly around. "Poor *thing,*" she murmured, almost tenderly, "he doesn't know what to do. He just *does* need somebody to look after him." She stood there looking at his back. He had a back a good deal like the back of her chum's father at home. Indeed there were various things about him suggested "home." Did one want one's own jeered at? One might see crudities one's self, but was one going to have supercilious outsiders coughing those sham coughs behind their hypocritical hands?

"For seven hundred francs," she heard the suave voice saying.

Seven hundred francs! Virginia's national pride, or, more accurately, her national rage, was lashed into action. It was with very red cheeks that the small American stepped stormily to the rescue of her countryman.

"Seven hundred francs for *that?*" she jeered, right in the face of the enraged manager and stiffening clerks. "Seven hundred francs—indeed!

Last year's model — a hideous colour, and"— picking it up, running it through her fingers and tossing it contemptuously aside — "abominable stuff!"

"Gee, but I'm grateful to you!" he breathed, again wiping his brow. "You know, I was a little leery of it myself."

The manager, quivering with rage and glaring uglily, stepped up to Virginia. "May I ask —?"

But the fat man stepped in between — he was well qualified for that position. "Cut it out, partner. The young lady's a friend of *mine* — see? She's looking out for me — not you. I don't want your stuff, anyway." And taking Virginia serenely by the arm he walked away.

"This was no place to buy dresses," said she crossly.

"Well, I wish I knew where the places *were* to buy things," he replied, humbly, forlornly.

"Well, what do you want to buy?" demanded she, still crossly.

"Why, I want to buy some nice things for my wife. Something the real thing from Paris, you know. I came over from London on purpose. But Lord," — again wiping his brow — "a fellow doesn't know where to *go*."

"Oh well," sighed Virginia, long-sufferingly, "I see I'll just have to take you. There doesn't seem any way out of it. It's evident you can't go *alone. Seven hundred francs!*"

"I suppose it was too much," he conceded meekly. "I tell you I *will* be grateful if you'll just stay by me a little while. I never felt so up against it in all my life."

"Now, a very nice thing to take one's wife from Paris," began Virginia didactically, when they reached the sidewalk, "is lace."

"L—ace? Um! Y—es, I suppose lace is all right. Still it never struck me there was anything so very *lively* looking about lace."

"'Lively looking' is not the final word in wearing apparel," pronounced Virginia in teacher-to-pupil manner. "Lace is always in good taste, never goes out of style, and all women care for it. I will take you to one of the lace shops."

"Very well," acquiesced he, truly chastened. "Here, let's get in this cab."

Virginia rode across the Seine looking like one pondering the destinies of nations. Her companion turned several times to address her, but it would have been as easy for a soldier to slap a general on the back. Finally she turned to him.

"Now when we get there," she instructed, "don't seem at all interested in things. Act—oh, bored, you know, and seeming to want to get me away. And when they tell the price, no matter what they say, just—well sort of groan and hold your head and act as though you are absolutely overcome at the thought of such an outrage."

"U — m. You have to do that here to get — lace?"

"You have to do that here to get *anything* — at the price you should get it. You, and people who go shopping the way you do, bring discredit upon the entire American nation."

"That so? Sorry. Never meant to do that. All right, Young Lady, I'll do the best I can. Never did act that way, but suppose I can, if the rest of them do."

"Groan and hold my head," she heard him murmuring as they entered the shop.

He proved an apt pupil. It may indeed be set down that his aptitude was their undoing. They had no sooner entered the shop than he pulled out his watch and uttered an exclamation of horror at the sight of the time. Virginia could scarcely look at the lace, so insistently did he keep waving the watch before her. His contempt for everything shown was open and emphatic. It was also articulate. Virginia grew nervous, seeing the real red showing through in the Frenchwoman's cheeks. And when the price was at last named — a price which made Virginia jubilant — there burst upon her outraged ears something between a jeer and a howl of rage, the whole of it terrifyingly done in the form of a groan; she looked at her companion to see him holding up his hands and wobbling his head as though it had been suddenly loosened from his spine, cast one look at the Frenchwoman — then fled, followed by her groaning compatriot.

"I didn't mean you to act like *that!*" she stormed.

"Why, I did just what you told me to! Seemed to me I was following directions to the letter. Don't think for a minute *I'm* going to bring discredit on the American nation! Not a bad scheme — taking out my watch that way, was it?"

"Oh, beautiful *scheme.* I presume you notice, however, that we have no lace."

They walked half a block in silence. "Now I'll take you to another shop," she then volunteered, in a turning the other cheek fashion, "and here please do nothing at all. Please just — sit."

"Sort of as if I was feeble-minded, eh?"

"Oh, don't *try* to look feeble-minded," she begged, alarmed at seeming to suggest any more parts; "just sit there — as if you were thinking of something very far away."

"Say, Young Lady, look here; this is very nice, being put on to the tricks of the trade, but the money end of it isn't cutting much ice, and isn't there any way you can just *buy* things — the way you do in Cincinnati? Can't you get their stuff without making a comic opera out of it?"

"No, you can't," spoke relentless Virginia; "not unless you want them to laugh and say 'Aren't Americans fools?' the minute the door is shut."

"Fools — eh? I'll show them a thing or two!"

"Oh, please show them nothing here! Please just — sit."

While employing her wiles to get for three hundred and fifty francs a yoke and scarf aggregating four hundred, she chanced to look at her American friend. Then she walked rapidly to the rear of the shop, buried her face in her handkerchief, and seemed making heroic efforts to sneeze. Once more he was following directions to the letter. Chin resting on hands, hands resting on stick, the huge American had taken on the beatific expression of a seventeen-year-old girl thinking of something "very far away." Virginia was long in mastering the sneeze.

On the sidewalk she presented him with the package of lace and also with what she regarded the proper thing in the way of farewell speech. She supposed it *was* hard for a man to go shopping alone; she could see how hard it would be for her own father; indeed it was seeing how difficult it would be for her father had impelled her to go with him, a stranger. She trusted his wife would like the lace; she thought it very nice, and a bargain. She was glad to have been of service to a fellow countryman who seemed in so difficult a position.

But he did not look as impressed as one to whom a farewell speech was being made should look. In fact, he did not seem to be hearing it. Once more, and in earnest this time, he appeared to be thinking of something very far away. Then all at once he came back, and it was in anything but a far-away voice he began, briskly: "Now look here, Young Lady, I don't doubt but this lace is great stuff. You say so, and I haven't seen man, woman or child on this side of the Atlantic knows as much as you do. I'm mighty grateful for the lace — don't you forget that, but just the same — well, now I'll tell you. I have a very special reason for wanting something a little livelier than lace. Something that seems to have Paris written on it in red letters — see? Now, where do you get the kind of hats you see some folks wearing, and where do you get the dresses — well, it's hard to describe 'em, but the kind they have in pictures marked 'Breezes from Paris'? You see — *S* — *ay!* — *what* do you think of *that?* "

"That" was in a window across the street. It was an opera cloak. He walked toward it, Virginia following. "Now *there,*" he turned to her, his large round face all aglow, "is what I want."

It was yellow; it was long; it was billowy; it was insistently and recklessly regal.

"That's the ticket!" he gloated.

"Of course," began Virginia, "I don't know anything about it. I am in a very strange position, not knowing what your wife likes or — or has. This is the kind of thing everything has to go *with* or one wouldn't — one couldn't —"

"Sure! Good idea. We'll just get everything to go with it."

"It's the sort of thing one doesn't see worn much outside of Paris — or New York. If one is — now my mother wouldn't care for that coat at all." Virginia took no little pride in that tactful finish.

"Can't sidetrack me!" he beamed. "I *want* it. Very thing I'm after, Young Lady."

"Well, of course you will have no difficulty in buying the coat without me," said she, as a dignified version of "I wash my hands of you." "You can do here as you said you wished to do, simply go in and pay what they ask. There would be no use trying to get it cheap. They would know that anyone who wanted it would" — she wanted to say "have more money than they knew what to do with," but contented herself with, "be able to pay for it."

But when she had finished she looked at him; at first she thought she wanted to laugh, and then it seemed that wasn't what she wanted to do after all. It was like saying to a small boy who was one beam over finding a tin horn: "Oh well, take the horn if you want to, but you can't haul your little red waggon while you're blowing the horn." There seemed something peculiarly inhuman about taking the waggon just when he had found the horn. Now if the waggon were broken, then to take away the horn would leave the luxury of grief. But let not shadows fall upon joyful moments.

With the full ardour of her femininity she entered into the purchasing of the yellow opera cloak. They paid for that decorative garment the sum of two thousand five hundred francs. It seemed it was embroidered, and the lining was — anyway, they paid it.

And they took it with them. He was going to " take no chances on losing it." He was leaving Paris that night and held that during his stay he had been none too impressed with either Parisian speed or Parisian veracity.

Then they bought some " Breezes from Paris," a dress that would " go with " the coat. It was violet velvet, and contributed to the sense of doing one's uttermost; and hats —" the kind you see some folks wearing." One was the rainbow done into flowers, and the other the kind of black hat to outdo any rainbow. " If you could just give me some idea what type your wife is," Virginia was saying, from beneath the willow plumes. " Now you see this hat quite overpowers me. Do you think it will overpower her? "

" Guess not. Anyway, if it don't look right on her head she may enjoy having it around to look at."

Virginia stared out at him. The *oddest* man! As if a hat were any good at all if it didn't look right on one's head!

Upon investigation — though yielding to his

taste she was still vigilant as to his interests — Virginia discovered a flaw in one of the plumes. The sylph in the trailing gown held volubly that it did not *fait rien;* the man with the open purse said he couldn't see that it figured much, but the small American held firm. That must be replaced by a perfect plume or they would not take the hat. And when she saw who was in command the sylph as volubly acquiesced that *naturellement* it must be *tout à fait* perfect. She would send out and get one that would be oh! so, so, *so* perfect. It would take half an hour.

"Tell you what we'll do," Virginia's friend proposed, opera cloak tight under one arm, velvet gown as tight under the other, "I'm tired — hungry — thirsty; feel like a ham sandwich — and something. I'm playing you out, too. Let's go out and get a bite and come back for the so, so, *so* perfect hat."

She hesitated. But he had the door open, and if he stood holding it that way much longer he was bound to drop the violet velvet gown. She did not want him to drop the velvet gown and furthermore, she *would* like a cup of tea. There came into her mind a fortifying thought about the relative deaths of sheep and lambs. If to be killed for the sheep were indeed no worse than being killed for the lamb, and if a cup of tea went with the sheep and nothing at all with the lamb —?

So she agreed. "There's a nice little tea-shop

right round the corner. We girls often go there."

"Tea? Like tea? All right, then"— and he started manfully on.

But as she entered the tea-shop she was filled with keen sense of the desirableness of being slain for the lesser animal. For, cosily installed in their favourite corner, were "the girls."

Virginia had explained to these friends some three hours before that she could not go with them that afternoon as she must attend a musicale some friends of her mother's were giving. Being friends of her mother's, she expatiated, she would have to go.

Recollecting this, also for the first time remembering the musicale, she bowed with the *hauteur* of self-consciousness.

Right there her friend contributed to the tragedy of a sheep's death by dropping the yellow opera cloak. While he was stooping to pick it up the violet velvet gown slid backward and Virginia had to steady it until he could regain position. The staring in the corner gave way to tittering — and no dying sheep had ever held its head more haughtily.

The death of this particular sheep proved long and painful. The legs of Virginia's friend and the legs of the tea-table did not seem well adapted to each other. He towered like a human mountain over the dainty thing, twisting now this way and now that. It seemed Providence — or at least so much of it as was represented by the management of that shop

— had never meant fat people to drink tea. The table was rendered further out of proportion by having a large box piled on either side of it.

Expansively, and not softly, he discoursed of these things. What did they think a fellow was to do with his *knees?* Didn't they sell tea enough to afford any decent chairs? Did all these women pretend to really *like* tea?

Virginia's sense of humour rallied somewhat as she viewed him eating the sandwiches. Once she had called them doll-baby sandwiches; now that seemed literal: tea-cups, *petit gâteau,* the whole service gave the fancy of his sitting down to a tea-party given by a little girl for her dollies.

But after a time he fell silent, looking around the room. And when he broke that pause his voice was different.

"These women here, all dressed so fine, nothing to do but sit around and eat this folderol, *they* have it easy — don't they?"

The bitterness in it, and a faint note of wistfulness, puzzled her. Certainly *he* had money.

"And the husbands of these women," he went on; "lots of 'em, I suppose, didn't always have so much. Maybe some of these women helped out in the early days when things weren't so easy. Wonder if the men ever think how lucky they are to be able to get it back at 'em?"

She grew more bewildered. Wasn't he "getting

it back?" The money he had been spending that day!

"Young Lady," he said abruptly, "you must think I'm a queer one."

She murmured feeble protest.

"Yes, you must. Must wonder what I want with all this stuff, don't you?"

"Why, it's for your wife, isn't it?" she asked, startled.

"Oh yes, but you must wonder. You're a shrewd one, Young Lady; judging the thing by me, you must wonder."

Virginia was glad she was not compelled to state her theory. Loud and common and impossible were terms which had presented themselves, terms which she had fought with kind and good-natured and generous. Their purchases she had decided were to be used, not for a knock, but as a crashing pound at the door of the society of his town. For her part, Virginia hoped the door would come down.

"And if you knew that probably this stuff would never be worn at all, that ten to one it would never do anything more than lie round on chairs — then you *would* think I was queer, wouldn't you?"

She was forced to admit that that would seem rather strange.

"Young Lady, I believe I'll tell you about it. Never do talk about it to hardly anybody, but I feel as if you and I were pretty well acquainted — we've been through so much together."

She smiled at him warmly; there was something so real about him when he talked that way.

But his look then frightened her. It seemed for an instant as though he would brush the tiny table aside and seize some invisible thing by the throat. Then he said, cutting off each word short: "Young Lady, what do you think of this? I'm worth more 'an a million dollars — and my wife gets up at five o'clock every morning to do washing and scrubbing."

"Oh, it's not that she *has* to," he answered her look, "but she *thinks* she has to. See? Once we were poor. For twenty years we were poor as dirt. Then she did have to do things like that. Then I struck it. Or rather, it struck me. Oil. Oil on a bit of land I had. I had just sense enough to make the most of it; one thing led to another — well, you're not interested in that end of it. But the fact is that now we're rich. Now she could have all the things that these women have — Lord A'mighty she could lay abed every day till noon if she wanted to! But — you see? — it *got* her — those hard, lonely, grinding years *took* her. She's" — he shrunk from the terrible word and faltered out — "her mind's not — "

There was a sobbing little flutter in Virginia's throat. In a dim way she was glad to see that the girls were going. She *could* not have them laughing at him — now.

"Well, you can about figure out how it makes me

feel," he continued, and looking into his face now it was as though the spirit redeemed the flesh. "You're smart. You can see it without my callin' your attention to it. Last time I went to see her I had just made fifty thousand on a deal. And I found her down on her knees thinking she was scrubbing the floor!"

Unconsciously Virginia's hand went out, following the rush of sympathy and understanding. "But can't they — restrain her?" she murmured.

"Makes her worse. Says she's got it to do — frets her to think she's not getting it done."

"But isn't there some *way?*" she whispered. "Some way to make her *know?*"

He pointed to the large boxes. "That," he said simply, "is the meaning of those. It's been seven years — but I keep on trying."

She was silent, the tears too close for words. And she had thought it cheap ambition! — vulgar aspiration — silly show — vanity!

"Suppose you thought I was a queer one, talking about lively looking things. But you see now? Thought it might attract her attention, thought something real gorgeous like this might impress money on her. Though I don't know," — he seemed to grow weary as he told it; "I got her a lot of diamonds, thinking they might interest her, and she thought she'd stolen 'em, and they had to take them away."

Still the girl did not speak. Her hand was shading her eyes.

"But there's nothing like trying. Nothing like keeping right on trying. And anyhow — a fellow likes to think he's taking his wife something from Paris."

They passed before her in their heartbreaking folly, their tragic uselessness, their lovable absurdity and stinging irony — those things they had bought that afternoon: an *opera cloak* — a *velvet dress* — *those hats* — *red silk stockings*.

The mockery of them wrung her heart. Right there in the tea-shop Virginia was softly crying.

"Oh, now that's too bad," he expostulated clumsily. "Why, look here, Young Lady, I didn't mean you to take it so hard."

When she had recovered herself he told her much of the story. And the thing which revealed him — glorified him — was less the grief he gave to it than the way he saw it. "It's the cursed unfairness of it," he concluded. "When you consider it's all because she did those things — when you think of her bein' bound to 'em for life just because she was *too faithful doin' 'em* — when you think that now — when I could give her everything these women have got! — she's got to go right on worrying about baking the bread and washing the dishes — did it for me when I was poor — and now with me rich she can't get *out* of it — and I *can't reach* her — oh, it's *rotten!* I tell you it's *rotten!* Sometimes I can just hear my money *laugh* at me! Sometimes I get to going round and round in a circle about it till it seems I'm going crazy myself."

"I think you are a — a noble man," choked Virginia.

That disconcerted him. "Oh Lord — don't think *that.* No, Young Lady, don't try to make any plaster saint out of *me.* My life goes on. I've got to eat, drink and be merry. I'm built that way. But just the same my heart on the inside's pretty sore, Young Lady. I want to tell you that the whole inside of my heart is *sore as a boil!*"

They were returning for the hats. Suddenly Virginia stopped, and it was a soft-eyed and gentle Virginia who turned to him after the pause. "There are lovely things to be bought in Paris for women who aren't well. Such soft, lovely things to wear in your room. Not but what I think these other things are all right. As you say, they may — interest her. But they aren't things she can use just now, and wouldn't you like her to have some of those soft lovely things she could actually wear? They might help most of all. To wake in the morning and find herself in something so beautiful —"

"Where do you get 'em?" he demanded promptly.

And so they went to one of those shops which have, more than all the others, enshrined Paris in feminine hearts. And never was lingerie selected with more loving care than that which Virginia picked out that afternoon. A tear fell on one particularly lovely *robe de nuit* — so soothingly soft, so caressingly luxurious, it seemed that surely it might help bring release from the bondage of those crushing years.

As they were leaving they were given two packages. "Just the kimona thing you liked," he said, "and a trinket or two. Now that we're such good friends, you won't feel like you did this morning."

"And if I don't want them myself, I might send them to my mother," Virginia replied, a quiver in her laugh at her own little joke.

He had put her in her cab; he had tried to tell her how much he thanked her; they had said good-bye and the *cocher* had cracked his whip when he came running after her. "Why, Young Lady," he called out, "we don't know each other's *names*."

She laughed and gave hers. "Mine's William P. Johnson," he said. "Part French and part Italian. But now look here, Young Lady — or I mean, Miss Clayton. A fellow at the hotel was telling me something last night that made me *sick*. He said American girls sometimes got awfully up against it here. He said one actually starved last year. Now, I don't like that kind of business. Look here, Young Lady, I want you to promise that if you — you or any of your gang — get up against it you'll cable William P. Johnson, of Cincinnati, Ohio."

The twilight grey had stolen upon Paris. And there was a mist which the street lights only penetrated a little way — as sometimes one's knowledge of life may only penetrate life a very little way. Her cab stopped by a blockade, she watched the burly back of William P. Johnson disappearing into the mist. The red box which held the yellow opera cloak she could see longer than all else.

"You never can tell," murmured Virginia. "It just goes to show that you never can tell."

And whatever it was you never could tell had brought to Virginia's girlish face the tender knowingness of the face of a woman.

II

THE PLEA

SENATOR HARRISON concluded his argument and sat down. There was no applause, but he had expected none. Senator Dorman was already saying "Mr. President?" and there was a stir in the crowded galleries, and an anticipatory moving of chairs among the Senators. In the press gallery the reporters bunched together their scattered papers and inspected their pencil-points with earnestness. Dorman was the best speaker of the Senate, and he was on the popular side of it. It would be the great speech of the session, and the prospect was cheering after a deluge of railroad and insurance bills.

"I want to tell you," he began, "why I have worked for this resolution recommending the pardon of Alfred Williams. It is one of the great laws of the universe that every living thing be given a chance. In the case before us that law has been violated. This does not resolve itself into a question of second chances. The boy of whom we are speaking has never had his first."

Senator Harrison swung his chair half-way around and looked out at the green things which were again coming into their own on the State-house grounds. He knew — in substance — what Senator Dorman would say without hearing it, and he was a little tired of the whole affair. He hoped that one way or other they would finish it up that night, and go ahead with something else. He had done what he could, and now the responsibility was with the rest of them. He thought they were shouldering a great deal to advocate the pardon in the face of the united opposition of Johnson County, where the crime had been committed. It seemed a community should be the best judge of its own crimes, and that was what he, as the Senator from Johnson, had tried to impress upon them.

He knew that his argument against the boy had been a strong one. He rather liked the attitude in which he stood. It seemed as if he were the incarnation of outraged justice attempting to hold its own at the floodgates of emotion. He liked to think he was looking far beyond the present and the specific and acting as guardian of the future — and the whole. In summing it up that night the reporters would tell in highly wrought fashion of the moving appeal made by Senator Dorman, and then they would speak dispassionately of the logical argument of the leader of the opposition. There was more satisfaction to self in logic than in mere eloquence. He was even a little proud of his unpopularity. It seemed sacrificial.

He wondered why it was Senator Dorman had thrown himself into it so whole-heartedly. All during the session the Senator from Maxwell had neglected personal interests in behalf of this boy, who was nothing to him in the world. He supposed it was as a sociological and psychological experiment. Senator Dorman had promised the Governor to assume guardianship of the boy if he were let out. The Senator from Johnson inferred that as a student of social science his eloquent colleague wanted to see what he could make of him. To suppose the interest merely personal and sympathetic would seem discreditable.

"I need not dwell upon the story," the Senator from Maxwell was saying, "for you all are familiar with it already. It is said to have been the most awful crime ever committed in the State. I grant you that it was, and then I ask you to look for a minute into the conditions leading up to it.

"When the boy was born, his mother was instituting divorce proceedings against his father. She obtained the divorce, and remarried when Alfred was three months old. From the time he was a mere baby she taught him to hate his father. Everything that went wrong with him she told him was his father's fault. His first vivid impression was that his father was responsible for all the wrong of the universe.

"For seven years that went on, and then his

mother died. His stepfather did not want him. He was going to Missouri, and the boy would be a useless expense and a bother. He made no attempt to find a home for him; he did not even explain — he merely went away and left him. At the age of seven the boy was turned out on the world, after having been taught one thing — to hate his father. He stayed a few days in the barren house, and then new tenants came and closed the doors against him. It may have occurred to him as a little strange that he had been sent into a world where there was no place for him.

"When he asked the neighbours for shelter, they told him to go to his own father and not bother strangers. He said he did not know where his father was. They told him, and he started to walk — a distance of fifty miles. I ask you to bear in mind, gentlemen, that he was only seven years of age. It is the age when the average boy is beginning the third reader, and when he is shooting marbles and spinning tops.

"When he reached his father's house he was told at once that he was not wanted there. The man had remarried, there were other children, and he had no place for Alfred. He turned him away; but the neighbours protested, and he was compelled to take him back. For four years he lived in this home, to which he had come unbidden, and where he was never made welcome.

"The whole family rebelled against him. The father satisfied his resentment against the boy's dead mother by beating her son, by encouraging his wife to abuse him, and inspiring the other children to despise him. It seems impossible such conditions should exist. The only proof of their possibility lies in the fact of their existence.

"I need not go into the details of the crime. He had been beaten by his father that evening after a quarrel with his stepmother about spilling the milk. He went, as usual, to his bed in the barn; but the hay was suffocating, his head ached, and he could not sleep. He arose in the middle of the night, went to the house, and killed both his father and stepmother.

"I shall not pretend to say what thoughts surged through the boy's brain as he lay there in the stifling hay with the hot blood pounding against his temples. I shall not pretend to say whether he was sane or insane as he walked to the house for the perpetration of the awful crime. I do not even affirm it would not have happened had there been some human being there to lay a cooling hand on his hot forehead, and say a few soothing, loving words to take the sting from the loneliness, and ease the suffering. I ask you to consider only one thing: he was eleven years old at the time, and he had no friend in all the world. He knew nothing of sympathy; he knew only injustice."

Senator Harrison was still looking out at the budding things on the State-house grounds, but in a vague way he was following the story. He knew when the Senator from Maxwell completed the recital of facts and entered upon his plea. He was conscious that it was stronger than he had anticipated — more logic and less empty exhortation. He was telling of the boy's life in reformatory and penitentiary since the commission of the crime,— of how he had expanded under kindness, of his mental attainments, the letters he could write, the books he had read, the hopes he cherished. In the twelve years he had spent there he had been known to do no unkind nor mean thing; he responded to affection — craved it. It was not the record of a degenerate, the Senator from Maxwell was saying.

A great many things were passing through the mind of the Senator from Johnson. He was trying to think who it was that wrote that book, "Put Yourself in His Place." He had read it once, and it bothered him to forget names. Then he was wondering why it was the philosophers had not more to say about the incongruity of people who had never had any trouble of their own sitting in judgment upon people who had known nothing but trouble. He was thinking also that abstract rules did not always fit smoothly over concrete cases, and that it was hard to make life a matter of rules, anyway.

Next he was wondering how it would have been

with the boy Alfred Williams if he had been born in Charles Harrison's place; and then he was working it out the other way and wondering how it would have been with Charles Harrison had he been born in Alfred Williams's place. He wondered whether the idea of murder would have grown in Alfred Williams's heart had he been born to the things to which Charles Harrison was born, and whether it would have come within the range of possibility for Charles Harrison to murder his father if he had been born to Alfred Williams's lot. Putting it that way, it was hard to estimate how much of it was the boy himself, and how much the place the world had prepared for him. And if it was the place prepared for him more than the boy, why was the fault not more with the preparers of the place than with the occupant of it? The whole thing was very confusing.

"This page," the Senator from Maxwell was saying, lifting the little fellow to the desk, "is just eleven years of age, and he is within three pounds of Alfred Williams's weight when he committed the murder. I ask you, gentlemen, if this little fellow should be guilty of a like crime to-night, to what extent would you, in reading of it in the morning, charge him with the moral discernment which is the first condition of moral responsibility? If Alfred Williams's story were this boy's story, would you deplore that there had been no one to check the childish passion, or would you say it was the inborn instinct of the murderer? And suppose again this were Alfred Williams at the age of eleven, would you not be willing to look into the future and say if he spent twelve years in penitentiary and reformatory, in which time he developed the qualities of useful and honourable citizenship, that the ends of justice would then have been met, and the time at hand for the world to begin the payment of her debt?"

Senator Harrison's eyes were fixed upon the page standing on the opposite desk. Eleven was a younger age than he had supposed. As he looked back upon it and recalled himself when eleven years of age — his irresponsibility, his dependence — he was unwilling to say what would have happened if the world had turned upon him as it had upon Alfred Williams. At eleven his greatest grievance was that the boys at school called him "yellow-top." He remembered throwing a rock at one of them for doing it. He wondered if it was criminal instinct prompted the throwing of the rock. He wondered how high the percentage of children's crimes would go were it not for countermanding influences. It seemed the great difference between Alfred Williams and a number of other children of eleven had been the absence of the countermanding influence.

There came to him of a sudden a new and moving thought. Alfred Williams had been cheated of his boyhood. The chances were he had never gone swimming, nor to a ball game, or maybe never to a circus. It might even be that he had never owned a dog. The Senator from Maxwell was right when he said the boy had never been given his chance, had been defrauded of that which has been a boy's heritage since the world itself was young.

And the later years — how were they making it up to him? He recalled what to him was the most awful thing he had ever heard about the State penitentiary: they never saw the sun rise down there, and they never saw it set. They saw it at its meridian, when it climbed above the stockade, but as it rose into the day, and as it sank into the night, it was denied them. And there, at the penitentiary, they could not even look up at the stars. It had been years since Alfred Williams raised his face to God's heaven and knew he was part of it all. The voices of the night could not penetrate the little cell in the heart of the mammoth stone building where he spent his evenings over those masterpieces with which, they said, he was more familiar than the average member of the Senate. When he read those things Victor Hugo said of the vastness of the night, he could only look around at the walls that enclosed him and try to reach back over the twelve years for some satisfying conception of what night really was.

The Senator from Johnson shuddered: they had taken from a living creature the things of life, and all because in the crucial hour there had been no one to say a staying word. Man had cheated him of the things that were man's, and then shut him away from the world that was God's. They had made for him a life barren of compensations.

There swept over the Senator a great feeling of self-pity. As representative of Johnson County, it was he who must deny this boy the whole great world without, the people who wanted to help him, and what the Senator from Maxwell called "his chance." If Johnson County carried the day, there would be something unpleasant for him to consider all the remainder of his life. As he grew to be an older man he would think of it more and more — what the boy would have done for himself in the world if the Senator from Johnson had not been more logical and more powerful than the Senator from Maxwell.

Senator Dorman was nearing the end of his argument. "In spite of the undying prejudice of the people of Johnson County," he was saying, "I can stand before you to-day and say that after an unsparing investigation of this case I do not believe I am asking you to do anything in violation of justice when I beg of you to give this boy his chance."

It was going to a vote at once, and the Senator from Johnson County looked out at the budding things and wondered whether the boy down at the penitentiary knew the Senate was considering his case that afternoon. It was without vanity he wondered whether what he had been trained to think of as an all-wise providence would not have preferred that Johnson County be represented that session by a less able man.

A great hush fell over the Chamber, for ayes and noes followed almost in alternation. After a long minute of waiting the secretary called, in a tense voice:

"Ayes, 30; Noes, 32."

The Senator from Johnson had proven too faithful a servant of his constituents. The boy in the penitentiary was denied his chance.

The usual things happened: some women in the galleries, who had boys at home, cried aloud; the reporters were fighting for occupancy of the telephone booths, and most of the Senators began the perusal of the previous day's Journal with elaborate interest. Senator Dorman indulged in none of these feints. A full look at his face just then told how much of his soul had gone into the fight for the boy's chance, and the look about his eyes was a little hard on the theory of psychological experiment.

Senator Harrison was looking out at the budding trees, but his face too had grown strange, and he seemed to be looking miles beyond and years ahead. It seemed that he himself was surrendering the voices of the night, and the comings and goings of the sun. He would never look at them — feel them — again without remembering he was keeping one of his fellow creatures away from them. He wondered at his own presumption in denying any living thing participation in the universe. And all the while there were before him visions of the boy who sat in the cramped cell with the volume of a favourite poet before him, trying to think how it would seem to be out under the stars.

The stillness in the Senate-Chamber was breaking; they were going ahead with something else. It seemed to the Senator from Johnson that sun, moon, and stars were wailing out protest for the boy who wanted to know them better. And yet it was not sun, moon, and stars so much as the unused swimming hole and the uncaught fish, the unattended ball game, the never-seen circus, and, above all, the unowned dog, that brought Senator Harrison to his feet.

They looked at him in astonishment, their faces seeming to say it would have been in better taste for him to have remained seated just then.

"Mr. President," he said, pulling at his collar and looking straight ahead, "I rise to move a reconsideration."

There was a gasp, a moment of supreme quiet, and then a mighty burst of applause. To men of all parties and factions there came a single thought. Johnson was the leading county of its Congressional district. There was an election that fall, and Harrison was in the race. Those eight words meant to a surety he would not go to Washington, for the Senator from Maxwell had chosen the right word when he referred to the prejudice of Johnson County on the Williams case as "undying." The world throbs with such things at the moment of their doing — even though condemning them later, and the part of the world then packed within the Senate-Chamber shared the universal disposition.

The noise astonished Senator Harrison, and he looked around with something like resentment. When the tumult at last subsided, and he saw that he was expected to make a speech, he grew very red, and grasped his chair desperately.

The reporters were back in their places, leaning nervously forward. This was Senator Harrison's chance to say something worth putting into a panel by itself with black lines around it — and they were sure he would do it.

But he did not. He stood there like a schoolboy who had forgotten his piece — growing more and more red. "I — I think," he finally jerked out, "that some of us have been mistaken. I'm in favour now of — of giving him his chance."

They waited for him to proceed, but after a helpless look around the Chamber he sat down. The president of the Senate waited several minutes for him to rise again, but he at last turned his chair around and looked out at the green things on the State-house grounds, and there was nothing to do but go ahead with the second calling of the roll. This time it stood 50 to 12 in favour of the boy.

A motion to adjourn immediately followed — no one wanted to do anything more that afternoon. They all wanted to say things to the Senator from Johnson; but his face had grown cold, and as they were usually afraid of him, anyhow, they kept away. All but Senator Dorman — it meant too much with him. "Do you mind my telling you," he said, tensely, "that it was as fine a thing as I have ever known a man to do?"

The Senator from Johnson moved impatiently. "You think it 'fine,'" he asked, almost resentfully, "to be a coward?"

"Coward?" cried the other man. "Well, that's scarcely the word. It was — heroic!"

"Oh no," said Senator Harrison, and he spoke wearily, "it was a clear case of cowardice. You see," he laughed, "I was afraid it might haunt me when I am seventy."

Senator Dorman started eagerly to speak, but the other man stopped him and passed on. He was seeing it as his constituency would see it, and it humiliated him. They would say he had not the courage of his convictions, that he was afraid of the unpopularity, that his judgment had fallen victim to the eloquence of the Senator from Maxwell.

But when he left the building and came out into the softness of the April afternoon it began to seem different. After all, it was not he alone who leaned to the softer side. There were the trees — they were permitted another chance to bud; there were the birds — they were allowed another chance to sing; there was the earth — to it was given another chance to yield. There stole over him a tranquil sense of unison with Life.

III

FOR LOVE OF THE HILLS

"SURE you're done with it?"

"Oh, yes," replied the girl, the suggestion of a smile on her face, and in her voice the suggestion of a tear. "Yes; I was just going."

But she did not go. She turned instead to the end of the alcove and sat down before a table placed by the window. Leaning her elbows upon it she looked about her through a blur of tears.

Seen through her own eyes of longing, it seemed that almost all of the people whom she could see standing before the files of the daily papers were homesick. The reading-room had been a strange study to her during those weeks spent in fruitless search for the work she wanted to do, and it had likewise proved a strange comfort. When tired and disconsolate and utterly sick at heart there was always one thing she could do — she could go down to the library and look at the paper from home. It was not that she wanted the actual news of Denver. She did not care in any vital way what the city officials were doing, what buildings were going up, or who was leaving town. She was only indifferently interested in the fires and the murders. She wanted the comforting companionship of that paper from home.

It seemed there were many to whom the papers offered that same sympathy, companionship, whatever it might be. More than anything else it perhaps gave to them — the searchers, drifters — a sense of anchorage. She would not soon forget the day she herself had stumbled in there and found the home paper. Chicago had given her nothing but rebuffs that day, and in desperation, just because she must go somewhere, and did not want to go back to her boarding-place, she had hunted out the city library. It was when walking listlessly about in the big reading-room it had occurred to her that perhaps she could find the paper from home; and after that when things were their worst, when her throat grew tight and her eyes dim, she could always comfort herself by saying: "After a while I'll run down and look at the paper."

But to-night it had failed her. It was not the paper from home to-night; it was just a newspaper. It did not inspire the belief that things would be better to-morrow, that it must all come right soon. It left her as she had come — heavy with the consciousness that in her purse was eleven dollars, and that that was every cent she had in the whole world.

It was hard to hold back the tears as she dwelt upon the fact that it was very little she had asked of Chicago. She had asked only a chance to do the work for which she was trained, in order that she might go to the art classes at night. She had read in the papers of that mighty young city of the Middle West — the heart of the continent— of its brawn and its brain and its grit. She had supposed that Chicago, of all places, would appreciate what she wanted to do. The day she drew her hard-earned one hundred dollars from the bank in Denver — how the sun had shone that day in Denver, how clear the sky had been, and how bracing the air! — she had quite taken it for granted that her future was assured. And now, after tasting for three weeks the cruelty of indifference, she looked back to those visions with a hard little smile.

She rose to go, and in so doing her eyes fell upon the queer little woman to whom she had yielded her place before the Denver paper. Submerged as she had been in her own desolation she had given no heed to the small figure which came slipping along beside her beyond the bare thought that she was queer-looking. But as her eyes rested upon her now there was something about the woman which held her.

She was a strange little figure. An old-fashioned shawl was pinned tightly about her shoulders, and she was wearing a queer, rusty little bonnet. Her hair was rolled up in a small knot at the back of her head. She did not look as though she belonged in Chicago. And then, as the girl stood there looking at her, she saw the thin shoulders quiver, and after a minute the head that was wearing the rusty bonnet went down into the folds of the Denver paper.

The girl's own eyes filled, and she turned to go. It seemed she could scarcely bear her own unhappiness that day, without coming close to the heartache of another. But when she reached the end of the alcove she glanced back, and the sight of that shabby, bent figure, all alone before the Denver paper, was not to be withstood.

" I am from Colorado, too," she said softly, laying a hand upon the bent shoulders.

The woman looked up at that and took the girl's hand in both of her thin, trembling ones. It was a wan and a troubled face she lifted, and there was something about the eyes which would not seem to have been left there by tears alone.

" And do you have a pining for the mountains? " she whispered, with a timid eagerness. " Do you have a feeling that you want to see the sun go down behind them to-night and that you want to see the darkness come stealing up to the tops? "

The girl half turned away, but she pressed the woman's hand tightly in hers. " I know what you mean," she murmured.

" I wanted to see it so bad," continued the woman, tremulously, " that something just drove me here to this paper. I knowed it was here because my nephew's wife brought me here one day and we come across it. We took this paper at home for more 'an twenty years. That's why I come. 'Twas the closest I could get."

"I know what you mean," said the girl again, unsteadily.

"And it's the closest I will ever get!" sobbed the woman.

"Oh, don't say that," protested the girl, brushing away her own tears, and trying to smile; "you'll go back home some day."

The woman shook her head. "And if I should," she said, "even if I should, 'twill be too late."

"But it couldn't be too late," insisted the girl. "The mountains, you know, will be there forever."

"The mountains will be there forever," repeated the woman, musingly; "yes, but not for me to see." There was a pause. "You see,"—she said it quietly—"I'm going blind."

The girl took a quick step backward, then stretched out two impulsive hands. "Oh, no, no you're not! Why—the doctors, you know, they do everything now."

The woman shook her head. "That's what I thought when I come here. That's why I come. But I saw the biggest doctor of them all to-day—they all say he's the best there is—and he said right out 'twas no use to do anything. He said 'twas—hopeless."

Her voice broke on that word. "You see," she hurried on, "I wouldn't care so much, seems like I wouldn't care 't all, if I could get there first! If I could see the sun go down behind them just one night! If I could see the black shadows come slippin' over 'em just once! And then, if just one morning — just once! — I could get up and see the sunlight come a streamin' — oh, you know how it looks! You know what 't is I want to see!"

"Yes; but why can't you? Why not? You won't go — your eyesight will last until you get back home, won't it?"

"But I can't go back home; not now."

"Why not?" demanded the girl. "Why can't you go home?"

"Why, there ain't no money, my dear," she explained, patiently. "It's a long way off — Colorado is, and there ain't no money. Now, George — George is my brother-in-law — he got me the money to come; but you see it took it all to come here, and to pay them doctors with. And George — he ain't rich, and it pinched him hard for me to come — he says I'll have to wait until he gets money laid up again, and — well he can't tell just when 't will be. He'll send it soon as he gets it," she hastened to add.

"But what are you going to do in the meantime? It would cost less to get you home than to keep you here."

"No, I stay with my nephew here. He's willin' I should stay with him till I get my money to go home."

"Yes, but this nephew, can't he get you the money? Doesn't he know," she insisted, heatedly, "what it means to you?"

"He's got five children, and not much laid up. And then, he never seen the mountains. He doesn't know what I mean when I try to tell him about gettin' there in time. Why, he says there's many a one living back in the mountains would like to be livin' here. He don't understand — my nephew don't," she added, apologetically.

"Well, *someone* ought to understand!" broke from the girl. "I understand! But —" she did her best to make it a laugh —"eleven dollars is every cent I've got in the world!"

"Don't!" implored the woman, as the girl gave up trying to control the tears. "Now, don't you be botherin'. I didn't mean to make you feel so bad. My nephew says I ain't reasonable, and maybe I ain't."

The girl raised her head. "But you *are* reasonable. I tell you, you *are* reasonable!"

"I must be going back," said the woman, uncertainly. "I'm just making you feel bad, and it won't do no good. And then they may be stirred up about me. Emma — Emma's my nephew's wife — left me at the doctor's office 'cause she had some trading to do, and she was to come back there for me. And then, as I was sittin' there, the pinin' came over me so strong it seemed I just must get up and start!

And " — she smiled wanly — " this was far as I got."

" Come over and sit down by this table," said the girl, impulsively, " and tell me a little about your home back in the mountains. Wouldn't you like to? "

The woman nodded gratefully. " Seems most like getting back to them to find someone that knows about them," she said, after they had drawn their chairs up to the table and were sitting there side by side.

The girl put her rounded hand over on the thin, withered one. " Tell me about it," she said again.

" Maybe it wouldn't be much interesting to you, my dear. It's just a common life — mine is. You see, William and I — William was my husband — we went to Georgetown before it really was any town at all. Years and years before the railroad went through, we was there. Was you ever there? " she asked wistfully.

" Oh, very often," replied the girl. " I love every inch of that country! "

A tear stole down the woman's face. " It's most like being home to find someone that knows about it," she whispered.

" Yes, William and I went there when 'twas all new country," she went on, after a pause. " We worked hard, and we laid up a little money. Then, three years ago, William took sick. He was sick for a year, and we had to live up most of what we'd saved. That's why I ain't got none now. It ain't that William didn't provide."

The girl nodded.

"We seen some hard days. But we was always harmonious — William and I was. And William had a great fondness for the mountains. The night before he died he made them take him over by the window and he looked out and watched the darkness come stealin' over the daylight — you know how it does in them mountains. 'Mother,' he said to me — his voice was that low I could no more 'an hear what he said — 'I'll never see another sun go down, but I'm thankful I seen this one.'"

She was crying outright now, and the girl did not try to stop her.

"And that's the reason I love the mountains," she whispered at last. "It ain't just that they're grand and wonderful to look at. It ain't just the things them tourists sees to talk about. But the mountains has always been like a comfortin' friend to me. John and Sarah is buried there — John and Sarah is my two children that died of fever. And then William is there — like I just told you. And the mountains was a comfort to me in all those times of trouble. They're like an old friend. Seems like they're the best friend I've got on earth."

"I know what you mean," said the girl, brokenly. "I know all about it."

"And you don't think I'm just notional," she asked wistfully, "in pinin' to get back while — whilst I can look at them?"

The girl held the old hand tightly in hers with a clasp more responsive than words.

"It ain't but I'd know they was there. I could feel they was there all right, but"— her voice sank with the horror of it —"I'm 'fraid I might forget just how they look!"

"Oh, but you won't," the girl assured her. "You'll remember just how they look."

"I'm scared of it. I'm scared there might be something I'd forget. And so I just torment myself thinkin' — 'Now do I remember this? Can I see just how that looks?' That's the way I got to thinkin' up in the doctor's office, when he told me there was nothing to do, and I was so worked up it seemed I must get up and start!"

"You must try not to worry about it," murmured the girl. "You'll remember."

"Well, maybe so. Maybe I will. But that's why I want just one more look. If I could look once more I'd remember it forever. You see I'd look to remember it, and I would. And do you know — seems like I wouldn't mind going blind so much then? When I'd sit facin' them I'd just say to myself: 'Now I know just how they look. I'm seeing them just as if I had my eyes!' The doctor says my sight 'll just kind of slip away, and when I look my last look, when it gets dimmer and dimmer to me, I want the last thing I see to be them mountains where William and me worked and was so happy! Seems like I can't bear it to have my sight slip away here in Chicago, where there's nothing I want to look at! And then to have a little left — to have just a little left! — and to know I could see if I was there to look — and to know that when I get there 'twill be — Oh, I'll be rebellious-like here — and I'd be contented there! I don't want to be complainin' — I don't want to! — but when I've only got a little left I want it — oh, I want it for them things I want to see!"

"You will see them," insisted the girl passionately. "I'm not going to believe the world can be so hideous as that!"

"Well, maybe so," said the woman, rising. "But I don't know where 'twill come from," she added doubtfully.

She took her back to the doctor's office and left her in the care of the stolid Emma. "Seems most like I'd been back home," she said in parting; and the girl promised to come and see her and talk with her about the mountains. The woman thought that talking about them would help her to remember just how they looked.

And then the girl returned to the library. She did not know why she did so. In truth she scarcely knew she was going there until she found herself sitting before that same secluded table at which she and the woman had sat a little while before. For a long time she sat there with her head in her hands, tears falling upon a pad of yellow paper on the table before her.

Finally she dried her eyes, opened her purse, and counted her money. It seemed that out of her great desire, out of her great new need, there must be more than she had thought. But there was not, and she folded her hands upon the two five-dollar bills and the one silver dollar and looked hopelessly about the big room.

She had forgotten her own disappointments, her own loneliness. She was oblivious to everything in the world now save what seemed the absolute necessity of getting the woman back to the mountains while she had eyes to see them.

But what could she do? Again she counted the money. She could make herself, some way or other, get along without one of the five-dollar bills, but five dollars would not take one very close to the mountains. It was at that moment that she saw a man standing before the Denver paper, and noticed that another man was waiting to take his place. The one who was reading had a dinner pail in his hand. The clothes of the other told that he, too, was of the world's workers. It was clear to the girl that the man at the file was reading the paper from home; and the man who was ready to take his place looked as if waiting for something less impersonal than the news of the day.

The idea came upon her with such suddenness, so full born, that it made her gasp. They — the people who came to read the Denver paper, the people who loved the mountains and were far from them, the people who were themselves homesick and full of longing — were the people to understand.

It took her but a minute to act. She put the silver dollar and one five-dollar bill back in her purse. She clutched the other bill in her left hand, picked up a pencil, and began to write. She headed the petition: " To all who know and love the mountains," and she told the story with the simpleness of one speaking from the heart, and the directness of one who speaks to those sure to understand. "And so I found her here by the Denver paper," she said, after she had stated the tragic facts, " because it was the closest she could come to the mountains. Her heart is not breaking because she is going blind. It is breaking because she may never again look with seeing eyes upon those great hills which rise up about her home. We must do it for her simply because we would wish that, under like circumstances, someone would do it for us. She belongs to us because we understand.

" If you can only give fifty cents, please do not hold it back because it seems but little. Fifty cents will take her twenty miles nearer home — twenty miles closer to the things upon which she longs that her last seeing glance may fall."

After she had written it she rose, and, the five-dollar bill in one hand, the sheets of yellow paper in the other, walked down the long room to the desk at which one of the librarians sat. The girl's cheeks were very red, her eyes shining as she poured out the story. They mingled their tears, for the girl at the desk was herself young and far from home, and then they walked back to the Denver paper and pinned the sheets of yellow paper just above the file. At the bottom of the petition the librarian wrote: "Leave your money at the desk in this room. It will be properly attended to." The girl from Colorado then turned over her five-dollar bill and passed out into the gathering night.

Her heart was brimming with joy. "I can get a cheaper boarding place," she told herself, as she joined the home-going crowds, "and until something else turns up I'll just look around and see if I can't get a place in a store."

. . . .

One by one they had gathered around while the woman was telling the story. "And so, if you don't mind," she said, in conclusion, "I'd like to have you put in a little piece that I got to Denver safe, so's they can see it. They was all so worked up about when I'd get here. Would that cost much?" she asked timidly.

"Not a cent," said the city editor, his voice gruff with the attempt to keep it steady.

"You might say, if it wouldn't take too much room, that I was much pleased with the prospect of getting home before sundown to-night."

"You needn't worry but what we'll say it all," he assured her. "We'll say a great deal more than you have any idea of."

"I'm very thankful to you," she said, as she rose to go.

They sat there for a moment in silence. "When one considers," someone began, "that they were people who were pushed too close even to subscribe to a daily paper —"

"When one considers," said the city editor, "that the girl who started it had just eleven dollars to her name —" And then he, too, stopped abruptly and there was another long moment of silence.

After that he looked around at the reporters. "Well, it's too bad you can't all have it, when it's so big a chance, but I guess it falls logically to Raymond. And in writing it, just remember, Raymond, that the biggest stories are not written about wars, or about politics, or even murders. The biggest stories are written about the things which draw human beings closer together. And the chance to write them doesn't come every day, or every year, or every lifetime. And I'll tell you, boys, all of you, when it seems sometimes that the milk of human kindness has all turned sour, just think back to the little story you heard this afternoon."

. . . .

Slowly the sun slipped down behind the mountains; slowly the long purple shadows deepened to black; and with the coming of the night there settled over the everlasting hills, and over the soul of one who had returned to them, that satisfying calm that men call peace.

IV

FRECKLES M'GRATH

MANY visitors to the State-house made the mistake of looking upon the Governor as the most important personage in the building. They would walk up and down the corridors, hoping for a glimpse of some of the leading officials, when all the while Freckles McGrath, the real character of the Capitol, and by all odds the most illustrious person in it, was at once accessible and affable.

Freckles McGrath was the elevator boy. In the official register his name had gone down as William, but that was a mere concession to the constituents to whom the official register was sent out. In the newspapers — and he appeared with frequency in the newspapers — he was always "Freckles," and every one from the Governor down gave him that title, the appropriateness of which was stamped a hundred fold upon his shrewd, jolly Irish face.

Like every one else on the State pay-roll, Freckles was keyed high during this first week of the new session. It was a reform Legislature, and so imbued was it with the idea of reforming that there was grave danger of its forcing reformation upon everything in sight. It happened that the Governor was of the same faction of the party as that dominant in the Legislature; reform breathed through every nook and crevice of the great building.

But high above all else in importance towered the Kelley Bill. From the very opening of the session there was scarcely a day when some of Freckles' passengers did not in hushed whispers mention the Kelley Bill. From what he could pick up about the building, and what he read in the newspapers, Freckles put together a few ideas as to what the Kelley Bill really was. It was a great reform measure, and it was going to show the railroads that they did not own the State. The railroads were going to have to pay more taxes, and they were making an awful fuss about it; but if the Kelley Bill could be put through it would be a great victory for reform, and would make the Governor "solid" in the State.

Freckles McGrath was strong for reform. That was partly because the snatches of speeches he heard in the Legislature were more thrilling when for reform than when against it; it was partly because he adored the Governor, and in no small part because he despised Mr. Ludlow.

Mr. Ludlow was a lobbyist. Some of the members of the Legislature were Mr. Ludlow's property — or at least so Freckles inferred from conversation overheard at his post. There had been a great deal of talk that session about Mr. Ludlow's methods.

Freckles himself was no snob. Although he had heard Mr. Ludlow called disgraceful, and although he firmly believed he was disgraceful, he did not consider that any reason for not speaking to him. And so when Mr. Ludlow got in all alone one morning, and the occasion seemed to demand recognition of some sort, Freckles had chirped: "Good-morning!"

But the man, possibly deep in something else, simply knit together his brows and gave no sign of having heard. After that, Henry Ludlow, lobbyist, and Freckles McGrath, elevator boy, were enemies.

A little before noon, one day near the end of the session, a member of the Senate and a member of the House rode down together in the elevator.

"There's no use waiting any longer," the Senator was saying as they got in. "We're as strong now as we're going to be. It's a matter of Stacy's vote, and that's a matter of who sees him last."

Freckles widened out his ears and gauged the elevator for very slow running. Stacy had been written up in the papers as a wabbler on the Kelley Bill.

"He's all right now," pursued the Senator, "but there's every chance that Ludlow will see him before he casts his vote this afternoon, and then — oh, I don't know!" and with a weary little flourish of his hands the Senator stepped off.

Freckles McGrath sat wrapped in deep thought. The Kelley Bill was coming up in the Senate that afternoon. If Senator Stacy voted for it, it would pass. If he voted against it, it would fail. He would vote for it if he didn't see Mr. Ludlow; he wouldn't vote for it if he did. That was the situation, and the Governor's whole future, Freckles felt, was at stake.

The bell rang sharply, and he was vaguely conscious then that it had been ringing before. In the next half-hour he was very busy taking down the members of the Legislature. Strangely enough, Senator Stacy and the Governor went down the same trip, and Freckles beamed with approbation when he saw them walk out of the building together.

Stacy was one of the first of the senators to return. Freckles sized him up keenly as he stepped into the elevator, and decided that he was still firm. But there was a look about Senator Stacy's mouth which suggested that there was no use in being too sure of him. Freckles considered the advisability of bursting forth and telling him how much better it would be to stick with the reform fellows; but just as the boy got his courage screwed up to speaking point, Senator Stacy got off.

About ten minutes later Freckles had the elevator on the ground floor, and was sitting there reading a paper, when he heard a step that made him prick up his ears. The next minute Mr. Ludlow turned the corner. He was immaculately dressed, as usual, and his iron-grey moustache seemed to stand out just a little more pompously than ever. There was a sneering look in his eyes as he stepped into the car. It seemed to be saying: "They thought they could beat me, did they? Oh, they're easy, they are!"

Freckles McGrath slammed the door of the cage and started the car up. He did not know what he was going to do, but he had an idea that he did not want any other passenger. When half way between the basement and the first floor, he stopped the elevator. He must have time to think. If he took that man up to the Senate Chamber, he would simply strike the death-blow to reform! And so he knelt and pretended to be fixing something, and he thought fast and hard.

"Something broke?" asked an anxious voice.

Freckles looked around into Mr. Ludlow's face, and he saw that the eminent lobbyist was nervous.

"Yes," he said calmly. "It's acting queer. Something's all out of whack."

"Well, drop it to the basement and let me out," said Mr Ludlow sharply.

"Can't drop it," responded Freckles. "She's stuck."

Mr. Ludlow came and looked things over, but his knowledge did not extend to the mechanism of elevators.

"Better call someone to come and take us out," he said nervously.

Freckles straightened himself up. A glitter had

come into his small grey eyes, and red spots were burning in his freckled cheeks.

"I think she'll run now," he said.

And she did run. Never in all its history had that State-house elevator run as it ran then. It rushed past the first and second floors like a thing let loose, with an utter abandonment that caused the blood to forsake the eminent lobbyist's face.

"Stop it, boy!" he cried in alarm.

"Can't!" responded Freckles, his voice thick with terror. "Running away!" he gasped.

"Will it — fall?" whispered the lobbyist.

"I — I think so!" blubbered Freckles.

The central portion of the State-house was very high. Above that part of the building which was in use there was a long stretch leading to the tower. The shaft had been built clear up, though practically unused. Past floors used for store-rooms, past floors used for nothing at all, they went — the man's face white, the boy wailing out incoherent supplications. And then, within ten feet of the top of the shaft, and within a foot of the top floor of the building, the elevator came to a rickety stop. It wabbled back and forth; it did strange and terrible things.

"She's falling!" panted Freckles. "Climb!"

And Henry Ludlow climbed. He got the door open, and he clambered up. No sooner had the man's feet touched the solid floor than Freckles reached up and slammed the door of the cage. Why he did that he was not sure at the time. Later he felt that something had warned him not to give his prisoner's voice a full sweep down the shaft.

Henry Ludlow was far from dull. As he saw the quick but even descent of the car, he knew that he had been tricked. He would have been more than human had there not burst from him furious and threatening words. But what was the use? The car was going down — down — down, and there he was, perhaps hundreds of feet above any one else in the building — alone, tricked, beaten!

Of course he tried the door at the head of the winding stairway, knowing full well that it would be locked. They always kept it locked; he had heard one of the janitors asking for the keys to take a party up just a few days before. Perhaps he could get out on top of the building and make signals of distress. But the door leading outside was locked also. There he was — helpless. And below — well, below they were passing the Kelley Bill!

He rattled the grating of the elevator shaft. He made strange, loud noises, knowing all the while he could not make himself heard. And then at last, alone in the State-house attic, Henry Ludlow, eminent lobbyist, sat down on a box and nursed his fury.

Below, Freckles McGrath, the youngest champion of reform in the building, was putting on a bold front. He laughed and he talked and he whistled. He took people up and down with as much nonchalance as if he did not know that up at the top of that shaft angry eyes were straining themselves for a glimpse of the car, and terrible curses were descending, literally, upon his stubby red head.

It was a great afternoon at the State-house. Every one thronged to the doors of the Senate Chamber, where they were putting through the Kelley Bill. The speeches made in behalf of the measure were brief. The great thing now was not to make speeches; it was to reach " S " on roll-call before a man with iron-grey hair and an iron-grey moustache could come in and say something to the fair-haired member with the weak mouth who sat near the rear of the chamber.

Freckles was called away just as it went to a vote. When he came back Senator Kelley was standing out in the corridor, and a great crowd of men were standing around slapping him on the back. The Governor himself was standing on the steps of the Senate Chamber; his eyes were bright, and he was smiling.

Freckles turned his car back to the basement. He wanted to be all alone for a minute, to dwell in solitude upon the fact that it was he, Freckles McGrath, who had won this great victory for reform. It was he, Freckles McGrath, who had assured the Governor's future. Why, perhaps he had that afternoon made for himself a name which would be handed down in the histories!

Freckles was a kind little boy, and he knew that an elegant gentleman could not find the attic any too pleasant a place in which to spend the afternoon. So he decided to go up and get Mr. Ludlow. It took courage; but he had won his victory and this was no time for faltering.

There was something gruesome about the long ascent. He thought of stories he had read of lonely turrets in which men were beheaded, and otherwise made away with. It seemed he would never come to the top, and when at last he did it was to find two of the most awful-looking eyes he had ever seen — eyes that looked as though furies were going to escape from them — peering down upon him.

The sight of that car, moving smoothly and securely up to the top, and the sight of that audacious little boy with the freckled face and the bat-like eyes, that little boy who had played his game so well, who had wrought such havoc, was too much for Henry Ludlow's self-control. Words such as he had never used before, such as he would not have supposed himself capable of using, burst from him. But Freckles stood calmly gazing up at the infuriated lobbyist, and just as Mr. Ludlow was saying, "I'll beat your head open, you little brat!" he calmly reversed the handle and sent the car skimming smoothly to realms below. He was followed by an angry yell, and then by a loud request to return, but he heeded them not, and for some time longer the car made its usual rounds between the basement and the legislative chambers.

In just an hour Freckles tried it again. He sent the car to within three feet of the attic floor, and then peered through the grating, his face tied in a knot of interrogation. The eminent lobbyist stood there gulping down wrath and pride, knowing well enough what was expected of him.

"Oh — all right," he muttered at last, and with that much of an understanding Freckles sent the car up, opened the door, and Henry Ludlow stepped in.

No word was spoken between them until the light from the floor upon which the Senate Chamber was situated came in view. Then Freckles turned with a polite inquiry as to where the gentleman wished to get off.

"You may take me down to the office of the Governor," said Mr. Ludlow stonily, meaningly.

"Sure," said Freckles cheerfully. "Guess you'll find the Governor in his office now. He's been in the Senate most of the afternoon, watching 'em pass that Kelley Bill."

Mr. Ludlow's lips drew in tightly. He squared his shoulders, and his silence was tremendous.

In just fifteen minutes Freckles was sent for from the executive office.

"I demand his discharge!" Mr. Ludlow was saying as the elevator boy entered.

"It happens you're not running this building,"

the Governor returned with a good deal of acidity. "Though of course," he added with dignity, "the matter will be carefully investigated."

The Governor was one great chuckle inside, and his heart was full of admiration and gratitude; but would Freckles be equal to bluffing it through? Would the boy have the finesse, the nice subtlety, the real master hand, the situation demanded? If not, then — imp of salvation though he was — in the interest of reform, Freckles would have to go.

It was a very innocent looking boy who stood before him and looked inquiringly into his face.

"William," began the Governor — Freckles was pained at first, and then remembered that officially he was William — "this gentleman has made a very serious charge against you."

Freckles looked at Mr. Ludlow in a hurt way, and waited for the Governor to proceed.

"He says," went on the chief executive, "that you deliberately took him to the top of the building and wilfully left him there a prisoner all afternoon. Did you do that?"

"Oh, sir," burst forth Freckles, "I did the very best I could to save his life! I was willing to sacrifice mine for him. I —"

"You little liar!" broke in Ludlow.

The Governor held up his hand. "You had your chance. Let him have his."

"You see, Governor," began Freckles, as if anxious to set right a great wrong which had been done him, " the car is acting bad. The engineer said only this morning it needed a going over. When it took that awful shoot, I lost control of it. Maybe I'm to be discharged for losing control of it, but not " — Freckles sniffled pathetically — " but not for anything like what he says I done. Why Governor," he went on, ramming his knuckles into his eyes, " I ain't got nothing against him! What'd I take him to the attic for? "

" Of course not for money," sneered Mr. Ludlow.

The Governor turned on him sharply. " When you can bring any proof of that, I'll be ready to hear it. Until you can, you'd better leave it out of the question."

" Strange it should have happened this very afternoon," put in the eminent lobbyist.

The Governor looked at him with open countenance. " You were especially interested in something this afternoon? I thought you told me you had no vital interest here this session."

There was nothing to be said. Mr. Ludlow said nothing.

" Now, William," pursued the Governor, fearful in his heart that this would be Freckles' undoing, " why did you close the door of the shaft before you started down? "

" Well, you see, sir," began Freckles, still tremulously, " I'm so used to closin' doors. Closin' doors has become a kind of second nature with me. I've been told about it so many times. And up there, though I thought I was losin' my life, still I didn't neglect my duty."

The Governor put his hand to his mouth and coughed.

"And why," he went on, more secure now, for a boy who could get out of that could get out of anything, "why was it you didn't make some immediate effort to get Mr Ludlow down? Why didn't you notify someone, or do something about it?"

"Why, I supposed, of course, he walked down by the stairs," cried Freckles. "I never dreamed he'd want to trust the elevator after the way she had acted."

"The door was locked," snarled the eminent lobbyist.

"Well, now, you see, I didn't know that," explained Freckles expansively. "Late in the afternoon I took a run up just to test the car — and there you were! I never was so surprised in my life. I supposed, of course, sir, that you'd spent the afternoon in the Senate, along with everybody else."

Once more the Governor put his hand to his mouth.

"Your case will come before the executive council at its next meeting, William. And if anything like this should happen again, you will be discharged on the spot." Freckles bowed. "You may go now."

When he was almost at the door the Governor called to him.

"Don't you think, William," he said — the Governor felt that he and Freckles could afford to be generous — "that you should apologise to the gentleman for the really grave inconvenience to which you have been the means of subjecting him?"

Freckles' little grey eyes grew steely. He looked at Henry Ludlow, and there was an ominous silence. Then light broke over his face. "On behalf of the elevator," he said, "I apologise."

And a third time the Governor's hand was raised to his mouth.

The next week Freckles was wearing a signet ring; long and audibly had he sighed for a ring of such kind and proportions. He was at some pains in explaining to everyone to whom he showed it that it had been sent him by "a friend up home."

V

FROM A TO Z

THUS had another ideal tumbled to the rubbish heap! She seemed to be breathing the dust which the newly fallen had stirred up among its longer dead fellows. Certainly she was breathing the dust from somewhere.

During her senior year at the university, when people would ask: "And what are you going to do when you leave school, Miss Willard?" she would respond with anything that came to hand, secretly hugging to her mind that idea of getting a position in a publishing house. Her conception of her publishing house was finished about the same time as her class-day gown. She was to have a roll-top desk — probably of mahogany — and a big chair which whirled round like that in the office of the under-graduate dean. She was to have a little office all by herself, opening on a bigger office — the little one marked "Private." There were to be beautiful rugs — the general effect not unlike the library at the University Club — books and pictures and cultivated gentlemen who spoke often of Greek tragedies and the Renaissance. She was a little uncertain as to her duties, but had a general idea about getting down between nine and ten, reading the morning paper, cutting the latest magazine, and then "writing something."

Commencement was now four months past, and one of her professors had indeed secured for her a position in a Chicago "publishing house." This was her first morning and she was standing at the window looking down into Dearborn Street while the man who was to have her in charge was fixing a place for her to sit.

That the publishing house should be on Dearborn Street had been her first blow, for she had long located her publishing house on that beautiful stretch of Michigan Avenue which overlooked the lake. But the real insult was that this publishing house, instead of having a building, or at least a floor, all to itself, simply had a place penned off in a bleak, dirty building such as one who had done work in sociological research instinctively associated with a box factory. And the thing which fairly trailed her visions in the dust was that the partition penning them off did not extend to the ceiling, and the adjoining room being occupied by a patent medicine company, she was face to face with glaring endorsements of Dr. Bunting's Famous Kidney and Bladder Cure. Taken all in all there seemed little chance for Greek tragedies or the Renaissance.

The man who was "running things"— she buried her phraseology with her dreams — wore a skull cap, and his moustache dragged down below his chin. Just at present he was engaged in noisily pulling a most unliterary pine table from a dark corner to a place near the window. That accomplished, an ostentatious hunt ensued, resulting in the triumphant flourish of a feather duster. Several knocks at the table, and the dust of many months — perhaps likewise of many dreams — ascended to a resting place on the endorsement of Dr. Bunting's Kidney and Bladder Cure. He next produced a short, straight-backed chair which she recognised as brother to the one which used to stand behind their kitchen stove. He gave it a shake, thus delicately indicating that she was receiving special favours in this matter of an able-bodied chair, and then announced with brisk satisfaction: "So! Now we are ready to begin." She murmured a "Thank you," seated herself and her buried hopes in this chair which did not whirl round, and leaned her arms upon a table which did not even dream in mahogany.

In the *other* publishing house, one pushed buttons and uniformed menials appeared — noiselessly, quickly and deferentially. At this moment a boy with sandy hair brushed straight back in a manner either statesmanlike or clownlike — things were too involved to know which — shuffled in with an armful of yellow paper which he flopped down on the pine table. After a minute he returned with a warbled "Take Me Back to New York Town" and a paste-pot. And upon his third appearance he was practising gymnastics with a huge pair of shears, which he finally presented, grinningly.

There was a long pause, broken only by the sonorous voice of Dr. Bunting upbraiding someone for not having billed out that stuff to Apple Grove, and then the sandy-haired boy appeared bearing a large dictionary, followed by the man in the skull cap behind a dictionary of equal unwieldiness. These were set down on either side of the yellow paper, and he who was filling the position of cultivated gentleman pulled up a chair, briskly.

"Has Professor Lee explained to you the nature of our work?" he wanted to know.

"No," she replied, half grimly, a little humourously, and not far from tearfully, "he didn't — explain."

"Then it is my pleasure to inform you," he began, blinking at her importantly, "that we are engaged here in the making of a dictionary."

"A *dic* —?" but she swallowed the gasp in the laugh coming up to meet it, and of their union was born a saving cough.

"Quite an overpowering thought, is it not?" he agreed pleasantly. "Now you see you have before you the two dictionaries you will use most, and over in that case you will find other references. The main thing"— his voice sank to an impressive whisper — "is *not* to infringe the copyright. The publisher was in yesterday and made a little talk to the force, and he said that any one who handed in a piece of copy infringing the copyright simply employed that means of writing his own resignation. Neat way of putting it, was it not?"

"Yes, *wasn't* it — neat?" she agreed, wildly.

She was conscious of a man's having stepped in behind her and taken a seat at the table next hers. She heard him opening his dictionaries and getting out his paper. Then the man in the skull cap had risen and was saying genially: "Well, here is a piece of old Webster, your first 'take' — no copyright on this, you see, but you must modernise and expand. Don't miss any of the good words in either of these dictionaries. Here you have dictionaries, copy-paper, paste, and Professor Lee assures me you have brains — all the necessary ingredients for successful lexicography. We are to have some rules printed to-morrow, and in the meantime I trust I've made myself clear. The main thing"— he bent down and spoke it solemnly — "is *not* to infringe the copyright." With a cheerful nod he was gone, and she heard him saying to the man at the next table: "Mr. Clifford, I shall have to ask you to be more careful about getting in promptly at eight."

She removed the cover from her paste-pot and dabbled a little on a piece of paper. Then she tried the unwieldy shears on another piece of paper. She then opened one of her dictionaries and read studiously for fifteen minutes. That accomplished, she opened the other dictionary and pursued it for twelve minutes. Then she took the column of "old Webster," which had been handed her pasted on a piece of yellow paper, and set about attempting to commit it to memory. She looked up to be met with the statement that Mrs. Marjory Van Luce De Vane, after spending years under the so-called best surgeons of the country, had been cured in six weeks by Dr. Bunting's Famous Kidney and Bladder Cure. She pushed the dictionaries petulantly from her, and leaning her very red cheek upon her hand, her hazel eyes blurred with tears of perplexity and resentment, her mouth drawn in pathetic little lines of uncertainty, looked over at the sprawling warehouse on the opposite side of Dearborn Street. She was just considering the direct manner of writing one's resignation — not knowing how to infringe the copyright — when a voice said: "I beg pardon, but I wonder if I can help you any?"

She had never heard a voice like that before. Or, *had* she heard it? — and where? She looked at him, a long, startled gaze. Something made her think of the voice the prince used to have in long-ago dreams. She looked into a face that was dark and thin and — different. Two very dark eyes were looking at her kindly, and a mouth which was a baffling combination of things to be loved and things to be deplored was twitching a little, as though it would like to join the eyes in a smile, if it dared.

Because he saw both how funny and how hard it was, she liked him. It would have been quite different had he seen either one without the other.

"You can tell me how *not* to infringe the copyright," she laughed. "I'm not sure that I know what a copyright is."

He laughed — a laugh which belonged with his voice. "Mr. Littletree isn't as lucid as he thinks he is. I've been here a week or so, and picked up a few things you might like to know."

He pulled his chair closer to her table then and gave her a lesson in the making of copy. Edna Willard was never one-half so attractive as when absorbed in a thing which someone was showing her how to do. Her hazel eyes would widen and glisten with the joy of comprehending; her cheeks would flush a deeper pink with the coming of new light, her mouth would part in a child-like way it had forgotten to outgrow, her head would nod gleefully in token that she understood, and she had a way of pulling at her wavy hair and making it more wavy than it had been before. The man at the next table was a long time in explaining the making of a dictionary. He spoke in low tones, often looking at the figure of the man in the skull cap, who was sitting with his back to them, looking over copy. Once she cried, excitedly: "Oh — I *see!*" and he warned,

"S — h!" explaining, "Let him think you got it all from him. It will give you a better stand-in." She nodded, appreciatively, and felt very well acquainted with this kind man whose voice made her think of something — called to something — she did not just know what.

After that she became so absorbed in lexicography that when the men began putting away their things it was hard to realise that the morning had gone. It was a new and difficult game, the evasion of the copyright furnishing the stimulus of a hazard.

The man at the next table had been watching her with an amused admiration. Her child-like absorption, the way every emotion from perplexity to satisfaction expressed itself in the poise of her head and the pucker of her face, took him back over years emotionally barren to the time when he too had those easily stirred enthusiasms of youth. For the man at the next table was far from young now. His mouth had never quite parted with boyishness, but there was more white than black in his hair, and the lines about his mouth told that time, as well as forces more aging than time, had laid heavy hand upon him. But when he looked at the girl and told her with a smile that it was time to stop work, it was a smile and a voice to defy the most tell-tale face in all the world.

During her luncheon, as she watched the strange people coming and going, she did much wondering.

She wondered why it was that so many of the men at the dictionary place were very old men; she wondered if it would be a good dictionary — one that would be used in the schools; she wondered if Dr. Bunting had made a great deal of money, and most of all she wondered about the man at the next table whose voice was like — like a dream which she did not know that she had dreamed.

When she had returned to the straggling old building, had stumbled down the narrow, dark hall and opened the door of the big bleak room, she saw that the man at the next table was the only one who had returned from luncheon. Something in his profile made her stand there very still. He had not heard her come in, and he was looking straight ahead, eyes half closed, mouth set — no unsurrendered boyishness there now. Wholly unconsciously she took an impulsive step forward. But she stopped, for she saw, and felt without really understanding, that it was not just the moment's pain, but the revealed pain of years. Just then he began to cough, and it seemed the cough, too, was more than of the moment. And then he turned and saw her, and smiled, and the smile changed all.

As the afternoon wore on the man stopped working and turning a little in his chair sat there covertly watching the girl. She was just typically girl. It was written that she had spent her days in the happy ways of healthful girlhood. He supposed that a great many young fellows had fallen in love with her — nice, clean young fellows, the kind she would naturally meet. And then his eyes closed for a minute and he put up his hand and brushed back his hair; there was weariness, weariness weary of itself, in the gesture. He looked about the room and scanned the faces of the men, most of them older than he, many of them men whose histories were well known to him. They were the usual hangers on about newspaper offices; men who, for one reason or other — age, dissipation, antiquated methods — had been pitched over, men for whom such work as this came as a godsend. They were the men of yesterday — men whom the world had rushed past. She was the only one there, this girl who would probably sit here beside him for many months, with whom the future had anything to do. Youth! — Goodness! — Joy! — Hope! — strange things to bring to a place like this. And as if their alienism disturbed him, he moved restlessly, almost resentfully, bit his lips nervously, moistened them, and began putting away his things.

As the girl was starting home along Dearborn Street a few minutes later, she chanced to look in a window. She saw that it was a saloon, but before she could turn away she saw a man with a white face — white with the peculiar whiteness of a dark face, standing before the bar drinking from a small glass. She stood still, arrested by a look such as she had never seen before: a panting human soul sobbingly fluttering down into something from which it had spent all its force in trying to rise. When she recalled herself and passed on, a mist which she could neither account for nor banish was dimming the clear hazel of her eyes.

The next day was a hard one at the dictionary place. She told herself it was because the novelty of it was wearing away, because her fingers ached, because it tired her back to sit in that horrid chair. She did not admit of any connection between her flagging interest and the fact that the place at the next table was vacant.

The following day he was still absent. She assumed that it was nervousness occasioned by her queer surroundings made her look around whenever she heard a step behind her. Where was he? Where had that look carried him? If he were in trouble, was there no one to help him?

The third day she did an unpremeditated thing. The man in the skull cap had been showing her something about the copy. As he was leaving, she asked: "Is the man who sits at the next table coming back?"

"Oh yes," he replied grimly, "he'll be back."

"Because," she went on, "if he wasn't, I thought I would take his shears. These hurt my fingers."

He made the exchange for her — and after that things went better.

He did return late the next morning. After he had taken his place he looked over at her and smiled. He looked sick and shaken — as if something that knew no mercy had taken hold of him and wrung body and soul.

"You have been ill?" she asked, with timid solicitude.

"Oh no," he replied, rather shortly.

He was quiet all that day, but the next day they talked about the work, laughed together over funny definitions they found. She felt that he could tell many interesting things about himself, if he cared to.

As the days went on he did tell some of those things — out of the way places where he had worked, queer people whom he had known. It seemed that words came to him as gifts, came freely, happily, pleased, perhaps, to be borne by so sympathetic a voice. And there was another thing about him. He seemed always to know just what she was trying to say; he never missed the unexpressed. That made it easy to say things to him; there seemed a certain at-homeness between his thought and hers. She accounted for her interest in him by telling herself she had never known any one like that before. Now Harold, the boy whom she knew best out at the university, why one had to *say* things to Harold to make him understand! And Harold never left one wondering — wondering what he had meant by that smile, what he had been going to say when he started to say something and stopped, wondering what it was about his face that one could not understand. Harold never could claim as his the hour after he had left her, and was one ever close to anyone with whom one did not spend some of the hours of absence? She began to see that hours spent together when apart were the most intimate hours of all.

And as Harold did not make one wonder, so he did not make one worry. Never in all her life had there been a lump in her throat when she thought of Harold. There was often a lump in her throat when the man at the next table was coughing.

One day, she had been there about two months, she said something to him about it. It was hard; it seemed forcing one's way into a room that had never been opened to one — there were several doors he kept closed.

"Mr. Clifford," she turned to him impetuously as they were putting away their things that night, "will you mind if I say something to you?"

He was covering his paste-pot. He looked up at her strangely. The closed door seemed to open a little way. "I can't conceive of 'minding' anything you might say to me, Miss Noah,"— he had called her Miss Noah ever since she, by mistake, had one day called him Mr. Webster.

"You see," she hurried on, very timid, now that

the door had opened a little, " you have been so good to me. Because you have been so good to me it seems that I have some right to — to — "

His head was resting upon his hand, and he leaned a little closer as though listening for something he wanted to hear.

" I had a cousin who had a cough like yours," — brave now that she could not go back — " and he went down to New Mexico and stayed for a year, and when he came back — when he came back he was as well as any of us. It seems so foolish not to "— her voice broke, now that it had so valiantly carried it — "not to — "

He looked at her, and that was all. But she was never wholly the same again after that look. It enveloped her being in a something which left her richer — different. It was a look to light the dark place between two human souls. It seemed for the moment that words would follow it, but as if feeling their helplessness — perhaps needlessness — they sank back unuttered, and at the last he got up, abruptly, and walked away.

One night, while waiting for the elevator, she heard two of the men talking about him. When she went out on the street it was with head high, cheeks hot. For nothing is so hard to hear as that which one has half known, and evaded. One never denies so hotly as in denying to one's self what one fears is true, and one never resents so bitterly as in resenting that which one cannot say one has the right to resent.

That night she lay in her bed with wide open eyes, going over and over the things they had said. "*Cure?*"— one of them had scoffed, after telling how brilliant he had been before he "went to pieces" — "why all the cures on earth couldn't help him! He can go just so far, and then he can no more stop himself — oh, about as much as an ant could stop a prairie fire!"

She finally turned over on her pillow and sobbed; and she wondered why — wondered, yet knew.

But it resulted in the flowering of her tenderness for him. Interest mounted to defiance. It ended in blind, passionate desire to "make it up" to him. And again he was so different from Harold; Harold did not impress himself upon one by upsetting all one's preconceived ideas.

She felt now that she understood better — understood the closed doors. He was — she could think of no better word than sensitive.

And that is why, several mornings later, she very courageously — for it did take courage — threw this little note over on his desk — they had formed a habit of writing notes to each other, sometimes about the words, sometimes about other things.

"IN-VI-TA-TION, *n.* That which Miss Noah extends to Mr. Webster for Friday evening, December second, at the house where she lives — hasn't she already told him where that is? It is the wish of Miss Noah to present Mr. Webster to various other Miss Noahs, all of whom are desirous of making his acquaintance."

She was absurdly nervous at luncheon that day, and kept telling herself with severity not to act like a high-school girl. He was late in returning that noon, and though there seemed a new something in his voice when he asked if he hadn't better sharpen her pencils, he said nothing about her new definition of invitation. It was almost five o'clock when he threw this over on her desk:

"AP-PRE-CI-A-TION, *n.* That sentiment inspired in Mr. Webster by the kind invitation of Miss Noah for Friday evening.

"RE-GRET, *n.* That which Mr. Webster experiences because, for reasons into which he cannot go in detail, it is impossible for him to accept Miss Noah's invitation.

"RE-SENT-MENT, *n.* That which is inspired in Mr. Webster by the insinuation that there are other Miss Noahs in the world."

Then below he had written: "Three hours later. Miss Noah, the world is queer. Some day you may find out — though I hope you never will — that it is frequently the things we most want to do that we must leave undone. Miss Noah, won't you go on bringing me as much of yourself as you can to Dearborn Street, and try not to think much about my not being able to know the Miss Noah of Hyde Park? And little Miss Noah — I thank you. There aren't words enough in this old book of ours to tell you how much — or why."

That night he hurried away with never a joke about how many words she had written that day. She did not look up as he stood there putting on his coat.

It was spring now, and the dictionary staff had begun on W.

They had written of Joy, of Hope and Life and Love, and many other things. Life seemed pressing just behind some of those definitions, pressing the harder, perhaps, because it could not break through the surface.

For it did not break through; it flooded just beneath.

How did she know that he cared for her? She could not possibly have told. Perhaps the nearest to actual proof she could bring was that he always saw that her overshoes were put in a warm place. And when one came down to facts, the putting of a girl's rubbers near the radiator did not necessarily mean love.

Perhaps then it was because there was no proof of it that she was most sure. For some of the most sure things in the world are things which cannot be proved.

It was only that they worked together and were

friends; that they laughed together over funny definitions they found, that he was kind to her, and that they seemed remarkably close together.

That is as far as facts can take it.

And just there — it begins.

For the force which rushes beneath the facts of life, caring nothing for conditions, not asking what one desires or what one thinks best, caring as little about a past as about a future — save its own future — the force which can laugh at man's institutions and batter over in one sweep what he likes to call his wisdom, was sweeping them on. And because it could get no other recognition it forced its way into the moments when he asked her for an eraser, when she wanted to know how to spell a word. He could not so much as ask her if she needed more copy-paper without seeming to be lavishing upon her all the love of all the ages.

And so the winter had worn on, and there was really nothing whatever to tell about it.

She was quiet this morning, and kept her head bent low over her work. For she had estimated the number of pages there were between W and Z. Soon they would be at Z; — and then? Then? Shyly she turned and looked at him; he too was bent over his work. When she came in she had said something about its being spring, and that there must be wild flowers in the woods. Since then he had not looked up.

Suddenly it came to her — tenderly, hotly, fearfully yet bravely, that it was she who must meet Z. She looked at him again, covertly. And she felt that she understood. It was the lines in his face made it clearest. Years, and things blacker, less easily surmounted than years — oh yes, that too she faced fearlessly — were piled in between. She knew now that it was she — not he — who could push them aside.

It was all very unmaidenly, of course; but maidenly is a word love and life and desire may crowd from the page.

Perhaps she would not have thrown it after all — the little note she had written — had it not been that when she went over for more copy-paper she stood for a minute looking out the window. Even on Dearborn Street the seductiveness of spring was in the air. Spring, and all that spring meant, filled her.

Because, way beyond the voice of Dr. Bunting she heard the songs of far-away birds, and because beneath the rumble of a printing press she could get the babble of a brook, because Z was near and life was strong, the woman vanquished the girl, and she threw this over to his desk:

"CHAFING-DISH, *n.* That out of which Miss Noah asks Mr. Webster to eat his Sunday night lunch tomorrow. All the other Miss Noahs are going to be away, and if Mr. Webster does not come, Miss

Noah will be all alone. Miss Noah does not like to be lonely."

She ate no lunch that day; she only drank a cup of coffee and walked around.

He did not come back that afternoon. It passed from one to two, from two to three, and then very slowly from three to four, and still he had not come.

He too was walking about. He had walked down to the lake and was standing there looking out across it.

Why not? — he was saying to himself — fiercely, doggedly. Over and over again — Well, *why not?*

A hundred nights, alone in his room, he had gone over it. Had not life used him hard enough to give him a little now? — longing had pleaded. And now there was a new voice —more prevailing voice — the voice of *her* happiness. His face softened to an almost maternal tenderness as he listened to that voice.

Too worn to fight any longer, he gave himself up to it, and sat there dreaming. They were dreams of joy rushing in after lonely years, dreams of stepping into the sunlight after long days in fog and cold, dreams of a woman before a fireplace — her arms about him, her cheer and her tenderness, her comradeship and her passion — all his to take! Ah, dreams which even thoughts must not touch — so wonderful and sacred they were.

A long time he sat there, dreaming dreams and

seeing visions. The force that rules the race was telling him that the one crime was the denial of happiness — his happiness, her happiness; and when at last his fight seemed but a puerile fight against forces worlds mightier than he, he rose, and as one who sees a great light, started back toward Dearborn Street.

On the way he began to cough. The coughing was violent, and he stepped into a doorway to gain breath. And after he had gone in there he realised that it was the building of Chicago's greatest newspaper.

He had been city editor of that paper once. Facts, the things he knew about himself, talked to him then. There was no answer.

It left him weak and dizzy and crazy for a drink. He walked on slowly, unsteadily, his white face set. For he had vowed that if it took the last nerve in his body there should be no more of that until after they had finished with Z. He knew himself too well to vow more. He was not even sure of that.

He did not turn in where he wanted to go; but resistance took the last bit of force that was in him. He was trembling like a sick man when he stepped into the elevator.

She was just leaving. She was in the little cloak room putting on her things. She was all alone in there.

He stepped in. He pushed the door shut, and

stood there leaning against it, looking at her, saying nothing.

"Oh — you are ill?" she gasped, and laid a frightened hand upon him.

The touch crazed him. All resistance gone, he swept her into his arms; he held her fiercely, and between sobs kissed her again and again. He could not let her go. He frightened her. He hurt her. And he did not care — he did not know.

Then he held her off and looked at her. And as he looked into her eyes, passion melted to tenderness. It was she now — not he; love — not hunger. Holding her face in his two hands, looking at her as if getting something to take away, his white lips murmured words too inarticulate for her to hear. And then again he put his arms around her — all differently. Reverently, sobbingly, he kissed her hair. And then he was gone.

He did not come out that Sunday afternoon, but Harold dropped in instead, and talked of some athletic affairs over at the university. She wondered why she did not go crazy in listening to him, and yet she could answer intelligently. It was queer — what one *could* do.

They had come at last to Z. There would be no more work upon the dictionary after that day. And it was raining — raining as in Chicago alone it knows how to rain.

They wrote no notes to each other now. It had

been different since that day. They made small effort to cover their raw souls with the mantle of commonplace words.

Both of them had tried to stay away that last day. But both were in their usual places.

The day wore on eventlessly. Those men with whom she had worked, the men of yesterday, who had been kind to her, came up at various times for little farewell chats. The man in the skull cap told her that she had done excellent work. She was surprised at the ease with which she could make decent reply, thinking again that it was queer — what one could do.

He was moving. She saw him lay some sheets of yellow paper on the desk in front. He had finished with his "take." There would not be another to give him. He would go now.

He came back to his desk. She could hear him putting away his things. And then for a long time there was no sound. She knew that he was just sitting there in his chair.

Then she heard him get up. She heard him push his chair up to the table, and then for a minute he stood there. She wanted to turn toward him; she wanted to say something — do something. But she had no power.

She saw him lay an envelope upon her desk. She heard him walking away. She knew, numbly, that his footsteps were not steady. She knew that he had stopped; she was sure that he was looking back. But still she had no power.

And then she heard him go.

Even then she went on with her work; she finished her "take" and laid down her pencil. It was finished now — and he had gone. Finished? — *Gone?* She was tearing open the envelope of the letter.

This was what she read:

"Little dictionary sprite, sunshine vender, and girl to be loved, if I were a free man I would say to you — Come, little one, and let us learn of love. Let us learn of it, not as one learns from dictionaries, but let us learn from the morning glow and the evening shades. But Miss Noah, maker of dictionaries and creeper into hearts, the bound must not call to the free. They might fittingly have used my name as one of the synonyms under that word Failure, but I trust not under Coward.

"And now, you funny little Miss Noah from the University of Chicago, don't I know that your heart is blazing forth the assurance that you don't *care* for any of those things—the world, people, common sense—that you want just love? They made a grand failure of you out at your university; they taught you philosophy and they taught you Greek, and they've left you just as much the woman as women were five thousand years ago. Oh, I know all about you—you little girl whose hair tried so hard to be red. Your soul touched mine as we sat there writing words — words — words, the very words in which men try to tell things, and can't — and I know all about what you would do. But you shall not do it. Dear little copy maker, would a man standing out on the end of a slippery plank have any right to cry to someone on the shore — 'Come out here on this plank with me?' If he loved the someone on the shore, would he not say instead — 'Don't get on this plank?' Me get off the plank — come with you to the shore — you are saying? But you see, dear, you only know slippery planks as viewed from the shore — God grant you may never know them any other way!

"It was you, was it not, who wrote our definition of happiness? Yes, I remember the day you did it. You were so interested; your cheeks grew so very red, and you pulled and pulled at your wavy hair. You said it was such an important definition. And so it is, Miss Noah, quite the most important of all. And on the page of life, Miss Noah, may happiness be written large and unblurred for you. It is because I cannot help you write it that I turn away. I want at least to leave the page unspoiled.

"I carry a picture of you. I shall carry it always. You are sitting before a fireplace, and I think of that fireplace as symbolising the warmth and care and tenderness and the safety that will surround you. And sometimes as you sit there let a thought of me come for just a minute, Miss Noah —

not long enough nor deep enough to bring you any pain. But only think — I brought him happiness after he believed all happiness had gone. He was so grateful for that light which came after he thought the darkness had settled down. It will light his way to the end.

"We've come to Z, and it's good-bye. There is one thing I can give you without hurting you,— the hope, the prayer, that life may be very, very good to you."

The sheets of paper fell from her hands. She sat staring out into Dearborn Street. She began to see. After all, he had not understood her. Perhaps men never understood women; certainly he had not understood her. What he did not know was that she was willing to *pay* for her happiness — *pay* — pay any price that might be exacted. And anyway — she had no choice. Strange that he could not see that! Strange that he could not see the irony and cruelty of bidding her good-bye and then telling her to be happy!

It simplified itself to such an extent that she grew very calm. It would be easy to find him, easy to make him see — for it was so very simple — and then. . . .

She turned in her copy. She said good-bye quietly, naturally, rode down in the lumbering old elevator and started out into the now drenching rain toward the elevated trains which would take her to the West Side; it was so fortunate that she had heard him telling one day where he lived.

When she reached the station she saw that more people were coming down the stairs than were going up. They were saying things about the trains, but she did not heed them. But at the top of the stairs a man in uniform said: "Blockade, Miss. You'll have to take the surface cars."

She was sorry, for it would delay her, and there was not a minute to lose. She was dismayed, upon reaching the surface cars, to find she could not get near them; the rain, the blockade on the "L," had caused a great crowd to congregate there. She waited a long time, getting more and more wet, but it was impossible to get near the cars. She thought of a cab, but could see none, they too having all been pressed into service.

She determined, desperately, to start and walk. Soon she would surely get either a cab or a car. And so she started, staunchly, though she was wet through now, and trembling with cold and nervousness.

As she hurried through the driving rain she faced things fearlessly. Oh yes, she understood — everything. But if he were not well — should he not have her with him? If he had that thing to fight, did he not need her help? What did men think women were like? Did he think she was one to sit down and reason out what would be advantageous?

Better a little while with him on a slippery plank than forever safe and desolate upon the shore!

She never questioned her going; were not life and love too great to be lost through that which could be so easily put right?

The buildings were reeling, the streets moving up and down — that awful rain, she thought, was making her dizzy. Labouriously she walked on — more slowly, less steadily, a pain in her side, that awful reeling in her head.

Carriages returning to the city were passing her, but she had not strength to call to them, and it seemed if she walked to the curbing she would fall. She was not thinking so clearly now. The thing which took all of her force was the lifting of her feet and the putting them down in the right place. Her throat seemed to be closing up — and her side — and her head. . . .

Someone had her by the arm. Then someone was speaking her name; speaking it in surprise — consternation — alarm.

It was Harold.

It was all vague then. She knew that she was in a carriage, and that Harold was talking to her kindly. "You're taking me there?" she murmured.

"Yes — yes, Edna, everything's all right," he replied soothingly.

"Everything's all right," she repeated, in a whisper, and leaned her head back against the cushions.

They stopped after a while, and Harold was standing at the open door of the cab with something steaming hot which he told her to drink. "You need it," he said decisively, and thinking it would help her to tell it, she drank it down.

The world was a little more defined after that, and she saw things which puzzled her. "Why, it looks like the city," she whispered, her throat too sore now to speak aloud.

"Why sure," he replied banteringly; "don't you know we have to go through the city to get out to the South Side?"

"Oh, but you see," she cried, holding her throat, "but you see, it's the *other* way!"

"Not to-night," he insisted; "the place for you to-night is home. I'm taking you where you belong."

She reached over wildly, trying to open the door, but he held her back; she began to cry, and he talked to her, gently but unbendingly. "But you don't *understand!*" she whispered, passionately. "I've *got* to go!"

"Not to-night," he said again, and something in the way he said it made her finally huddle back in the corner of the carriage.

Block after block, mile after mile, they rode on in silence. She felt overpowered. And with submission she knew that it was Z. For the whole city was piled in between. Great buildings were in between, and thousands of men running to and fro on the streets; man, and all man had builded up, were in between. And then Harold — Harold who had always seemed to count for so little, had come and taken her away.

Dully, wretchedly — knowing that her heart would ache far worse to-morrow than it did to-night — she wondered about things. Did things like rain and street-cars and wet feet and a sore throat determine life? Was it that way with other people, too? Did other people have barriers — whole cities full of them — piled in between? And then did the Harolds come and take them where they said they belonged? Were there not *some* people strong enough to go where they wanted to go?

VI

THE MAN OF FLESH AND BLOOD

THE elements without were not in harmony with the spirit which it was desired should be engendered within. By music, by gay decorations, by speeches from prominent men, the board in charge of the boys' reformatory was striving to throw about this dedication of the new building an atmosphere of cheerfulness and good-will — an atmosphere vibrant with the kindness and generosity which emanated from the State, and the thankfulness and loyalty which it was felt should emanate from the boys.

Outside the world was sobbing. Some young trees which had been planted along the driveway of the reformatory grounds, and which were expected to grow up in the way they should go, were rocking back and forth in passionate insurrection. Fallen leaves were being spit viciously through the air. It was a sullen-looking landscape which Philip Grayson, he who was to be the last speaker of the afternoon, saw stretching itself down the hill, across the little valley, and up another little hill of that rolling prairie state. In his ears was the death wail of the summer. It seemed the spirit of out-of-doors was sending itself up in mournful, hopeless cries.

The speaker who had been delivering himself of pedantic encouragement about the open arms with which the world stood ready to receive the most degraded one, would that degraded one but come to the world in proper spirit, sat down amid perfunctory applause led by the officers and attendants of the institution, and the boys rose to sing. The brightening of their faces told that their work as performers was more to their liking than their position as auditors. They threw back their heads and waited with well-disciplined eagerness for the signal to begin. Then, with the strength and native music there are in some three hundred boys' throats, there rolled out the words of the song of the State.

There were lips which opened only because they must, but as a whole they sang with the same heartiness, the same joy in singing, that he had heard a crowd of public-school boys put into the song only the week before. When the last word had died away it seemed to Philip Grayson that the sigh of the world without was giving voice to the sigh of the world within as the well-behaved crowd of boys sat down to resume their duties as auditors.

And then one of the most important of the professors from the State University was telling them about the kindness of the State: the State had provided for them this beautiful home; it gave them comfortable clothing and nutritious food; it furnished that fine gymnasium in which to train their bodies, books and teachers to train their minds; it provided those fitted to train their souls, to work against the unfortunate tendencies — the professor stumbled a little there — which had led to their coming. The State gave liberally, gladly, and in return it asked but one thing: that they come out into the world and make useful, upright citizens, citizens of which any State might be proud. Was that asking too much? the professor from the State University was saying.

The sobbing of the world without was growing more intense. Many pairs of eyes from among the auditors were straying out to where the summer lay dying. Did they know — those boys whom the State classed as unfortunates — that out of this death there would come again life? Or did they see but the darkness — the decay — of to-day?

The professor from the State University was putting the case very fairly. There were no flaws — seemingly — to be picked in his logic. The State had been kind; the boys were obligated to good citizenship. But the coldness! — comfortlessness! — of it all. The open arms of the world! — how mocking in its abstractness. What did it mean? Did it mean that they — the men who uttered the phrase so easily — would be willing to give these boys aid, friendship when they came out into the world? What would they say, those boys whose ears were filled with high-sounding, non-committal phrases, if some man were to stand before them and say, "And so, fellows, when you get away from this place, and are ready to get your start in the world, just come around to my office and I'll help you get a job?" At thought of it there came from Philip Grayson a queer, partly audible laugh, which caused those nearest him to look his way in surprise.

But he was all unconscious of their looks of inquiry, absorbed in the thoughts that crowded upon him. How far away the world — his kind of people — must seem to these boys of the State Reform School. The speeches they had heard, the training that had been given them, had taught them — unconsciously perhaps, but surely — to divide the world into two great classes: the lucky and the unlucky, those who made speeches and those who must listen, the so-called good and the so-called bad; perhaps — he smiled a little at his own cynicism — those who were caught and those who were not.

There came to him these words of a poet of whom he used to be fond:

In men whom men pronounce as ill,
I find so much of goodness still;
In men whom men pronounce divine,
  I find so much of sin and blot;
I hesitate to draw the line
  Between the two, when God has not.

When God has not! He turned and looked out

at the sullen sky, returning — as most men do at times — to that conception of his childhood that somewhere beyond the clouds was God. God! Did God care for the boys of the State Reformatory? Was that poet of the western mountains right when he said that God was not a drawer of lines, but a seer of the good that was in the so-called bad, and of the bad in the so-called good, and a lover of them both?

If that was God, it was not the God the boys of the reformatory had been taught to know. They had been told that God would forgive the wicked, but it had been made clear to them — if not in words, in implications — that it was they who were the wicked. And the so-called godly men, men of such exemplary character as had been chosen to address them that afternoon, had so much of the spirit of God that they, too, were willing to forgive, be tolerant, and — he looked out at the bending trees with a smile — disburse generalities about the open arms of the world.

What would they think — those three hundred speech-tired boys — if some man who had been held before them as exemplary were to rise and lay bare his own life — its weaknesses, its faults, perhaps its crimes — and tell them there was weakness and there was strength in every human being, and that the world-old struggle of life was to overcome one's weakness with one's strength.

The idea took strange hold on him. It seemed the method of the world — at any rate it had been the method of that afternoon — for the men who stood before their fellows with clean hands to plant themselves on the far side of a chasm of conventions, or narrow self-esteem, or easily won virtue, and cry to those beings who struggled on the other side of that chasm — to those human beings whose souls had never gone to school: "Look at us! Our hands are clean, our hearts are pure. See how beautiful it is to be good! Come ye, poor sinners, and be good also." And the poor sinners, the untaught, birthmarked human souls, would look over at the self-acclaimed goodness they could see far across the chasm, and even though attracted to it (which, he grimly reflected, would not seem likely) the thing that was left with them was a sense of the width of the chasm.

He had a sense of needless waste, of unnecessary blight. He looked down at those three hundred faces and it was as if looking at human waste; and it was human stupidity, human complacency and cowardice kept those human beings human drift.

With what a smug self-satisfaction — under the mask of benevolence — the speakers of that afternoon had flaunted their virtue — their position! How condescendingly they had spoken of the home which we, the good, prepare for you, the bad, and what namby-pambyness there was, after all, in that sentiment which all of them had voiced — and now you must pay us back by being good!

Oh for a man of flesh and blood to stand up and tell how he himself had failed and suffered! For a man who could bridge that chasm with strong, broad, human understanding and human sympathies — a man who would stand among them pulse-beat to pulse-beat and cry out, "I know! I understand! I fought it and I'll help you fight it too!"

The sound of his own name broke the spell that was upon him. He looked to the centre of the stage and saw that the professor from the State University had seated himself and that the superintendent of the institution was occupying the place of the speaker. And the superintendent was saying:

"We may esteem ourselves especially fortunate in having him with us this afternoon. He is one of the great men of the State, one of the men who by high living, by integrity and industry, has raised himself to a position of great honour among his fellow men. A great party — may I say the greatest of all parties?— has shown its unbounded confidence in him by giving him the nomination for the governorship of the State. No man in the State is held in higher esteem to-day than he. And so it is with special pleasure that I introduce to you that man of the future — Philip Grayson."

The superintendent sat down then, and he himself — Philip Grayson — was standing in the place where the other speakers had stood. It was with a rush which almost swept away his outward show of calm that it came to him that he — candidate for the governorship — was well fitted to be that man of flesh and blood for whom he had sighed. That he himself was within grasp of an opportunity to get beneath the jackets and into the very hearts and souls of those boys, and make them feel that a man of sins and virtues, of weaknesses and strength, a man who had had much to conquer, and for whom the fight would never be finally won, was standing before them stripped of his coat of conventions and platitudes, and in nakedness of soul and sincerity of heart was talking to them as a man who understood.

Almost with the inception of the idea was born the consciousness of what it might cost. And as in answer to the silent, blunt question, Is it worth it? there looked up at him three hundred pairs of eyes — eyes behind which there was good as well as bad, eyes which had burned with the fatal rush of passion, and had burned, too, with the hot tears of remorse — eyes which had opened on a hostile world.

And then the eyes of Philip Grayson could not see the eyes which were before him, and he put up his hand to break the mist — little caring what the men upon the platform would think of him, little thinking what effect the words which were crowding into his heart would have upon his candidacy. But one thing was vital to him now: to bring upon that ugly chasm the levelling forces of a common humanity, and to make those boys who were of his clay feel that a being who had fallen and risen again, a fellow being for whom life would always mean a falling and a rising again, was standing before them, and — not as the embodiment of a distant goodness, not as a pattern, but as one among them, verily as man to man — was telling them a few things which his own life had taught him were true.

It was his very consecration which made it hard to begin. He was fearful of estranging them in the beginning, of putting between them and him that very thing he was determined there should not be.

"I have a strange feeling," he said, with a winning little smile, "that if I were to open my heart to-day, just open it clear up the way I'd like to if I could, that you boys would look into it, and then jump back in a scared kind of way and cry, 'Why — that's me!' You would be a little surprised — wouldn't you? — if you could look back and see the kind of boy I was, and find I was much the kind of boy you are?

"Do you know what I think? I think hypocrisy is the worst thing in the world. I think it's worse than stealing, or lying, or any of the other bad things you can name. And do you know where I think lots of the hypocrisy comes from? I think it comes from the so-called self-made men — from the real good men, the men who say 'I haven't got one bad thing charged up to my account.'

"Now the men out campaigning for me call me a self-made man. Your superintendent just now spoke of my integrity, of the confidence reposed in me, and all that. But do you know what is the honest truth? If I am any kind of a man worth mentioning, if I am deserving of any honour, any confidence, it is not because I was born with my heart filled with good and beautiful things, for I was not. It is because I was born with much in my heart that we call the bad, and because, after that bad had grown stronger and stronger through the years it was unchecked, and after it had brought me the great shock, the great sorrow of my life, I began then, when older than you boys are now, to see a little of that great truth which you can put briefly in these words: 'There is good and there is bad in every human heart, and it is the struggle of life to conquer the bad with the good.' What I am trying to say is, that if I am worthy any one's confidence to-day, it is because, having seen that truth, I have been able, through never ceasing trying, through slow conquering, to crowd out some of the bad and make room for a little of the good.

"You see," he went on, three hundred pairs of eyes hard upon him now, "some of us are born to a harder struggle than others. There are people who would object to my saying that to you, even if I believed it. They would say you would make the fact of being born with much against which to struggle an excuse for being bad. But look here a minute; if you were born with a body not as strong as other boys' bodies, if you couldn't run as far, or jump as high, you wouldn't be eternally saying, 'I can't be expected to do much; I wasn't born right.' Not a bit of it! You'd make it your business to get as strong as you could, and you wouldn't make any parade of the fact that you weren't as strong as you should be. We don't like people who whine, whether it's about weak bodies or weak souls.

"I've been sitting here this afternoon wondering what to say to you boys. I had intended telling some funny stories about things which happened to me when I was a boy. But for some reason a serious mood has come over me, and I don't feel just like those stories now. I haven't been thinking of the funny side of life in the last half-hour. I've been thinking of how much suffering I've endured since the days when I, too, was a boy."

He paused then; and when he went on his voice tested to the utmost the silence of the room: "There is lots of sorrow in this old world. Maybe I'm on the wrong track, but as I see it to-day human beings are making a much harder thing of their existence than there is any need of. There are millions and millions of them, and year after year, generation after generation, they fight over the same old battles, live through the same old sorrows. Doesn't it seem all wrong that after the battle has been fought a million times it can't be made a little easier for those who still have it before them?

"If a farmer had gone over a bad road, and the next day saw another farmer about to start over the same road, wouldn't he send him back? Doesn't it seem too bad that in things which concern one's whole life people can't be as decent as they are about things which involve only an inconvenience? Doesn't it seem that when we human beings have so much in common we might stand together a little better? I'll tell you what's the matter. Most of the people of this world are coated round and round with self-esteem, and they're afraid to admit any understanding of the things which aren't good. Suppose the farmer had thought it a disgrace to admit he had been over that road, and so had said: 'From what I have read in books, and from what I have learned in a general way, I fancy that road isn't good.' Would the other farmer have gone back? I rather think he would have said he'd take his chances. But you see the farmer said he *knew;* and how did he know? Why, because he'd been over the road himself."

As he paused again, looking at them, he saw it all with a clarifying simplicity. He himself knew life for a fine and beautiful thing. He had won for himself some of the satisfactions of understanding, certain rare delights of the open spirit. He wanted to free the spirits of these boys to whom he talked; wanted to show them that spirits could free themselves, indicate to them that self-control and self-development carried one to pleasures which sordid self-indulgences had no power to bestow. It was a question of getting the most from life. It was a matter of happiness.

It was thus he began, slowly, the telling of his life's story:

"I was born with strange, wild passions in my heart. I don't know where they came from; I only know they were there. I resented authority. If someone who had a right to dictate to me said, 'Philip, do this,' then Philip would immediately begin to think how much he would rather do the other thing. And," he smiled a little, and some of the boys smiled with him in anticipation, "it was the other thing which Philip usually did.

"I didn't go to a reform school, for the very good reason that there wasn't any in the State where I lived." Some of the boys smiled again, and he could hear the nervous coughing of one of the party managers sitting close to him. "I was what you would call a very bad boy. I didn't mind any one. I was defiant — insolent. I did bad things just because I knew they were bad, and — and I took a great deal of satisfaction out of it."

The sighing of the world without was the only

sound which vibrated through the room. "I say," he went on, "that I got a form of satisfaction from it. I did not say I got happiness; there is a vast difference between a kind of momentary satisfaction and that thing — that most precious of all things — which we call happiness. Indeed, I was very far from happy. I had hours when I was so morose and miserable that I hated the whole world. And do you know what I thought? I thought there was no one in all the world who had the same kind of things surging up in his heart that I did. I thought there was no one else with whom it was as easy to be bad, or as hard to be good. I thought that no one understood. I thought that I was all alone.

"Did you ever feel like that? Did you ever feel that no one else knew anything about such feelings as you had? Did you ever feel that here was you, and there was the rest of the world, and that the rest of the world didn't know anything about you, and was just generally down on you? Now that's the very thing I want to talk away from you to-day. You're not the only one. We're all made of the same kind of stuff, and there's none of us made of stuff that's flawless. We all have a fight; some an easy one, and some a big one, and if you have formed the idea that there is a kind of dividing-line in the world, and that on the one side is the good, and on the other side the bad, why, all I can say is that you have a wrong notion of things.

"Well, I grew up to be a man, and because I hadn't fought against any of the stormy things in my heart they kept growing stronger and stronger. I did lots of wild, ugly things, things of which I am bitterly ashamed. I went to another place, and I fell in with the kind of fellows you can imagine I felt at home with. I had been told when I was a boy that it was wrong to drink and gamble. I think that was the chief reason I took to drink and gambling."

There was another cough, more pronounced this time, from the party manager, and the superintendent was twisting uneasily in his seat. It was the strangest speech that had ever been delivered at the boys' reformatory. The boys were leaning forward — self-forgetful, intent. "One night I was playing cards with a crowd of my friends, and one of the men, the best friend I had, said something that made me mad. There was a revolver right there which one of the men had been showing us. Some kind of a demon got hold of me, and without so much as a thought I picked up that revolver and fired at my friend."

The party manager gave way to an exclamation of horror, and the superintendent half rose from his seat. But before any one could say a word Philip Grayson continued, looking at the half-frightened faces before him: "I suppose you wonder why I am not in the penitentiary. I had been drinking, and

I missed my aim; and I was with friends, and it was hushed up."

He rested his hand upon the table, and looked out at the sullen landscape. His voice was not steady as he went on: "It's not an easy thing to talk about, boys. I never talked about it to any one before in all my life. I'm not telling it now just to entertain you or to create a sensation. I'm telling it," his voice grew tense in its earnestness, "because I believe that this world could be made a better and a sweeter place if those who have lived and suffered would not be afraid to reach out their hands and cry: 'I know that road — it's bad! I steered off to a better place, and I'll help you steer off, too.'"

There was not one of the three hundred pairs of eyes but was riveted upon the speaker's colourless face. The masks of sullenness and defiance had fallen from them. They were listening now — not because they must, but because into their hungry and thirsty souls was being poured the very sustenance for which — unknowingly — they had yearned.

"We sometimes hear people say," resumed the candidate for Governor, "that they have lived through hell. If by that they mean they've lived through the deepest torments the human heart can know, then I can say that I, too, have lived through hell. What I suffered after I went home that night no one in this world will ever know. Words couldn't tell it; it's not the kind of thing words can come anywhere near. My whole life spread itself out before me; it was not a pleasant thing to look at. But at last, boys, out of the depths of my darkness, I began to get a little light. I began to get some understanding of the battle which it falls to the lot of some of us human beings to wage. There was good in me, you see, or I wouldn't have cared like that, and it came to me then, all alone that terrible night, that it is the good which lies buried away somewhere in our hearts must fight out the bad. And so — all alone, boys — I began the battle of trying to get command of my own life. And do you know — this is the truth — it was with the beginning of that battle I got my first taste of happiness. There is no finer feeling in this world than the sense of coming into mastery of one's self. It is like opening a door that has shut you in. Oh, you don't do it all in a minute. This is no miracle I'm talking about. It's a fight. But it's a fight that can be won. It's a fight that's gloriously worth the winning. I'm not saying to you, 'Be good and you'll succeed.' Maybe you won't succeed. Life as we've arranged it for ourselves makes success a pretty tough proposition. But that doesn't alter the fact that it pays to be a decent sort. You and I know about how much happiness there is in the other kind of thing. And there *is* happiness in feeling you're doing what you can to develop what's in you. Success or failure, it brings a sense of having done your part,— that bully sense of having put up the best fight you could."

He leaned upon the table then, as though very weary. "I don't know, I am sure, what the people of my State will think of all this. Perhaps they won't want a man for their Governor who once tried to kill another man. But," he looked around at them with that smile of his which got straight to men's hearts, "there's only one of me, and there are three hundred of you, and how do I know but that in telling you of that stretch of bad road ahead I've made a dozen Governors this very afternoon!"

He looked from row to row of them, trying to think of some last word which would leave them with a sense of his sincerity. What he did say was: "And so, boys, when you get away from here, and go out into the world to get your start, if you find the arms of that world aren't quite as wide open as you were told they would be, if there seems no place where you can get a hold, and you are saying to yourself, 'It's no use — I'll not try,' before you give up just remember there was one man who said he knew all about it, and give that one man a chance to show he meant what he said. So look me up, if luck goes all against you, and maybe I can give you a little lift." He took a backward step, as though to resume his seat, and then he said, with a dry little smile which took any suggestion of heroics from what had gone before, "If I'm not at the State-house, you'll find my name in the directory of the city where your programme tells you I live."

He sat down, and for a moment there was silence. Then, full-souled, heart-given, came the applause. It was not led by the attendants this time; it was the attendants who rose at last to stop it. And when the clapping of the hands had ceased, many of those hands were raised to eyes which had long been dry.

The exercises were drawn to a speedy close, and he found the party manager standing by his side. "It was very grand," he sneered, "very high-sounding and heroic, but I suppose you know," jerking his hand angrily toward a table where a reporter for the leading paper of the opposition was writing, "that you've given them the winning card."

As he replied, in far-off tone, "I hope so," the candidate for Governor was looking, not at the reporter who was sending out a new cry for the opposition, but into those faces aglow with the light of new understanding and new-born hopes. He stood there watching them filing out into the corridor, craning their necks to throw him a last look, and as he turned then and looked from the window it was to see that the storm had sobbed itself away, and that along the driveway of the reformatory grounds the young trees — unbroken and unhurt — were rearing their heads in the way they should go.

VII

HOW THE PRINCE SAW AMERICA

THEY began work at seven-thirty, and at ten minutes past eight every hammer stopped. In the Senate Chamber and in the House, on the stairways and in the corridors, in every office from the Governor's to the custodian's they laid down their implements and rose to their feet. A long whistle had sounded through the building. There was magic in its note.

"What's the matter with you fellows?" asked the attorney-general, swinging around in his chair.

"Strike," declared one of the men, with becoming brevity.

"Strike of what?"

"Carpet-Tackers' Union Number One," replied the man, kindly gathering up a few tacks.

"Never heard of it."

"Organised last night," said the carpet-tacker, putting on his coat.

"Well I'll —" he paused expressively, then inquired: "What's your game?"

"Well, you see, boss, this executive council that runs the State-house has refused our demands."

"What are your demands?"

"Double pay."

"Double pay! Now how do you figure it out that you ought to have double pay?"

"Rush work. You see we were under oath, or pretty near that, to get every carpet in the State-house down by four o'clock this afternoon. Now you know yourself that rush work is hard on the nerves. Did you ever get rush work done at a laundry and not pay more for it? We was anxious as anybody to get the Capitol in shape for the big show this afternoon. But there's reason in all things."

"Yes," agreed his auditor, "there is."

The man looked at him a little doubtfully. "Our president — we elected Johnny McGuire president last night — went to the Governor this morning with our demands."

The Governor's fellow official smiled — he knew the Governor pretty well. "And he turned you down?"

The striker nodded. "But there's an election next fall; maybe the turning down will be turned around."

"Maybe so — you never can tell. I don't know just what power Carpet-Tackers' Union Number One will wield, but the Governor's pretty solid, you know, with Labour as a whole."

That was true, and went home. The striker rubbed his foot uncertainly across the floor, and took courage from its splinters. "Well, there's one thing sure. When Prince Ludwig and his train load of big guns show up at four o'clock this afternoon they'll find bare floors, and pretty bum bare floors, on deck at this place."

The attorney-general rubbed his own foot across the splintered, miserable boards. "They are pretty bum," he reflected. "I wonder," he added, as the man was half-way out of the door, "what Prince Ludwig will think of the American working-man when he arrives this afternoon?"

"Just about as much," retorted the not-to-be-downed carpet-tacker, "as he does about American generosity. And he may think a few things," he added weightily, "about American independence."

"Oh, he's sure to do that," agreed the attorney-general.

He joined the crowd in the corridor. They were swarming out from all the offices, all talking of the one thing. "It was a straight case of hold-up," declared the Governor's secretary. "They supposed they had us on the hip. They were getting extra money as it was, but you see they just figured it out we'd pay anything rather than have these wretched floors for the reception this afternoon. They thought the Governor would argue the question, and then give in, or, at any rate, compromise. They never intended for one minute that the Prince should find bare floors here. And I rather think," he concluded, " that they feel a little done up about it themselves."

" What's the situation? " asked a stranger within the gates.

" It's like this," a newspaper reporter told him; " about a month ago there was a fire here and the walls and carpets were pretty well knocked out with smoke and water. The carpets were mean old things anyway, so they voted new ones. And I want to tell you " — he swelled with pride — " that the new ones are beauties. The place'll look great when we get 'em down. Well, you know Prince Ludwig and his crowd cross the State on their way to the coast, and of course they were invited to stop. Last week Billy Patton — he's running the whole show — declined the invitation on account of lack of time, and then yesterday comes a telegram saying the Prince himself insisted on stopping. You know he's keen about Indian dope — and we've got Indian traditions to burn. So Mr. Bill Patton had to make over his schedule to please the Prince, and of course we were all pretty tickled about it, for more reasons than one. The telegram didn't come until five o'clock yesterday afternoon, but you know what a hummer the Governor is when he gets a start. He made up his mind this building should be put in shape within twenty-four hours. They engaged a whole lot of fellows to work on the carpets to-day. Then what did they do but get together last night —

well, you know the rest. Pretty bum-looking old shack just now, isn't it?" and the reporter looked around ruefully.

It was approaching the hour for the legislature to convene, and the members who were beginning to saunter in swelled the crowd — and the indignation — in the rotunda.

The Governor, meanwhile, had been trying to get other men, but Carpet-Tackers' Union Number One had looked well to that. The biggest furniture dealer in the city was afraid of the plumbers. "Pipes burst last night," he said, "and they may not do a thing for us if we get mixed up in this. Sorry — but I can't let my customers get pneumonia."

Another furniture man was afraid of the teamsters. For one reason or another no one was disposed to respond to the Macedonian cry, and when the Governor at last gave it up and walked out into the rotunda he was about as disturbed as he permitted himself to get. "It's the idea of lying down," he said. "I'd do anything — anything! — if I could only think what to do."

A popular young member of the House overheard the remark. "By George, Governor," he burst forth, after a minute's deep study — "say — by Jove, I say, let's do it ourselves!"

They all laughed, but the Governor's laugh stopped suddenly, and he looked hard at the young man.

"Why not?" the young legislator went on. "It's a big job, but there are a lot of us. We've all put down carpets at home; what are we afraid to tackle it here for?"

Again the others laughed, but the Governor did not. "Say, Weston," he said, "I'd give a lot — I tell you I'd give a lot — if we just could!"

"Leave it to me!" — and he was lost in the crowd.

The Governor's eyes followed him. He had always liked Harry Weston. He was the very sort to inspire people to do things. The Governor smiled knowingly as he noted the men Weston was approaching, and his different manner with the various ones. And then he had mounted a few steps of the stairway, and was standing there facing the crowd.

"Now look here," he began, after silence had been obtained, "this isn't a very formal meeting, but it's a mighty important one. It's a clear case of Carpet-Tackers' Union against the State. What I want to know is — Is the State going to lie down?"

There were loud cries of "No!" — "Well, I should say not!"

"Well, then, see here. The Governor's tried for other men and can't get them. Now the next thing I want to know is — What's the matter with us?"

They didn't get it for a minute, and then everybody laughed.

"It's no joke! You've all put down carpets at home; what's the use of pretending you don't know how to do it? Oh yes — I know, bigger building, and all that, but there are more of us, and the principle of carpet-tacking is the same, big building or little one. Now my scheme is this — Every fellow his own carpet-tacker! The Governor's office puts down the Governor's carpet; the Secretary's office puts down the Secretary's carpet; the Senate puts down the Senate carpet — and we'll look after our little patch in the House!"

"But you've got more fellows than anybody else," cried a member of the Senate.

"Right you are, and we'll have an over-flow meeting in the corridors and stairways. The House, as usual, stands ready to do her part," — that brought a laugh for the Senators, and from them.

"Now get it out of your heads this is a joke. The carpets are here; the building is full of able-bodied men; the Prince is coming at four — by his own request, and the proposition is just this: Are we going to receive him in a barn or in a palace? Let's hear what Senator Arnold thinks about it."

That was a good way of getting away from the idea of its being a joke. Senator Arnold was past seventy. Slowly he extended his right arm and tested his muscle. "Not very much," he said, "but enough to drive a tack or two." That brought applause and they drew closer together, and the atmosphere warmed perceptibly. "I've fought for the State in more ways than one," — Senator Arnold was a distinguished veteran of the Civil War —" and if I can serve her now by tacking down carpets, then it's tacking down carpets I'm ready to go at. Just count on me for what little I'm worth."

Someone started the cry for the Governor. "Prince Ludwig is being entertained all over the country in the most lavish manner," he began, with his characteristic directness in stating a situation. "By his own request he is to visit our Capitol this afternoon. I must say that I, for one, want to be in shape for him. I don't like to tell him that we had a labour complication and couldn't get the carpets down. Speaking for myself, it is a great pleasure to inform you that the carpet in the Governor's office will be in proper shape by four o'clock this afternoon."

That settled it. Finally Harry Weston made himself heard sufficiently to suggest that when the House and Senate met at nine o'clock motions to adjourn be entertained. "And as to the rest of you fellows," he cried, "I don't see what's to hinder your getting busy right now!"

There were Republicans and there were Democrats; there were friends and there were enemies; there were good, bad and — no, there were no indifferent. An unprecedented harmony of thought, a millennium-like unity of action was born out of that sturdy cry — Every man his own carpet-tacker! The Secretary of State always claimed that he drove the first tack, but during the remainder of his life the Superintendent of Public Instruction also contended hotly for that honour. The rivalry as to who would do the best job, and get it done most quickly, became intense. Early in the day Harry Weston made the rounds of the building and announced a fine of one-hundred dollars for every wrinkle. There were pounded fingers and there were broken backs, but slowly, steadily and good-naturedly the State-house carpet was going down. It was a good deal bigger job than they had anticipated, but that only added zest to the undertaking. The news of how the State officials were employing themselves had spread throughout the city, and guards were stationed at every door to keep out people whose presence would work more harm than good. All assistance from women was courteously refused. "This is solemn business," said the Governor, in response to a telephone from some of the fair sex, "and the introduction of the feminine element might throw about it a social atmosphere which would result in loss of time. And then some of the boys might feel called upon to put on their collars and coats."

Stretch — stretch — stretch, and tack — tack — tack, all morning long it went on, for the State-house was large — oh, very large. There should have been a Boswell there to get the good things, for the novelty of the situation inspired wit even in minds where wit had never glowed before. Choice bits which at other times would fairly have gone on official record were now passed almost unnoticed, so great was the surfeit. Instead of men going out to lunch, lunch came in to them. Bridget Haggerty, who by reason of her long connection with the boarding-house across the street was a sort of unofficial official of the State, came over and made the coffee and sandwiches, all the while calling down blessings on the head of every mother's son of them, and announcing in loud, firm tones that while all five of her boys belonged to the union she'd be after tellin' them what she thought of this day's work!

It was a United States Senator who did the awful trick, and, to be fair, the Senator did not think of it as an awful trick at all. He came over there in the middle of the morning to see the Governor, and in a few hurried words — it was no day for conversation — was told what was going on. It was while standing out in the corridor watching the perspiring dignitaries that the idea of his duty came to him, and one reason he was sure he was right was the way in which it came to him in the light of a duty. Here was America in undress uniform! Here was — not a thing arranged for show, but absolutely the thing itself! Prince Ludwig had come with a sincere desire to see America. Every one knew that he was not seeing it at all. He would go back with memories of bands and flags and people all dressed up standing before him making polite speeches. But would he carry back one small whiff of the spirit of the country? Again Senator Bruner looked about him. The Speaker of the House was just beginning laying the stair carpet; a judge of the Supreme Court was contending hotly for a better hammer. "It's an insult to expect any decent man to drive tacks with a hammer like this," he was saying. Here were men — real, live men, men with individuality, spirit. When the Prince had come so far, wasn't it too bad that he should not see anything but uniforms and cut glass and dress suits and other externals and non-essentials? Senator Bruner was a kind man; he was a good fellow; he was hospitable — patriotic. He decided now in favour of the Prince.

He had to hurry about it, for it was almost twelve then. One of the vice-presidents of the road lived there, and he was taken into confidence, and proved an able and eager ally. They located the special train bearing the Prince and ordered it stopped at the next station. The stop was made that Senator Patton might receive a long telegram from Senator Bruner. "I figure it like this," the Senator told the vice-president. "They get to Boden at a quarter of one and were going to stop there an hour. Then they were going to stop a little while at Creyville. I've told Patton the situation, and that if he wants to do the right thing by the Prince he'll cut out those stops and rush right through here. That will bring him in — well, they could make it at a quarter of two. I've told him I'd square it with Boden and Creyville. Oh, he'll do it all right."

And even as he said so came the reply from Patton: "Too good to miss. Will rush through. Arrive before two. Have carriage at Water Street."

"That's great!" cried the Senator. "Trust Billy Patton for falling in with a good thing. And he's right about missing the station crowd. Patton can always go you one better," he admitted, grinningly.

They had luncheon together, and they were a good deal more like sophomores in college than like a United States Senator and a big railroad man. "You don't think there's any danger of their getting through too soon?" McVeigh kept asking, anxiously.

"Not a bit," the Senator assured him. "They can't possibly make it before three. We'll come in just in time for the final skirmish. It's going to be a jolly rush at the last."

They laid their plans with skill worthy of their training. The State library building was across from the Capitol, and they were connected by tunnel. "I never saw before," said the Senator, "what that tunnel was for, but I see now what a great thing it is. We'll get him in at the west door of the library — we can drive right up to it, you know, and then we walk him through the tunnel. That's a stone floor" — the Senator was chuckling with every sentence — "so I guess they won't be carpeting it. There's a little stairway running up from the tunnel — and say, we must telephone over and arrange about those keys. There'll be a good deal of climbing, but the Prince is a good fellow, and won't mind. It wouldn't be safe to try the elevator, for Harry Weston would be in it taking somebody a bundle of tacks. The third floor is nothing but store rooms; we'll not be disturbed up there, and we can look right down the rotunda and see the whole show. Of course we'll be discovered in time; some one is sure to look up and see us, but we'll fix it so they won't see us before we've had our fun, and it strikes me, McVeigh, that for two old fellows like you and me we've put the thing through in pretty neat shape."

It was a very small and unpretentious party which stepped from the special at Water Street a little before two. The Prince was wearing a long coat and an automobile cap and did not suggest anything at all formidable or unusual. "You've saved the country," Senator Patton whispered in an aside. "He was getting bored. Never saw a fellow jolly up so in my life. Guess he was just spoiling for some fun.

Said it would be really worth while to see somebody who wasn't looking for him."

Senator Bruner beamed. "That's just the point. He's caught my idea exactly."

It went without a hitch. "I feel," said the Prince, as they were hurrying him through the tunnel, "that I am a little boy who has run away from school. Only I have a terrible fear that at any minute some band may begin to play, and somebody may think of making a speech."

They gave this son of a royal house a seat on a dry-goods box, so placed that he could command a good view, and yet be fairly secure. The final skirmish was on in earnest. Two State Senators — coatless, tieless, collarless, their faces dirty, their hair rumpled, were finishing the stair carpet. The chairman of the appropriations committee in the House was doing the stretching in a still uncarpeted bit of the corridor, and a member who had recently denounced the appropriations committee as a disgrace to the State was presiding at the hammer. They were doing most exquisitely harmonious team work. A railroad and anti-railroad member who fought every time they came within speaking distance of one another were now in an earnest and very chummy conference relative to a large wrinkle which had just been discovered on the first landing. Many men were standing around holding their backs, and many others were deeply absorbed in nursing their fingers. The doors of the offices were all open, and there was a general hauling in of furniture and hanging of pictures. Clumsy but well-meaning fingers were doing their best with "finishing touches." The Prince grew so excited about it all that they had to keep urging him not to take too many chances of being seen.

"And I'll tell you," Senator Bruner was saying, "it isn't only because I knew it would be funny that I wanted you to see it; but — well, you see America isn't the real America when she has on her best clothes and is trying to show off. You haven't seen anybody who hasn't prepared for your coming, and that means you haven't seen them as they are at all. Now here we are. This is us! You see that fellow hanging a picture down there? He's president of the First National Bank. Came over a little while ago, got next to the situation, and stayed to help. And — say, this is good! Notice that red-headed fellow just getting up from his knees? Well, he's president of the teamsters' union — figured so big in a strike here last year. I call that pretty rich! He's the fellow they are all so afraid of, but I guess he liked the idea of the boys doing it themselves, and just sneaked in and helped.— There's the Governor. He's a fine fellow. He wouldn't be held up by anybody — not even to get ready for a Prince, but he's worked like a Trojan all day to make things come his way. Yes sir — this is the sure-enough thing.

Here you have the boys off dress parade. Not that we run away from our dignity every day, but — see what I mean? "

"I see," replied the Prince, and he looked as though he really did.

"You know — say, dodge there! Move back! No — too late. The Governor's caught us. Look at him!"

The Governor's eyes had turned upward, and he had seen. He put his hands on his back — he couldn't look up without doing that — and gave a long, steady stare. First, Senator Bruner waved; then Senator Patton waved; then Mr. McVeigh waved; and then the Prince waved. Other people were beginning to look up. "They're all on," laughed Patton, "let's go down."

At first they were disposed to think it pretty shabby treatment. "We worked all day to get in shape," grumbled Harry Weston, "and then you go ring the curtain up on us before it's time for our show to begin."

But the Prince made them feel right about it. He had such a good time that they were forced to concede the move had been a success. And he said to the Governor as he was leaving: "I see that the only way to see America is to see it when America is not seeing you."

VIII

THE LAST SIXTY MINUTES

"NINE — ten —" The old clock paused as if in dramatic appreciation of the situation, and then slowly, weightily, it gave the final stroke, "Eleven!"

The Governor swung his chair half-way round and looked the timepiece full in the face. Already the seconds had begun ticking off the last hour of his official life. On the stroke of twelve another man would be Governor of the State. He sat there watching the movement of the minute hand.

The sound of voices, some jovial, some argumentative, was borne to him through the open transom. People were beginning to gather in the corridors, and he could hear the usual disputes about tickets of admission to the inaugural.

His secretary came in just then with some letters. "Could you see Whitefield now?" he asked. "He's waiting out here for you."

The old man looked up wearily. "Oh, put him off, Charlie. Tell him you can talk to him about whatever it is he wants to know."

The secretary had his hand on the knob, when the Governor added, "And, Charlie, keep everybody out, if you can. I'm — I've got a few private matters to go over."

The younger man nodded and opened the door. He half closed it behind him, and then turned to say, "Except Francis. You'll want to see him if he comes in, won't you?"

He frowned and moved impatiently as he answered, curtly: "Oh, yes."

Francis! Of course it never occurred to any of them that he could close the door on Francis. He drummed nervously on his desk, then suddenly reached down and, opening one of the drawers, tossed back a few things and drew out a newspaper. He unfolded this and spread it out on the desk. Running across the page was the big black line, "Real Governors of Some Western States," and just below, the first of the series, and played up as the most glaring example of nominal and real in governorship, was a sketch of Harvey Francis.

He sat there looking at it, knowing full well that it would not contribute to his peace of mind. It did not make for placidity of spirit to be told at the end of things that he had, as a matter of fact, never been anybody at all. And the bitterest part of it was that, looking back on it now, getting it from the viewpoint of one stepping from it, he could see just how true was the statement: "Harvey Francis has been the real Governor of the State; John Morrison his mouthpiece and figurehead."

He walked to the window and looked out over the January landscape. It may have been the snowy hills, as well as the thoughts weighing him down, that carried him back across the years to one snowy afternoon when he stood up in a little red schoolhouse and delivered an oration on "The Responsibilities of Statesmanship." He smiled as the title came back to him, and yet — what had become of the spirit of that seventeen-year-old boy? He had meant it all then; he could remember the thrill with which he stood there that afternoon long before and poured out his sentiments regarding the sacredness of public trusts. What was it had kept him, when his chance came, from working out in his life the things he had so fervently poured into his schoolboy oration?

Someone was tapping at the door. It was an easy, confident tap, and there was a good deal of reflex action in the Governor's "Come in."

"Indulging in a little meditation?"

The Governor frowned at the way Francis said it, and the latter went on, easily: "Just came from a row with Dorman. Everybody is holding him up for tickets, and he — poor young fool — looks as though he wanted to jump in the river. Takes things tremendously to heart — Dorman does."

He lighted a cigar, smiling quietly over that youthful quality of Dorman's. "Well," he went on, leaning back in his chair and looking about the room, " I thought I'd look in on you for a minute. You see I'll not have the *entrée* to the Governor's office by afternoon." He laughed, the easy, good-humoured laugh of one too sophisticated to spend emotion uselessly.

It was he who fell into meditation then, and the Governor sat looking at him; a paragraph from the newspaper came back to him: " Harvey Francis is the most dangerous type of boss politician. His is not the crude and vulgar method that asks a man what his vote is worth. He deals gently and tenderly with consciences. He knows how to get a man without fatally injuring that man's self-respect."

The Governor's own experience bore out the summary. When elected to office as State Senator he had cherished old-fashioned ideas of serving his constituents and doing his duty. But the very first week Francis had asked one of those little favours of him, and, wishing to show his appreciation of support given him in his election, he had granted it. Then various courtesies were shown him; he was let in on a " deal," and almost before he realised it, it seemed definitely understood that he was a " Francis man."

Francis roused himself and murmured: " Fools! — amateurs."

" Leyman? " ventured the Governor.

" Leyman and all of his crowd! "

" And yet," the Governor could not resist, " in

another hour this same fool will be Governor of the State. The fool seems to have won."

Francis rose, impatiently. "For the moment. It won't be lasting. In any profession, fools and amateurs may win single victories. They can't keep it up. They don't know *how*. Oh, no," he insisted, cheerfully, "Leyman will never be re-elected. Fact is, I'm counting on this contract business we've saved up for him getting in good work." He was moving toward the door. "Well," he concluded, with a curious little laugh, "see you upstairs."

The Governor looked at the clock. It pointed now to twenty-five minutes past eleven. The last hour was going fast. In a very short time he must join the party in the anteroom of the House. But weariness had come over him. He leaned back in his chair and closed his eyes.

He was close upon seventy, and to-day looked even older than his years. It was not a vicious face, but it was not a strong one. People who wanted to say nice things of the Governor called him pleasant or genial or kindly. Even the men in the appointive offices did not venture to say he had much force.

He felt it to-day as he never had before. He had left no mark; he had done nothing, stood for nothing. Never once had his personality made itself felt. He had signed the documents; Harvey Francis had always "suggested"—the term was that man's own—the course to be pursued. And the "suggestions" had ever dictated the policy that would throw the most of influence or money to that splendidly organised machine that Francis controlled.

With an effort he shook himself free from his cheerless retrospect. There was a thing or two he wanted to get from his desk, and his time was growing very short. He found what he wanted, and then, just as he was about to close the drawer, his eye fell on a large yellow envelope.

He closed the drawer; but only to reopen it, take out the envelope and remove the documents it contained; and then one by one he spread them out before him on the desk.

He sat there looking down at them, wondering whether a man had ever stepped into office with as many pitfalls laid for him. During the last month they had been busy about the old State-house setting traps for the new Governor. The "machine" was especially jubilant over those contracts the Governor now had spread out before him. The convict labour question was being fought out in the State just then — organised labour demanding its repeal; country taxpayers insisting that it be maintained. Under the system the penitentiary had become self-supporting. In November the contracts had come up for renewal; but on the request of Harvey Francis the matter had been put off from time to time, and still remained open. Just the week before,

Francis had put it to the Governor something like this:

"Don't sign those contracts. We can give some reason for holding them off, and save them up for Leyman. Then we can see that the question is agitated, and whatever he does about it is going to prove a bad thing for him. If he doesn't sign, he's in bad with the country fellows, the men who elected him. Don't you see? At the end of his administration the penitentiary, under you self-sustaining, will have cost them a pretty penny. We've got him right square!"

The clock was close to twenty minutes of twelve, and he concluded that he would go out and join some of his friends he could hear in the other room. It would never do for him to go upstairs with a long, serious face. He had had his day, and now Leyman was to have his, and if the new Governor did better than the old one, then so much the better for the State. As for the contracts, Leyman surely must understand that there was a good deal of rough sailing on political waters.

But it was not easy to leave the room. Walking to the window he again stood there looking out across the snow, and once more he went back now at the end of things to that day in the little red schoolhouse which stood out as the beginning.

He was called back from that dreaming by the sight of three men coming up the hill. He smiled faintly in anticipation of the things Francis and the rest of them would say about the new Governor's arriving on foot. Leyman had requested that the inaugural parade be done away with — but one would suppose he would at least dignify the occasion by arriving in a carriage. Francis would see that the opposing papers handled it as a grand-stand play to the country constituents.

And then, forgetful of Francis, and of the approaching ceremony, the old man stood there by the window watching the young man who was coming up to take his place. How firmly the new Governor walked! With what confidence he looked ahead at the State-house. The Governor — not considering the inconsistency therein — felt a thrill of real pride in thought of the State's possessing a man like that.

Standing though he did for the things pitted against him, down in his heart John Morrison had all along cherished a strong admiration for that young man who, as District Attorney of the State's metropolis, had aroused the whole country by his fearlessness and unquestionable sincerity. Many a day he had sat in that same office reading what the young District Attorney was doing in the city close by — the fight he was making almost single-handed against corruption, how he was striking in the high places fast and hard as in the low, the opposition, threats, and time after time there had been that same secret thrill at thought of there being a man like that. And when the people of the State, convinced that here was one man who would serve *them*, began urging the District Attorney for chief executive, Governor Morrison, linked with the opposing forces, doing all he could to bring about Leyman's defeat, never lost that secret feeling for the young man, who, unbacked by any organisation, struck blow after blow at the machine that had so long dominated the State, winning in the end that almost incomprehensible victory.

The new Governor had passed from sight, and a moment later his voice came to the ear of the lonely man in the executive office. Some friends had stopped him just outside the Governor's door with a laughing "Here's hoping you'll do as much for us in the new office as you did in the old," and the new Governor replied, buoyantly: "Oh, but I'm going to do a great deal more!"

The man within the office smiled a little wistfully and with a sigh sat down before his desk. The clock now pointed to thirteen minutes of twelve; they would be asking for him upstairs. There were some scraps of paper on his desk and he threw them into the waste-basket, murmuring: "I can at least give him a clean desk."

He pushed his chair back sharply. A clean desk! The phrase opened to deeper meanings. . . . Why not clean it up in earnest? Why not give him a square deal — a real chance? Why not *sign the contracts?*

Again he looked at the clock — not yet ten minutes of twelve. For ten minutes more he was Governor of the State! Ten minutes of real governorship! Might it not make up a little, both to his own soul and to the world, for the years he had weakly served as another man's puppet? The consciousness that he could do it, that it was not within the power of any man to stop him, was intoxicating. Why not break the chains now at the last, and just before the end taste the joy of freedom?

He took up his pen and reached for the inkwell. With trembling, excited fingers he unfolded the contracts. He dipped his pen into the ink; he even brought it down on the paper; and then the tension broke. He sank back in his chair, a frightened, broken old man.

"Oh, no," he whispered; "no, not now. It's —" his head went lower and lower until at last it rested on the desk — "too late."

When he raised his head and grew more steady, it was only to see the soundness of his conclusion. He had not the right now in the final hour to buy for himself a little of glory. It would only be a form of self-indulgence. They would call it, and perhaps rightly, hush money to his conscience. They would say he went back on them only when he was through with them. Oh, no, there would be no more strength in it than in the average deathbed repentance. He would at least step out with consistency.

He folded the contracts and put them back into the envelope. The minute hand now pointed to seven minutes to twelve. Some one was tapping at the door, and the secretary appeared to say they were waiting for him upstairs. He replied that he would be there in a minute, hoping that his voice did not sound as strange to the other man as it had to himself.

Slowly he walked to the door leading into the corridor. This, then, was indeed the end; this the final stepping down from office! After years of what they called public service, he was leaving it all now with a sense of defeat and humiliation. A lump was in the old man's throat; his eyes were blurred. "But you, Frank Leyman," he whispered passionately, turning as if for comfort to the other man, "it will be different with you! They'll not get you — not you!"

It lifted him then as a great wave — this passionate exultation that here was one man whom corruption could not claim as her own. Here was one human soul not to be had for a price! There flitted before him again a picture of that seventeen-year-old boy in the little red schoolhouse, and close upon it came the picture of this other young man against whom all powers of corruption had been turned in vain. With the one it had been the emotional luxury of a sentiment, a thing from life's actualities apart; with the other it was a force that dominated all things else, a force over which circumstances and design could not prevail. "I know all about it," he was saying. "I know about it all! I know how easy it is to fall! I know how fine it is to stand!"

His sense of disappointment in his own empty, besmirched career was almost submerged then as he projected himself on into the career of this other man who within the hour would come there in his stead. How glorious was his opportunity, how limitless his possibilities, and how great to his own soul the satisfaction the years would bring of having done his best!

It had all changed now. That passionate longing to vindicate himself, add one thing honourable and fine to his own record, had altogether left him, and with the new mood came new insight and what had been an impulse centred to a purpose.

It pointed to three minutes to twelve as he walked over to his desk, unfolded the contracts, and one by one affixed his signature. In a dim way he was conscious of how the interpretation of his first motive would be put upon it, how they would call him traitor and coward; but that mattered little. The very fact that the man for whom he was doing it would never see it as it was brought him no pang. And when he had carefully blotted the papers, affixed the seal and put them away, there was in his heart the clean, sweet joy of a child because he had been able to do this for a man in whom he believed.

The band was playing the opening strains as he closed the door behind him and started upstairs.

IX

"OUT THERE"

THE old man held the picture up before him and surveyed it with admiring but disapproving eye. "No one that comes along this way 'll have the price for it," he grumbled. "It 'll just set here 'till doomsday."

It did seem that the picture failed to fit in with the rest of the shop. A persuasive young fellow who claimed he was closing out his stock let the old man have it for what he called a song. It was only a little out-of-the-way store which subsisted chiefly on the framing of pictures. The old man looked around at his views of the city, his pictures of cats and dogs and gorgeous young women, his flaming bits of landscape. "Don't belong in here," he fumed, "any more 'an I belong in Congress."

And yet the old man was secretly proud of his acquisition. He seemed all at once to be lifted from his realm of petty tradesman to that of patron of art. There was a hidden dignity in his scowling as he shuffled about pondering the least ridiculous place for the picture.

It is not fair to the picture to try repainting it in words, for words reduce it to a lithograph. It was a bit of a pine forest, through which there exuberantly rushed an unspoiled little mountain stream. Chromos and works of art may deal with kindred subjects. There is just that one difference of dealing with them differently. "It ain't what you *see*, so much as what you can guess is there," was the thought it brought to the old man who was dusting it. "Now this frame ain't three feet long, but it wouldn't surprise me a bit if that timber kept right on for a hundred miles. I kind of suspect it's on a mountain — looks cool enough in there to be on a mountain. Wish I was there. Bet they never see no such days as we do in Chicago. Looks as though a man might call his soul his own — out there."

He began removing some views of Lincoln Park and some corpulent Cupids in order to make room in the window for the new picture. When he went outside to look at it he shook his head severely and hastened in to take away some ardent young men and women, some fruit and flowers and fish which he had left thinking they might "set it off." It was evident that the new picture did not need to be "set off." "And anyway," he told himself, in vindication of entrusting all his goods to one bottom, "I might as well take them out, for the new one makes them look so kind of sick that no one would have them, anyhow." Then he went back to mounting views with the serenity of one who stands for the finer things.

His clamorous little clock pointed to a quarter of six when he finally came back to the front of the store. It was time to begin closing up for the night, but for the minute he stood there watching the crowd of workers coming from the business district not far away over to the boarding-house region, a little to the west. He watched them as they came by in twos and threes and fours: noisy people and worn-out people, people hilarious and people sullen, the gaiety and the weariness, the acceptance and the rebellion of humanity — he saw it pass. "As if any of *them* could buy it," he pronounced severely, adding, contemptuously, "or wanted to."

The girl was coming along by herself. He watched her as she crossed to his side of the street, thinking it was too bad for a poor girl to be as tired as that. She was dressed like many of the rest of them, and yet she looked different — like the picture and the chromo. She turned an indifferent glance toward the window, and then suddenly she stood there very still, and everything about her seemed to change. "For all the world," he told himself afterward, "as if she'd found a long-lost friend, and was 'fraid to speak for fear it was too good to be true."

She did seem afraid to speak — afraid to believe. For a minute she stood there right in the middle of the sidewalk, staring at the picture. And when she came toward the window it was less as if coming than as if drawn. What she really seemed to want to do was to edge away; yet she came closer, as close as she could, her eyes never leaving the picture, and then fear, or awe, or whatever it was made her look so queer gave way to wonder — that wondering which is ready to open the door to delight. She looked up and down the street as one rubbing one's eyes to make sure of a thing, and then it all gave way to a joy which lighted her pale little face like — "Well, like nothing I ever saw before," was all the old man could say of it. "Why, she'd never know if the whole fire department was to run right up here on the sidewalk," he gloated. Just then she drew herself up for a long breath. "See?" he chuckled, delightedly. "She knows it has a smell!" She looked toward the door, but shook her head. "Knows she can't pay the price," he interpreted her. Then she stepped back and looked at the number above the door. "Coming again," he made of that; "ain't going to run no chances of losing the place." And then for a long time she stood there before the picture, so deeply and so strangely quiet that he could not translate her. "I can't just get the run of it," was his bewildered conclusion. "I don't see why it should make anybody act like *that*." And yet he must have understood more than he knew, for suddenly he was seeing her through a blur of tears.

As he began shutting up for the night he was so

excited about the way she looked when she finally turned away that it never occurred to him to be depressed about her inability to pay the price.

He kept thinking of her, wondering about her, during the next day. At a little before six he took up his station near the front window. Once more the current of workers flowed by. "I'm an old fool," he told himself, irritated at the wait; "as if it makes any difference whether she comes or not — when she can't buy it, anyhow. She's just as big a fool as I am — liking it when she can't have it, only I'm the biggest fool of all — caring whether she likes it or not." But just then the girl passed quickly by a crowd of girls who were ahead of her and came hurrying across the street. She was walking fast, and looked excited and anxious. "Afraid it might be gone," he said — adding, grimly: "Needn't worry much about that."

She came up to the picture as some people would enter a church. And yet the joy which flooded her face is not well known to churches. "I'll tell you what it's like" — the old man's thoughts stumbling right into the heart of it —"it's like someone that's been wandering round in a desert country all of a sudden coming on a spring. She's *thirsty* — she's drinking it in — she can't get enough of it. It's — it's the water of life to her!" And then, ashamed of saying a thing that sounded as if it were out of a poem, he shook his shoulders roughly as if to shake off a piece of sentiment unbecoming his age and sex.

He went to the door and watched her as she passed away. "I'll bet she'd never tip the scale to one hundred pounds," he decided. "Looks like a good wind could blow her away." She stooped a little, and just as she passed from sight he saw that she was coughing.

Then the old man made what he prided himself was a great deduction. "She's been there, and she wants to go back. This kind of takes her back for a minute, and when she gets the breath of it she ain't so homesick."

All through those July days he watched each night for the frail-looking little girl who liked the picture of the pines. She would always come hurrying across the street in the same eager way, an eagerness close to the feverish. But the tenseness would always relax as she saw the picture. "She never looks quite so wilted down when she goes away as she does when she comes," the old man saw. "Upon my soul, I believe she really *goes* there. It's — oh, Lord "— irritated at getting beyond his depth — "*I* don't know!"

He never called it anything now but "Her Picture." One day at just ten minutes of six he took it out of the window. "Seems kind of mean," he admitted, "but I just want to find out how much she does think of it."

And when he found out he told himself that of all

the mean men God had ever let live, he was the meanest. The girl came along in the usual hurried, anxious fashion. And when she saw the empty window he thought for a minute she was going to sink right down there on the sidewalk. Everything about her seemed to give way — as if something from which she had been drawing had been taken from her. The luminousness gone from her face, there were cruel revelations. " Blast my *soul!* " the old man muttered angrily, not far from tearfully. She looked up and down the noisy, dirty, parched street, then back to the empty window. For a minute she just stood there — that was the worst minute of all. And then — accepting — she turned and walked slowly away, walked as the too-weary and the too-often disappointed walk.

It was with not wholly steady hand that the old man hastened to replace the picture, all the while telling himself what he thought of himself: more low-down than the cat who plays with the mouse, meaner than the man who'd take the bone from the dog, less to be loved than the man who would kick over the child's play-house, only to be compared with the brute who would snatch the cup of water from the dying — such were the verdicts he pronounced. He thought perhaps she would come back, and stayed there until almost seven, waiting for her, though pretending it was necessary that he take down and then put up again the front curtains. All the next day he was restless and irritable. As if to make up to the girl for the contemptible trick he had played he spent a whole hour that afternoon arranging a tapestry background for the picture. "She'll think," he told himself, "that this was why it was out, and won't be worried about its being gone again. This will just be a little sign to her that it's here to stay."

He began his watch that night at half-past five. After fifteen minutes the thought came to him that she might be so disheartened she would go home by another street. He became so gloomily certain she would do this that he was jubilant when he finally saw her coming along on the other side — coming purposelessly, shorn of that eagerness which had always been able, for the moment, to vanquish the tiredness. But when she came to the place where she always crossed the street she only stood there an instant and then, a little more slowly, a little more droopingly, walked on. She had given up! She was not coming over!

But she did come. After she had gone a few steps she hesitated again and this time started across the street. "That's right," approved the old man, "never give up the ship!"

She passed the store as if she were not going to look in; she seemed trying not to look, but her head turned — and she saw the picture. First her body seemed to stiffen, and then something — he couldn't make out whether or not it was a sob — shook her, and as she came toward the picture on her white, tired face were the tears.

" Don't you worry," he murmured affectionately to her retreating form, " it won't never be gone again."

The very next week he was put to the test. The kind of lady who did not often pass along that street entered the shop and asked to see the picture in the window. He looked at her suspiciously. Then he frowned at her, as he stood there, fumbling. *Her* picture! What would she think? What would she do? Then a crafty smile stole over his face and he walked to the window and got the picture. " The price of this picture, madame," he said, haughtily, " is forty dollars,"—adding to himself, " That'll fix her."

But the lady made no comment, and stood there holding the picture up before her. " I will take it," she said, quietly.

He stared at her stupidly. Forty dollars! Then it must be that the picture was better than the young man had known. " Will you wrap it, please? " she asked. " I will take it with me."

He turned to the back of the store. Forty dollars! — he kept repeating it in dazed fashion. And they had raised the rent on him, and the papers said coal would be high that winter — those facts seemed to have something to do with forty dollars. *Forty dollars!* — it was hammering at him, overwhelmed him, too big a sum to contend with. With long, grim stroke he tore off the wrapping paper; stoically he began folding it. But something was the matter. The paper would not go on right. Three times he took it off, and each time he could not help looking down at the picture of the pines. And each time the forest seemed to open a little farther; each time it seemed bigger — bigger even than forty dollars; it seemed as if it *knew things* — things more important than even coal and rent. And then the strangest thing of all happened: the forest faded away into its own shadowy distances, and in its place was a noisy, crowded, sun-baked street, and across the street was eagerly hurrying an anxious little girl, a frail little wisp of a girl who probably should not be crossing hot, noisy streets at all — then a light in tired eyes, a smile upon a worn face, relief as from a cooling breeze — and *anyway*, suddenly furious at the lady, furious at himself — "he'd be gol-*darned* if it wasn't *her* picture!"

He walked firmly back to the front of the store. "I forgot at first," he said, brusquely, "that this picture belongs to someone else."

The lady looked at him in astonishment. "I do not understand," she said.

"There's nothing to understand," he fairly shouted, "except that it belongs to someone else!"

She turned away, but came back to him. "I

will give you fifty dollars for it," she said, in her quiet way.

"Madame," he thundered at her, "you can stand there and offer me five hundred dollars, and I'm here to tell you that this picture is not for sale. Do you *hear?*"

"I certainly do," replied the lady, and walked from the store.

He was a long time in cooling off. "I tell you," he stormed to a very blue Lake Michigan he was putting into a frame, "it's hers — it's *hern* — and anybody that comes along here with any nonsense is just going to hear from *me!*"

In the days which followed he often thought to go out and speak to her, but perhaps the old man had a restraining sense of values. He planned some day to go out and tell her the picture was hers, but that seemed a silly thing to tell her, for surely she knew it anyway. He worried a good deal about her cough, which seemed to be getting worse, and he had it all figured out that when cold weather came he would have her come in where it was warm, and take her look in there. He felt that he knew all about her, and though he did not know her name, though he had never heard her speak one word, in some ways he felt closer to her than to any one else in the world.

Yet if the old man had known just how it was with the girl it is altogether unlikely that he would have understood. It would have mystified and disappointed him had he known that she had never seen a pine forest or a mountain in her life. Indeed there was a great deal about the little girl which the old man, together with almost all the rest of the world, would not have understood.

Not that the surface facts about her were either incomprehensible or interesting. The tale of her existence would sound much like that of a hundred other girls in the same city. Inquiry about her would have developed the facts that she did typewriting for a land company, that she did not seem to have any people, and lived at a big boarding-house. At the boarding-house they would have told you that she was a nice little thing, quiet as a mouse, and that it was too bad she had to work, for she seemed more than half sick. There the story would have rested, and the real things about her would not have been touched.

She worked for the Chicago branch of a big Northwestern land company. They dealt in the lands of Idaho, Montana, Oregon and Washington. The things she sat at her typewriter and wrote were of the wonders of that great country: the great timber lands, the valleys and hills, towering mountain peaks and rushing rivers. She typewrote "literature" telling how there was a chance for every man out there, how the big, exhaustless land was eager to yield of its store to all who would come and seek. Day after day she wrote those things telling how the sick were made well and the poor were made rich, how it was a land of indescribable wonders which the feeble pen could not hope to portray.

And the girl with whom almost everything in life had gone wrong came to think of Out There as the place where everything was right. It was the far country where there was no weariness nor loneliness, the land where one did not grow tired, where one never woke up in the morning too tired to get up, where no one went to bed at night too tired to go to sleep. The street-cars did not ring their gongs so loud Out There, the newsboys had pleasant voices, and there were no elevated trains. It was a pure, high land which knew no smoke nor dirt, a land where great silences drew one to the heart of peace, where the people in the next room did not come in and bang things around late at night. Out There was a wide land where buildings were far apart and streets were not crowded. Even the horses did not grow tired Out There. Oh, it was a land where dreams came true — a beautiful land where no one ate prunes, where the gravy was never greasy and the potatoes never burned. It was a land of flowers and birds and lovely people — a land of wealth and health and many smiles.

Her imagination made use of it all. She knew how men were reclaiming the desert of Idaho, of the tremendous undeveloped wealth of what had been an almost undiscovered State. She thrilled to the poetry of irrigation. Often when hot and tired and dusty her fancy would follow the little mountain stream from its birth way up in the clouds, her imagination rushing with it through sweetening forest and tumbling with it down cooling rocks until finally strong, bold, wise men guided it to the desert which had yearned for it through all the years, and the grateful desert smiled rich smiles of grain and flowers. She could make it more like a story than any story in any book. And she could always breathe better in thinking of the pine forests of Oregon. There was something liberating — expanding — in just the thought of them. She dreamed cooling dreams about them, dreams of their reaching farther than one's fancy could reach, big widening dreams of their standing there serene in the consciousness of their own immensity. They stood to her for a beautiful idea: the idea of space, of room — room for everybody, and then much more room! Even one's understanding grew big as one turned to them.

And she loved to listen for the Pacific Ocean, coming from incomprehensible distances and unknowable countries, now rushing with passion to the wild coast of Oregon, again stealing into the Washington harbours. She loved to address the letters to Portland, Seattle, Spokane, Tacoma —all those pulsing, vivid cities of a country of big chances and big beauty. She loved to picture Seattle, a city builded upon many hills — how wonderful that a city should be builded upon hills! — in Chicago there was nothing that could possibly be thought of as a hill. And she loved to shut her eyes and let the great mountain peak grow in the distance, as one could see it from Portland — how noble a thing to see a mountain peak from a city! Sometimes she trembled before that consciousness of a mountain. Often when so tired she scarcely knew what she was doing she found she was saying her prayers to a mountain. Indeed, Out There seemed the place to send one's prayers — for was it not a place where prayers were answered?

During that summer when the West was overrun with tourists who grumbled about everything from the crowded trains to the way in which sea-foods were served, this little girl sat in one of the hot office buildings of Chicago and across the stretch of miles drew to herself the spirit of that country of coming days. Thousands rode in Pullman cars along the banks of the Columbia — saw, and felt not; she sat before her typewriter in a close, noisy room and heard the cooling rush of waters and got the freeing message of the pines. In some rare moments when she rose from the things about her to the things of which she dreamed she possessed the whole great land, and as the sultry days sapped of her meagre strength, and the bending over the typewriter cramped an already too cramped chest she clung with a more and more passionate tenacity to the bigness and the beauty and rightness of things Out There. And it was so kind to her — that land of deep breaths and restoring breezes. It never shut her out. It always kept itself bigger and more wonderful than one could ever hope to fancy it.

And the night she found the picture she knew that it was all really so. That was why it was so momentous a night. The picture was a dream visualised — a dreamer vindicated. They had pictures in the office, of course — some pictures trying to tell of that very kind of a place. But those were just pictures; this *proved* it, told what it meant. It told that she had been right, and there was joy in knowing that she had known. She clung to the picture as one would to that which proves as real all one has long held dear, loved it as the dreamer loves that which secures him in his dreaming.

She came to think of it as her own abiding place. Often when too tired for long wings of fancy she would just sink down in the deep, cool shadows of the pines, beside the little river which one knew so well was the gift of distant snows. It rested her most of all; it quieted her.

She smiled sometimes to think how no one in the office knew about it, wondered what they would think if they knew. Often she would find someone in the office looking at her strangely. She used to wonder about it a little.

And then one day Mr. Osborne sent for her to come into his office. He acted so queerly. As she came in and sat down near his desk he swung his chair around and sat there with his back to her. After that he got up and walked to the window.

The head stenographer had complained of her cough. She said she did not think it right either to the girl or to the rest of them for her to be there. She said she hated to speak of it, but could not stand it any longer. That had been the week before, and ever since he had been putting it off. But now he could put it off no longer; the head stenographer was valuable, and besides he knew that she was right.

And so he told her — this was all he could think of just then — that they were contemplating some changes in the office, and for a time would have less desk room. If he sent her machine to her home, would she be willing to do her work there for a while? Hers was the kind of work that could be done at home.

She was sorry, for she wondered if she could find a place in her room for the typewriter, and it did not seem there would be air enough there to last her all day long. And she had grown fond of the office, with its "literature" and pictures and maps and the men who had just come from Out There coming in every once in a while. It was a bond — a place to touch realities. But of course there was nothing for her to do but comply, and she made no comment on the arrangement.

She pushed her chair back and rose to go. "Are you alone in the world?" he asked abruptly then.

"Yes; I — oh yes."

It was too much for him. "How would you like," he asked recklessly, "to have me get you transportation out West?"

She sank back in her chair. Every particle of colour had left her face. Her deep eyes had grown almost wild. "Oh," she gasped —"you can't mean — you don't think —"

"You wouldn't want to go?"

"I mean"— it was but a whisper —"it would be — too wonderful."

"You would like it then?"

She only nodded; but her lips were parted, her eyes glowing. He wondered why he had never seen before how different looking and — yes, beautiful, in a strange kind of way — she was.

"I see you have a cold," he said, "and I think you would get along better out there. I'll see if I can fix up the transportation, and get something with our people in one of the towns that would be good for you."

She leaned back in her chair and sat there smiling at him. Something in the smile made him say, abruptly: "That's all; you may go now, and I'll send a boy with your machine."

She walked through the streets as one who had already found another country. More than one turned to look at her. She reached her room at last and pulling her one little chair up to the window sat staring out across the alley at the brick wall across from her. But she was not seeing a narrow alley and a high brick wall. She was seeing rushing rivers and mighty forests and towering peaks. She leaned back in her chair — an indulgence less luxurious than it sounds, as the chair only reached the middle of her back — and looked out at the high brick wall and saw a snow-clad range of hills. But she was tired; this tremendous idea was too much for her; the very wonder of it was exhausting. She lay down on her bed — radiant, but languid. Soon she heard a rush of waters. At first it was only someone filling the bath-tub, but after a while it was the little stream which flowed through her forest. And then she was not lying on a lumpy bed; she was sinking down under pine trees — all so sweet and still and cool. But an awful thing was happening! — the forest was on fire — it was choking and burning her! She awoke to find smoke from the building opposite pouring into her room; flies were buzzing about, and her face and hands were hot.

She did little work in the next few days. It was hard to go on with the same work when waiting for a thing which was to make over one's whole life. The stress of dreams changing to hopes caused a great languor to come over her. And her chair was not right for her typewriter, and the smoke came in all the time. Strangely enough Out There seemed farther away. Sometimes she could not go there at all; she supposed it was because she was really going.

At the close of the week she went to the office with her work. She was weak with excitement as she stepped into the elevator. Would Mr. Osborne have the transportation for her? Would he tell her when she was to go?

But she did not see Mr. Osborne at all. When she asked for him the clerk just replied carelessly that he was not there. She was going to ask if he had left any message for her, but the telephone rang then and the man to whom she was talking turned away. Someone was sitting at her old desk, and they did not seem to be making the changes they had contemplated; everyone in the office seemed very busy and uncaring, and because she knew her chin was trembling she turned away.

She had a strange feeling as she left the office: as if standing on ground which quivered, an impulse to reach out her hand and tell someone that something must be done right away, a dreadful fear that she was going to cry out that she could not wait much longer.

All at once she found that she was crossing the

street, and saw ahead the little art store with the wonderful picture which proved it was all really so. In the same old way, her step quickened. It would show her again that it was all just as she had thought it was, and if that were true, then it must be true also that Mr. Osborne was going to get her the transportation. It would prove that everything was all right.

But a cruel thing happened. It failed her. It was just as beautiful — but something a long way off, impossible to reach. Try as she would, she could not get *into* it, as she used to. It was only a picture; a beautiful picture of some pine trees. And they were very far away, and they had nothing at all to do with her.

Through the window, at the back of the store, she saw the old man standing with his back to her. She thought of going in and asking to sit down — she wanted to sit down — but perhaps he would say something cross to her — he was such a queer looking old man — and she knew she would cry if anything cross was said to her. That he had watched for her each night, that he had tried and tried to think of a way of finding her, that he would have been more glad to see her than to see anyone in the world, would have been kinder to her than anyone on earth would have been — those were the things she did not know. And so — more lonely than she had ever been before — she turned away.

On Monday she felt she could wait no longer. It did not seem that it would be *safe*. She got ready to go to see Mr. Osborne, but the getting ready tired her so that she sat a long time resting, looking out at the high brick wall beyond which there was nothing at all. She was counting the blocks, thinking of how many times she would have to cross the street. But just then it occurred to her that she could telephone.

When she came back upstairs she crept up on the bed and lay there very still. The boy had said that Mr. Osborne was away and would be gone two weeks. No one in the office had heard him say anything about her transportation.

All through the day she lay there, and what she saw before her was a narrow alley and a high brick wall. She had lost her mountains and her forests and her rivers and her lakes. She tried to go out to them in the same old way — but she could not get beyond the high brick wall. She was shut in. She tried to draw them to her, but they could not come across the wall. It shut them out. She tried to pray to the great mountain which one could see from Portland. But even prayers could get no farther than the wall.

Late that afternoon, because she was so shut in that she was choking, because she was consumed with the idea that she must claim her country now or lose it forever, she got up and started for the picture. It was a long, long way to go, and dreadful things were in between — people who would bump against her, hot, uneven streets, horses that might run over her — but she must make the journey. She must make it because the things that she lived on were slipping from her — and she was choking — sinking down — and all alone.

Step by step, never knowing just how her foot was going to make the next step, sick with the fear that people were going to run into her — the streets going up and down, the buildings round and round, she did go; holding to the window casings for the last few steps — each step a terrible chasm which she was never sure she was going to be able to cross — she was there at last. And in the window as she stood there, swayingly, was a dark, blurred thing which might have been anything at all. She tried to remember why she had come. What *was* it —? And then she was sinking down into an abyss.

That the hemorrhage came then, that the old man came out and found her and tenderly took her in, that he had her taken where she should have been taken long before, that the doctors said it was too late, and that soon their verdict was confirmed — those are the facts which would seem to tell the rest of the story. But deep down beneath facts rests truth, and the truth is that this is a story with the happiest kind of a happy ending. What facts would call the breeze from an electric fan was in truth the gracious breath of the pines. And when the nurse said "She's going," she was indeed going, but to a land of great spaces and benign breezes, a land of deep shadows and rushing waters. For a most wondrous thing had happened. She had called to the mountain, and the mountain had heard her voice; and because it was so mighty and so everlasting it drew her to itself, across high brick walls and past millions of hurrying, noisy people — oh, a most triumphant flight! And the mountain said — "I give you this whole great land. It is yours because you have loved it so well. Hills and valleys and rivers and forests and lakes — it is all for you." Yes, the nurse was quite right; she was going: going for a long sweet sleep beneath trees of many shadows, beside clear waters which had come from distant snows — really going "Out There."

X

THE PREPOSTEROUS MOTIVE

THE Governor was sitting alone in his private office with an open letter in his hand. He was devoutly and gloomily wishing that some other man was just then in his shoes. The Governor had not devoted a large portion of his life to nursing a desire of that nature, for he was a man in whose soul the flame of self-satisfaction glowed cheeringly; but just now there were reasons, and he deemed them ample, for deploring that he had been made chief executive of his native State.

Had he chosen to take you into his confidence — a thing the Governor would assuredly choose not to do — he would have told you there were greater things in the world than the governorship of that State. He might have suggested a seat in the Senate of the United States as one of those things. It was of the United States Senate his Excellency was thinking as he sat there alone moodily deploring the gubernatorial shoes.

The senior Senator was going to die. He differed therein from his fellows in that he was going to die soon, almost immediately. He had reached the tottering years even at the time of his reëlection, and it had never been supposed that his life would outstretch his term. He had been sent back, not for another six years of service, but to hold out the leader of the Boxers, as they called themselves — the younger and unorthodox element of the party in the State, an element growing to dangerous proportions. It was only by returning the aged Senator, whom they held it would be brutal to turn down after a life of service to the party, that the "machine" won the memorable fight of the previous winter.

From the viewpoint of the machine, the Governor was the senior Senator's logical successor. Had it not been for the heavy inroads of the Boxers, his Excellency would even then have been sitting in the Senate Chamber at Washington. It had not been considered safe to nominate the Governor. Had his supporters conceded that the time was at hand for a change, there would have been a general clamour for the leader of the Boxers — Huntington, undeniably the popular man of the State. And so they concocted a beautiful sentiment about "rounding out the veteran's career," and letting him "die with his boots on"; and through the omnipotence of sentiment, they won.

Down in his heart the venerable Senator was not seeking to die with his boots on. He would have preferred sitting in a large chair before the fire and reading quietly of what other men were doing in the Senate of the United States. But they told him he must sacrifice that wish, for if he retired he would be succeeded by a dangerous man. And the old man, believing them, had gone dutifully back into the arena.

Now it seemed that a power outside man's control was declaring against the well-laid plans of the machine. As the machine saw things, the time was not ripe for the senior Senator to die. He had just entered upon his new term, and the Governor himself had but lately stepped into a second term. They had assumed that the Senator would live on for at least two years, but now they heard that he was likely to die almost at once. His Excellency could not very well name himself for the vacancy, and it seemed dangerous just then to risk a call of the Assembly. They dared not let the Governor appoint a weaker man, even if he would consent to do so, for they would need the best they had to put up against the leader of the Boxers. With the Governor, they believed they could win, but the question of appointing him had suddenly become a knotty one.

The Governor himself was bowed with chagrin. He saw now that he had erred in taking a second term, and he was not the man to enjoy reviewing his mistakes. As he sat there reading and rereading the letter which told him that the work of the senior Senator was almost done, he said to himself that it was easy enough to wrestle with men, but a harder thing to try one's mettle with fate. He spent a gloomy and unprofitable day.

Late in the afternoon a telegram reached the executive office. Styles was coming to town that night, and wanted to see the Governor at the hotel. Things always cleared when Styles came to town; and so, though still unable to foresee the outcome, he brightened at once.

Styles was a railroad man, and rich. People to whom certain things were a sealed book said that it was nice of Mr. Styles to take an interest in politics when he had so many other things on his mind, and that he must be a very public-spirited man. That he took an interest in politics, no one familiar with the affairs of the State would deny. The orthodox papers painted him as a public benefactor, but the Boxers arrayed him with hoofs and horns.

The Governor and Mr. Styles were warm friends. It was said that their friendship dated from mere boyhood, and that the way the two men had held together through all the vicissitudes of life was touching and beautiful — at least, so some people observed. There were others whose eyebrows went up when the Governor and Mr. Styles were mentioned in their Damon and Pythias capacity.

That night, in the public benefactor's room at the hotel, the Governor and his old friend had a long talk. When twelve o'clock came they were still talking; more than that, the Governor was excitedly pacing the floor.

"I tell you, Styles," he expostulated, "I don't like it! It doesn't put me in a good light. It's too apparent, and I'll suffer for it, sure as fate. Mark my words, we'll all suffer for it!"

Mr. Styles was sitting in an easy attitude before the table. The public benefactor never paced the floor; it did not seem necessary. He smoked in silence for a minute; then raised himself a little in his chair.

"Well, have you anything better to offer?"

"No, I haven't," replied the Governor, tartly; "but it seems to me you ought to have."

Styles sank back in his chair and for several minutes more devoted himself to the art of smoking. There were times when this philanthropic dabbler in politics was irritating.

"I think," he began presently, "that you exaggerate the unpleasant features of the situation. It will cause talk, of course; but isn't it worth it? You say it's unheard of; maybe, but so is the situation, and wasn't there something in the copy-books about meeting new situations with new methods? If you have anything better to offer, produce it; if not, we've got to go ahead with this. And really, I don't see that it's so bad. You have to go South to look after your cotton plantation; you find now that it's going to take more time than you feel you should take from the State; you can't afford to give it up; consequently, you withdraw in favor of the Lieutenant-Governor. We all protest, but you say Berriman is a good man, and the State won't suffer, and you simply can't afford to go on. Well, we can keep the Senator's condition pretty quiet here; and after all, he's sturdy, and may live on to the close of the year. After due deliberation Berriman appoints you. A little talk? — Yes. But it's worth a little talk. It seems to me the thing works out very smoothly."

When Tom Styles leaned back in his chair and declared a thing worked out very smoothly, that thing was quite likely to go. In three days the Governor went South. When he returned, the newspaper men were startled by the announcement that business considerations which he could not afford to overlook demanded his withdrawal from office. Previous to this time the Lieutenant-Governor and Mr. Styles had met and the result of their meeting was not made a matter of public record.

As the Governor had anticipated, many things were said. Inquiries were made into the venerable Senator's condition — which, the orthodox papers declared, was but another example of the indecency of the Boxer journals. The Governor went to his cotton plantation. The Lieutenant-Governor went into office, and was pronounced a worthy successor to a good executive. The venerable Senator continued to live. As Mr. Styles had predicted, the gossip soon quieted into a friendly hope that the Governor would realise large sums with his cotton.

It was late in the fall when the senior Senator finally succumbed. The day the papers printed the story of his death, they printed speculative editorials on his probable successor. When the bereaved family commented with bitterness on this ill-concealed haste, they were told that it was politics — enterprise — life.

The old man's remains lay in state in the rotunda of the State Capitol, and the building was draped in mourning. Many came and looked upon the quiet face; but far more numerous than those who gathered at his bier to weep were those who assembled in secluded corners to speculate on the wearing of his toga. It was politics — enterprise — life.

Mr. Styles told the Lieutenant-Governor to be deliberate. There was no need of an immediate appointment, he said. And so for a time things went on about the State-house much as usual, save that the absorbing topic was the senatorial situation, and that every one was watching the new chief executive. The retired Governor now spent part of his time in the South, and part at home. The cotton plantation was not demanding all his attention, after all.

It could not be claimed that John Berriman had ever done any great thing. He was not on record as having ever risen grandly to an occasion; but there may have been something in the fact that an occasion admitting of a grand rising had never presented itself. Before he became Lieutenant-Governor, he had served inoffensively in the State Senate for two terms. No one had ever worked very hard for Senator Berriman's vote. He had been put in by the machine, and it had always been assumed that he was machine property.

Berriman himself had never given the matter of his place in the human drama much thought. He had an idea that it was proper for him to vote with his friends, and he always did it. Had he been called a tool, he would have been much ruffled; he merely trusted to the infallibility of the party.

The Boxers did not approach him now concerning the appointment of Huntington. That, of course, was a fixed matter, and they were not young and foolish enough to attempt to change it.

One day the Governor received a telegram from Styles suggesting that he "adjust that matter" immediately. He thought of announcing the appointment that very night, but the newspaper men had all left the building, and as he had promised that they should know of it as soon as it was made, he concluded to wait until the next morning.

Governor Berriman had a brother in town that week, attending a meeting of the State Agricultural Society. Hiram Berriman had a large farm in the southern part of the State. He knew but little of political methods, and had primitive ideas about honesty. There had always been a strong tie between the brothers, despite the fact that Hiram was fifteen years the Governor's senior. They talked of many things that night, and the hour was growing late. They were about to retire when the Governor remarked, a little sleepily:

"Well, to-morrow morning I announce the senatorial appointment."

"You do, eh?" returned the farmer.

"Yes, there's no need of waiting any longer, and it's getting on to the time the State wants two senators in Washington."

"Well, I suppose, John," Hiram said, turning a serious face to his brother, "that you've thought the matter all over, and are sure you are right?"

The Governor threw back his head with a scoffing laugh.

"I guess it didn't require much thought on my part," he answered carelessly.

"I don't see how you figure that out," contended Hiram warmly. "You're Governor of the State, and your own boss, ain't you?"

It was the first time in all his life that anyone had squarely confronted John Berriman with the question whether or not he was his own boss, and for some reason it went deep into his soul, and rankled there.

"Now see here, Hiram," he said at length, "there's no use of your putting on airs and pretending you don't understand this thing. You know well enough it was all fixed before I went in." The other man looked at him in bewilderment, and the Governor continued brusquely: "The party knew the Senator was going to die, and so the Governor pulled out and I went in just so the thing could be done decently when the time came."

The old farmer was scratching his head.

"That's it, eh? They got wind the Senator was goin' to die, and so the Governor told that lie about having to go South just so he could step into the dead man's shoes, eh?"

"That's the situation — if you want to put it that way."

"And now you're going to appoint the Governor?"

"Of course I am; I couldn't do anything else if I wanted to."

"Why not?"

"Why, look here, Hiram, haven't you any idea of political obligation? It's expected of me."

"Oh, it is, eh? Did you promise to appoint the Governor?"

"Why, I don't know that I exactly made any promises, but that doesn't make a particle of difference. The understanding was that the Governor was to pull out and I was to go in and appoint him. It's a matter of honour;" and Governor Berriman drew himself up with pride.

The farmer turned a troubled face to the fire.

"I suppose, then," he said finally, "that you all think the Governor is the best man we have for the United States Senate. I take it that in appointing him, John, you feel sure he will guard the interests of the people before everything else, and that the people — I mean the working people of this State — will always be safe in his hands; do you?"

"Oh, Lord, no, Hiram!" exclaimed the Governor irritably. "I don't think that at all!"

Hiram Berriman's brown face warmed to a dull red.

"You don't?" he cried. "You mean to sit there, John Berriman, and tell me that you don't think the man you're going to put in the United States Senate will be an honest man? What do you mean by saying you're going to put a dishonest man in there to make laws for the people, to watch over them and protect them? If you don't think he's a good man, if you don't think he's the best man the State has"— the old farmer was pounding the table heavily with his huge fist — "if you don't think that, in God's name, *why do you appoint him?*"

"I wish I could make you understand, Hiram," said the Governor in an injured voice, "that it's not for me to say."

"Why ain't it for you to say? Why ain't it, I want to know? Who's running you, your own conscience or some gang of men that's trying to steal from the State? Good *God*, I wish I had never lived to see the day a brother of mine put a thief in the United States Senate to bamboozle the honest, hard-working people of this State!"

"Hold on, please — that's a little too strong!" flamed the Governor.

"It ain't too strong. If a Senator ain't an honest man, he's a thief; and if he ain't lookin' after the welfare of the people, he's bamboozlin' them, and that's all there is about it. I don't know much about politics, but I ain't lived my life without learning a little about right and wrong, and it's a sorry day we've come to, John Berriman, if right and wrong don't enter into the makin' of a Senator!"

The Governor could think of no fitting response, so he held his peace. This seemed to quiet the irate farmer, and he surveyed his brother intently, and not unkindly.

"You're in a position now, John," he said, and there was a kind of homely eloquence in his serious voice, "to be a friend to the people. It ain't many of us ever get the chance of doin' a great thing. We work along, and we do the best we can with what comes our way, but most of us don't get the chance to do a thing that's goin' to help thousands of people, and that the whole country's goin' to say was a move for the right. You want to think of that, and when you're thinkin' so much about honour, you don't want to clean forget about honesty. Don't you stick to any foolish notions about bein' faithful to the party; it ain't the party that needs helpin'. No matter how you got where you are, you're Governor of the State right now, John, and your first duty is to the people of this State, not to Tom Styles or anybody else. Just you remember that when you're namin' your Senator in the morning."

It was long before the Governor retired. He sat there by the fireplace until after the fire had died down, and he was too absorbed to grow cold. He thought of many things. Like the man who had preceded him in office, he wished that some one else was just then encumbered with the gubernatorial shoes.

The next morning there was a heavy feeling in his head which he thought a walk in the bracing air might dispel, so he started on foot for the State-house. A light snow was on the ground, and there was something reassuring in the crispness of the morning. It would make a slave feel like a free man to drink in such air, he was thinking. Snatches of his brother's outburst of the night before kept breaking into his consciousness but curiously enough they did not greatly disturb him. He concluded that it was wonderful what a walk in the bracing air could do. From the foot of the hill he looked up at the State-house, for the first time in his experience seeing and thinking about it — not simply taking it for granted. There seemed a nobility about it — in the building itself, and back of that, in what it stood for.

As he walked through the corridor to his office he was greeted with cheerful, respectful salutations. His mood let him give the greetings a value they did not have and from that rose a sense of having the trust and goodwill of his fellows.

But upon reaching his desk he found another telegram from Styles. It was imperatively worded and as he read it the briskness and satisfaction went from his bearing. He walked to the window and stood there looking down at the city, and, as it had been in looking ahead at the State-house, he now looked out over the city really seeing and understanding it, not merely taking it for granted. He found himself wondering if many of the people in that city — in that State — looked to their Governor with the old-fashioned trust his brother had shown. His eyes dimmed; he was thinking of the satisfaction it would afford his children, if — long after he had gone — they could tell how a great chance had once come into their father's life, and how he had proved himself a man.

"Will you sign these now, Governor?" asked a voice behind him.

It was his secretary, a man who knew the affairs of the State well, and whom every one seemed to respect.

"Mr. Haines," he said abruptly, "who do you

think is the best man we have for the United States Senate?"

The secretary stepped back, dumfounded; amazed that the question should be put to him, startled at that strange way of putting it. Then he told himself he must be discreet. Like many of the people at the State-house, in his heart Haines was a Boxer.

"Why, I presume," he ventured, "that the Governor is looked upon as the logical candidate, isn't he?"

"I'm not talking about logical candidates. I want to know who you think is the man who would most conscientiously and creditably represent this State in the Senate of the United States."

It was so simply spoken that the secretary found himself answering it as simply. "If you put it that way, Governor, Mr. Huntington is the man, of course."

"You think most of the people feel that way?"

"I know they do."

"You believe if it were a matter of popular vote, Huntington would be the new Senator?"

"There can be no doubt of that, Governor. I think they all have to admit that. Huntington is the man the people want."

"That's all, Mr. Haines. I merely wondered what you thought about it."

Soon after that Governor Berriman rang for a messenger boy and sent a telegram. Then he settled quietly down to routine work. It was about eleven when one of the newspaper men came in.

"Good-morning, Governor," he said briskly; "how's everything to-day?"

"All right, Mr. Markham. I have nothing to tell you to-day, except that I've made the senatorial appointment."

"Oh," laughed the reporter excitedly, "that's all, is it?"

"Yes," replied the Governor, smiling too; "that's all!"

The reporter looked at the clock. "I'll just catch the noon edition," he said, "if I telephone right away."

He was moving to the other room when the Governor called to him.

"See here, it seems to me you're a strange newspaper man!"

"How so?"

"Why, I tell you I've made a senatorial appointment — a matter of some slight importance — and you rush off never asking whom I've appointed."

The reporter gave a forced laugh. He wished the Governor would not detain him with a joke now when every second counted.

"That's right," he said, with strained pleasantness. "Well, who's the man?"

The Governor raised his head. "Huntington," he said quietly, and resumed his work.

"What?" gasped the reporter. "*What?*" Then he stopped in embarrassment, as if ashamed of being so easily taken in. "Guess you're trying to jolly me a little, aren't you, Governor?"

"Jolly you, Mr. Markham? I'm not given to 'jollying' newspaper reporters. Here's a copy of the telegram I sent this morning, if you are still sceptical. Really, I don't see why you think it so impossible. Don't you consider Mr. Huntington a fit man for the place?"

But for the minute the reporter seemed unable to speak. "May I ask," he fumbled at last, "why you did it?"

"I had but one motive, Mr. Markham. I thought the matter over and it seemed to me the people should have the man they wanted. I am with them in believing Huntington the best man for the place." He said it simply, and went quietly back to his work.

For many a long day politicians and papers continued the search for "the motive." Styles and his crowd saw it as a simple matter of selling out; they knew, of course, that it could be nothing else. After their first rage had subsided, and they saw there was nothing they could do, they wondered, sneeringly, why he did not "fix up a better story." That was a little *too* simple-minded. Did he think people were fools? And even the men who profited by the situation puzzled their brains for weeks trying to understand it. There was something behind it, of course.

XI

HIS AMERICA

HE HATED to see the reporter go. With the closing of that door it seemed certain that there was no putting it off any longer. But even when the man's footsteps were at last sounding on the stairway, he still clung to him.

"Father," he asked, fretfully, "why do you always talk to those fellows?"

Herman Beckman turned in his chair and stared at his son. Then he laughed. "Now, that's a fine question to come from the honour man of a law school! I hope, Fritz, that your oration to-night is going to have a little more sense in it than that."

The calling up of his oration made him reach out another clutching hand to the vanished reporter. "But it's farcical, father, to be always interviewed by a paper nobody reads."

"Nobody — *reads?*"

"Why, nobody cares anything about the *Leader.* It's dead."

Herman Beckman looked at his son sharply; something about him seemed strange. He decided that he was nervous about the commencement programme. Fritz had the one oration.

The boy had opened the drawer of his study table and was fingering some papers he had taken out.

"Sure you know it?" the man asked with affectionate parental anxiety.

"Oh, I know it all right," Fred answered grimly, and again the father decided that he was nervous about the thing. He wasn't just like himself.

The man walked to the window and stood looking across at the university buildings. Colleges had always meant much to Herman Beckman. The very day Fritz was born he determined that the boy was to go to college. It was good to witness the fulfilment of his dreams. He turned his glance to the comfortable room.

"Pretty decent comfortable sort of place, isn't it, father?" Fred asked, following his father's look and thought from the Morris chair to the student's lamp, and all those other things which nowadays seem an inevitable part of the acquirement of learning.

It made his father laugh. "Yes, my boy, I should call it decent — and comfortable." He grew thoughtful after that.

"Pretty different from the place you had, father?"

"Oh — me? My place to study was any place I could find. Sometimes on top of a load of hay, lots of times by the light of the logs. I've studied in some funny places, Fritz."

"Well, you *got* there, father!" the boy burst out with feeling. "By Jove, there aren't many of them *know* the things you know!"

"I know enough to know what I don't know," said the old man, a little sadly. "I know enough to know what I missed. I wanted to go to college. No one will ever know how I wanted to! I began to think I'd never feel right about it. But I have a notion that when I sit there to-night listening to you, Fritz, knowing that you're speaking for two hundred boys, half of whose fathers did go to college, I think I'm going to feel better about it then."

The boy turned away. Something in the kindly words seemed as the cut of a whip across his face.

"Well, Fritz," his father continued, getting into his coat, "I'll be going downtown. Leave you to put on an extra flourish or two." He laughed in proud parental fashion. "Anyway, I have some things to see about."

The boy stood up. "Father, I have something to tell you." He said it shortly and sharply.

The father stood there, puzzled.

"You won't like my oration to-night, father."

And still the man did not speak. The words would not have bothered him much — it was the boy's manner.

"In fact, father, you're going to be desperately disappointed in it."

The dull red was creeping into the man's cheeks.

He was one to have little patience with that thing of not doing one's work. "*Why* am I going to be disappointed? This is no time to shirk! You should —"

"Oh, you'll not complain of the time and thought I've put on it," the boy broke in with a short, hard laugh. "But, you see, father — you see"— his armour had slipped from him — "it doesn't express — your views."

"Did I ever *say* I wanted you to express 'my views'? Did I bring you up to be a mouthpiece of mine? Haven't I told you to *think?*" But with a long, sharp glance at his boy anger gave way. "Come, boy"— going over and patting him on the back —"brace up now. You're acting like a seven-year-old girl afraid to speak her first piece," and his big laugh rang out, eager to reassure.

"You won't see it! You won't believe it! I don't suppose you'll believe it when you hear it!" He turned away, overwhelmed by a sudden realisation of just how difficult was the thing that lay before him.

The man started toward his son, but instead he walked over and sat down at the opposite side of the table, waiting. He was beginning to see that there was something in this which he did not understand.

At last the boy turned to him, fighting back some things, taking on other things. He gazed at the care-worn, rugged face — face of a worker and a dreamer, reading in those lines the story of that life, seeing more clearly than he had ever seen before the beauty and futility of it. Here was the idealist, the man who would give his whole lifetime to a dream he had dreamed. He loved his father very tenderly as he looked at him, read him, then.

"Father," he asked quietly, "are you satisfied with your life?"

The man simply stared — waiting, seeking his bearings.

"You came to this country when you were nineteen years old — didn't you, father?" The man nodded. "And now you're — it's sixty-one, isn't it?"

Again he nodded.

"You've been in America, then, forty-two years. Father, do you think as much of it now as you did forty-two years ago?"

"I don't know what you mean," the man said, searching his son's quiet, passionate face. "I can't make you out, Fritz."

"My favourite story as a kid," the boy went on, "was to hear you tell of how you felt when your boat came sailing into New York Harbour, and you saw the first outlines of a country you had dreamed about all through your boyhood, which you had saved pennies for, worked nights for, ever since you were old enough to know the meaning of America. I mean," he corrected, significantly, "the meaning of what you thought was America.

"It's a bully story, father," he continued, with a smile at once tender and hard; "the simple German boy, born a dreamer, standing there looking out at the dim shores of that land he had idealised. If ever a man came to America bringing it rich gifts, that man was you!"

"Fritz," his father's voice was rendered harsh by mystification and foreboding, "tell me what you're talking about. Come to the point. Clear this up."

"I'm talking about American politics — your party — having ruined your life! I'm talking about working like a slave all your days and having nothing but a mortgaged farm at sixty-one! I'm talking about playing a losing game! I'm saying, *What's the use?* Father, I'm telling you that *I'm* going to join the other party and make some money!"

The man just sat there, staring.

"Well," the boy took it up defiantly, "why not?"

And then he moved, laid a not quite steady hand out upon the table. "My boy, you're not well. You've studied too hard. Now brace yourself up for to-night, and then we'll go down home and fix you up. What you need, Fritz," he said, trying to laugh, "is the hayfield."

"You're not *seeing* it!" The boy pushed back his chair and began moving about the room. "The only way I can brace myself up for to-night is to get so mad — father, usually you see things so easily! Don't you understand? It was my chance, my one moment, my time to strike. It will be years before I get such a hearing again. You see, father, the thing will be printed, and the men I want to have hear it, the men who *own this State*, will be there. One of them is to preside. And the story of it, the worth of it, to them, is that I'm your son. You see, after all," he seized at this wildly, "I'm getting my start on the fact that I'm your son."

"Go on," said the man; the brown of his wind-beaten face had yielded to a tinge of grey. "Just what is it you are going to say?"

"I call it 'The New America,' a lot of this talk about doing things, the glory of industrial America, the true Americans the men of constructive genius, the patriotism of railroad and factory building, a eulogy of railroad officials and corporation presidents," he rushed on with a laugh. "Singing the song of Capital. Father, can't you see *why?*"

The old man had risen. "Tell me this," he said. "None of it matters much, if you just tell me this: You *believe* these things? You've thought it all out for yourself — and you *feel* that way? You're honest, aren't you, Fritz?" He put that last in a whisper.

The boy made no reply; after a minute the man sank back to his chair. The years seemed coming to him with the minutes.

Fred was leaning against the wall. "Father," he said at last, "I hope you'll let me be a little roundabout. It's only fair to me to let me ramble on a little. I've got to put it all right before you or — or — You know, dad,"— he came back to his place by the table, "the first thing I remember very clearly is those men, your party managers, coming down to the farm one time and asking you to run for Governor. How many times is it you've run for Governor, father?" He put the question slowly.

"Five," said the man heavily.

"I don't know which time this was; but you didn't want to. You were sorry when you saw them coming. I heard some of the talk. You talked about your farm, what you wanted to do that summer, how you couldn't afford the time or the money. They argued that you owed it to the party — they always got you there; how no other man could hold down majorities as you could — a man like you giving the best years of his life to holding down majorities! They said you were the one man against whom no personal attack could be made. And when there was so much to fight, anyway — oh, I know that speech by heart! They've made great capital of your honesty and your clean life. In fact, they've held that up as a curtain behind which a great many things could go on. Oh, *you* didn't know about them; you were out in front of the curtain, but I haven't lived in this town without finding out that they needed your integrity and your clean record pretty bad!

"That was out on the side porch. Mother had brought out some buttermilk, and they drank it while they talked. You put up a good fight. Your time was money to you at that time of year; a man shouldn't neglect his farm — but you never yet could hold out against that 'needing-you' kind of talk. They knew there was no chance for your election. You knew it. But it takes a man of just your grit to put any snap into a hopeless campaign.

"Mother cried when you went to drive them back to town. You see, I remember all those things. She told about how hard you would work, and how it would do no good — that the State belonged to the other party. She talked about the farm, too, and the addition she had wanted for the house, and how now she wouldn't have it. Mother felt pretty bad that night. She's gone through a lot of those times."

There was a silence.

"You were away a lot that summer, and all fall. You looked pretty well used up when you came home, but you said that you had held down majorities splendidly."

Again there was silence. It was the silences that seemed to be saying the most.

"You had one term in Congress — that's the only thing you ever had. Then you did so much that they concentrated in your district and saw to it that you never got back. Julius Cæsar couldn't have been elected again," he laughed harshly.

"Father," the boy went on, after a pause, "you asked me if I were honest. There are two kinds of honesty. The primitive kind — like yours — and then the kind you develop for yourself. Do I believe the things I'm going to say to-night? No — not now. But I'll believe them more after I've heard the applause I'm sure to get. I'll believe them still more after I've had my first case thrown to me by our railroad friends who own this State. More and more after I've said them over in campaigning next fall, and pretty soon I'll be so sure I believe them that I really will believe them — and that," he concluded, flippantly, "is the new brand of American honesty. Why, any smart man can persuade himself he's not a hypocrite!"

"My *God!*" it wrenched from the man. "*This?* If you'd stolen money — killed a man — but hypocrisy, cant — the very thing I've fought hardest, hated most! You lived all your life with me to learn *this?*"

"I lived all my life with you to learn what pays, and what doesn't. I lived all my life with you to learn from failure the value of success."

"I never was sure I was a failure until this hour."

"Father! Can't you see —"

"Oh, don't *talk* to me!" cried the old man, rising,

reaching out his fist as though he would strike him. "Son of mine sitting there telling me he is fixing up a brand of honesty for himself!"

The boy grew quieter as self-restraint left his father. "I mean that — just that," he said at last. "Let a man either give or get. If he gives, let it be to the real thing. There are two Americas. The America of you dreamers — and then the real America. Yours is an idea — an idea quite as much as an ideal. I don't think you have the slightest comprehension of how far apart it is from the real America. The people who dream of it over in Europe are a great deal nearer it than you people who work for it here. Father, the spirit of this country flows in a strong, swift, resistless current. You never got into it at all. Your kind of idealists influence it about as much — about as much as red lights burned on the banks of the great river would influence the current of that river. You're not *of* it. You came here, throbbing with the love for America; and with your ideal America you've fought the real, and you've worked and you've believed and you've sacrificed. Father, *what's the use?* In this State, anyway, it's hopeless. It has been so through your lifetime; it will be through mine."

The man sat looking at him. He felt that he should say something, but the words did not come — held back, perhaps, by a sense of their uselessness. It was not so much what Fred said as it was the look in his eyes as he said it. There was nothing impetuous or youthful about that look, nothing to be laughed at or argued away. He had always felt that Fred had a mind which saw things straight, saw them in their right relations, and at that moment he had no words to plead for what Fred called the America of the dreamers.

"I'm of the second generation, dad," the boy went on, at length, "and the second generation has an ideal of its own, and that ideal is Success. It took us these forty years to come to understand the spirit of America. You were a dreamer who loved America. I'm an American. We've translated democracy and brotherhood and equality into enterprise and opportunity and success — and that's getting Americanised. Now, father," he sought refuge in the tone of every-day things, "you'll get used to it — won't you? I don't expect you to feel very good about it, but you aren't going to be broken up about it — are you? After all, father," laughing and moving about as if to break the seriousness of things, "there's nothing criminal about being one of the other fellows — is there? Just remember that there *are* folks who even think it's respectable!"

The father had risen and picked up his hat. "No, Fred," he said, with a sadness in which there was great dignity, "there is nothing criminal in it if a man's conviction sends him that way. But to me there is something — something too sad for words in a man's selling his own soul."

"Father! How extravagant! *Why* is it selling one's soul to sit down and figure out what's the best thing to do?" He hesitated, hating to add hurt to hurt, not wanting to say that his father's fight should have been with the revolutionists, that his life was ineffective because, seeing his dream from within a dream, his thinking had been muddled. He only said: "As I say, father, it's a question of giving or getting. I couldn't even give in your way. And I've seen enough of giving to want a taste of getting. I want to make things go — and I see my chance. Why father," he laughed, trying to turn it, "there's nothing so American as wanting to make things *go*."

He looked at him for a long minute. "My boy," he said, "I fear you are becoming so American that I am losing you."

"Father," the boy pleaded, affectionately, "now don't —"

The old man held up his hand. "You've tried to make me understand it," he said, "and succeeded. You can't complain of the way you've succeeded. I don't know why I don't argue with you — plead; there are things I could say — should say, perhaps — but something assures me it would be useless. I feel a good many years older than I did when I came into this room, but the reason for it is not that you're joining the other party. You know what I think of the men who control this State, the men with whom you desire to cast your lot, but I trust the years I've spent fighting them haven't made a bigot of me. It's not joining their party — it's *using* it — makes this the hardest thing I've been called upon to meet."

"Father, don't look like that! How do you think I am going to get up and speak to-night with *that* face before me?"

"You didn't think, did you," the man laughed bitterly, "that I would inspire you to your effort?"

The boy stood looking at his father, a strange new fire in his eyes.

"Yes," he said, quietly, tenderly, "you will inspire me. When I get up before those men to-night I'm going to see the picture of that boy straining for his first glimpse of New York Harbour. I'm going to think for just a minute of the things that boy brought with him — things he has never lost. And then I'll see you as you stand here now — it will be enough. What I need to do is to get mad. If I falter I'll just think of some of those times when you came home from your campaigns — how you looked — what you said. It will bring the inspiration. Father, I figure it out like this. We're going to get it back. We're going to get what's coming to us. There's another America than the America of you dreamers. To yours you have given; from mine I will get. And the irony of it — don't think I don't see the irony of it — is that I will be called the real American. Do you know what I'm going to do? I'm going to make the railroads of this State — oh, it sounds like schoolboy talk, but just give me a little time — I'm going to make the railroads of this State pay off every cent of that mortgage on your farm! Father," he finished, impetuously, in a last appeal, "you're broken up now, disappointed, but would you honestly want me to travel the road you've traveled?"

"My boy," answered the old man, and the tears came with it, "I wanted you to travel the road of an honest man."

Herman Beckman did not go to the commencement exercises that night. There was no train home until morning, so he had the night to spend in town. He was alone, for his friends assumed that he would be out at the university. But he preferred being alone.

He sat in his room at the hotel, reading. And he could read. Years of discipline stood him in good stead now. His life had taught him to read anywhere, at any time. He had never permitted himself the luxury of not being "in the mood." It was only the men who had gone to college who could do that. He *had* to read. He always carried some little book with him, for how did a man know that he might not have to wait an hour for a train somewhere? The man had a simple-minded veneration for knowledge. He wanted to know about things. And he had never learned to pretend that he didn't want to know. He quite lacked the modern art of flippancy. He believed in great books.

And so on the night that his son was being graduated from college he sat in his room at the hotel — cheap room in a mediocre hotel; he had never learned to feel at home in the rich ones — reading Marcus Aurelius. But his hand as he turned the pages trembled as the hand of a very old man. At midnight some reporters came in to ask him what he thought of his son's oration. They wanted a statement from him.

He told them that he had never believed the sins of a parent should be visited on a child, and that it was even so with the thought. He had always contended that a man should do his own thinking. The contention applied to his son.

"Gamey old brute!" was what one of the reporters said in the elevator.

He could not read Marcus Aurelius after that. He went to bed, but he did not sleep. Many things passed before him. His anticipations, his dreams for Fritz, had brought the warmest pleasure of his stern, unrelaxing life. There was a great emptiness tonight. What was a man to turn to, think about, when he seemed stripped, not only of the future, but of the past? He seemed called upon to readjust the whole of his life, giving up that which he had held dearest. What was left? Daylight found him turning it over and over.

In the morning he went home. He got away without seeing any of his friends.

He did not try to read this morning; somehow it seemed there was no use in trying to read any more. He watched the country through which they were passing, thinking of the hundreds of times he had ridden over it in campaigning. He wondered, vaguely, just how much money he had spent on railroad fare — he had never accepted mileage. Fred's "What's the use?" kept ringing in his ears. There was something about that phrase which made one feel very tired and old. It even seemed there was no use looking out to see how the crops were getting on. *What's the use? What's the use?* Was that a phrase one learned in college?

There had been two things to tell "mother" that night. The first was that he had stopped in town and told Claus Hansen he could have that south hundred and sixty he had been wanting for two years.

It was not easy to tell the woman who had worked shoulder to shoulder with him for thirty years, the woman who during those years had risen with him in the early morning and worked with him until darkness rescued the weary bodies, that in their old age they must surrender the fruit of their toil. They would have left just what they had started with. They had just held their own.

Coming down on the train he had made up his mind that if Hansen were in town he would tell him that he could have the land. He felt so very tired and old, so bowed down with Fred's "What's the use?" that he saw that he himself would never get the mortgage paid off. And Fred had said something about making the railroads pay it. He did not know just how the boy figured that out — indeed, he was getting a little dazed about the whole thing — but if Fritz had any idea of having the railroads pay off the mortgage on *his* farm — he couldn't forget how the boy looked when he said it, face white, eyes burning — he would see to it right now that there was no chance of that.

He tried not to look at the land as he drove past it on the way home. He wondered just how much campaign literature it had paid for. He wondered if he would ever get used to seeing Claus Hansen putting up his hay over there in that field.

He had felt so badly about telling mother that he told it very bluntly. And because he felt so sorry for her he said not one kind word, but just sat quiet, looking the other way.

She was clearing off the table. He heard her scraping out the potato dish with great care. Then she was coming over to him. She came awkwardly, hesitatingly — her life had not schooled her in meeting emotional moments beautifully — but she laid her hand upon him, patted him on the shoulder as one would a child. " Never mind, papa — never you mind. It will make it easier for us. There's enough left — and it will make it easier. We're getting on — we're —" There she broke off abruptly into a vigorous scolding of the dog, who was lifting covetous nostrils to a piece of meat.

That was all. And there was no woman in the country had worked harder. And Martha was ambitious; she liked land, and she did not like Claus Hansen's wife.

Yes, he had had a good wife.

Then there was that other thing to tell her — about Fritz. That was harder.

Mother had not gone up to the city to hear Fritz " speak " because her feet were bothering her, and she could not wear her shoes. He had had a vague idea of how disappointed she was, though she had said very little about it. Martha never had been one to say much about things. When he came back, of course she had wanted to know all about it, and he had put her off. Now he had to tell her.

It was much harder; and in the telling of it he broke down.

This time she did not come over and pat his shoulder. Perhaps Martha knew — likely she had never heard the word intuition, but, anyway, she knew — that it was beyond that.

It seemed difficult for her to comprehend. She was bewildered to find that Fritz could change parties all in a minute. She seemed to grasp, first of all, that it was disrespectful to his father. Some boys at school had been putting notions into his head.

But gradually she began to see it. Fritz wanted to make money. Fritz wanted to have it easier. And the other people did "have it easier."

It divided her feeling: sorry and indignant for the father, secretly glad and relieved for the boy. "He will have it easier than we had it, papa," she said at the last. "But it was not right of Fritz," she concluded, vaguely but severely.

As she washed the dishes Martha was thinking that likely Fritz's wife would have a hired girl.

Then Martha went up to bed. He said that he would come in a few minutes, but many minutes went by while he sat out on the side porch trying to think it out.

The moon was shining brightly down on that hundred and sixty which Claus Hansen was to have. And the moon, too, seemed to be saying: "What's the use?"

Well, what *was* the use? Perhaps, after all, the boy was right. What had it all amounted to? What was there left? What had he done?

Two Americas, Fred had said, and his but the America of the dreamers. He had always thought that he was fighting for the real. And now Fred said that he had never become an American at all.

From the time he was twelve years old he had

wanted to be an American. A queer old man back in the German village — an old man, he recalled strangely now, who had never been in America — told him about it. He told how all men were brothers in America, how the poor and the rich loved each other — indeed, how there were no poor and rich at all, but the same chance for every man who would work. He told about the marvellous resources of that distant America — gold in the earth, which men were free to go and get, hundreds upon hundreds of miles of untouched forests and great rivers — all for men to use, great cities no older than the men who were in them, which men at that present moment were *making* — every man his equal chance. He told of rich land which a man could have for nothing, which would be *his*, if he would but go and work upon it. In the heart of the little German boy there was kindled then a fire which the years had never put out. His cheeks grew red, his eyes bright and very deep as he listened to the story. He went home that night and dreamed of going to America. And through the years of his boyhood, penny by penny, he saved his money for America. It was his dream. It was the passion of his life. More plainly than the events of yesterday, he remembered his first glimpse of those wonderful shores — the lump in his throat, the passionate excitement, the uplift. Leaning over the railing of his boat, staring, searching, penetrating, worshipping, he lifted up his heart and sent out his pledge of allegiance to the new land. How he would love America, work for it, be true to it!

He had three dollars and sixty cents in his pocket when he stepped upon American soil. He wondered if any man had ever felt richer. For had he not reached the land where there was an equal chance for every man who would work, where men loved each other as brothers, and where the earth itself was so rich and so gracious in its offerings?

The old man crossed one leg over the other — slowly, stiffly. It made him tired and stiff now just to think of the work he had done between that day and this.

But there was something which he had always had — that something was *his* America. That had never wavered, though he soon learned that between it and realities were many things which were wrong and unfortunate. With the whole force and passion of his nature, with all his single mindedness — would some call it simple mindedness? — he threw himself into the fight against those things which were blurring men's vision of his America. No work, no sacrifice was too great, for America had enemies who called themselves friends, men who were striking heavy blows at that equal chance for every man. When he failed, it was because he did not know enough; he must work, he must study, he must think, in order to make more real to other men the

America which was in his heart. He must fight for it because it was his.

And now it seemed that the end had come; he was old, he was tired, he was not sure. Claus Hansen would have his land and his son would join hands with the things which he had spent his life in fighting. And far deeper and sadder and more bitter than that, he had not transmitted the America of his heart even to his own son. He was not leaving someone to fight for it in his stead, to win where he had failed. Fred saw in it but a place for gain. "I lived all my life with you to learn from failure the value of success." That was what he had given to his boy. Yes, that was what he had bequeathed to America. Could the failure, the futility of his life be more clearly revealed?

Twice Martha had called to him, but still he sat, smoking, thinking. There was much to think about to-night.

Finally, it was not thought, but visions. Too tired for conscious thinking, he gave himself up to what came — Fred's America, his America, the America of the dreamers — and the things which stood between. The America of the future —what would that America be?

At the last, taking form from many things which came and went, shaping itself slowly, form giving place to new form, he seemed to see it grow. Out beyond that land Claus Hansen was to have, a long way off, there rose the vision of the America of the future — an America of realities, and yet an America of dreams; for the dreamers had become the realists — or was it that the realists had become dreamers? In the manifold forms taken on and cast aside destroying dualism had made way for the strength and the dignity and harmony of unity. He watched it as breathlessly, as yearningly, as the nineteen-year-old boy had watched the other America taking shape in the distance some forty years before. "How did you come?" he whispered. "What are you?"

And the voice of that real America seemed to answer: "I came because for a long-enough time there were enough men who held me in their hearts. I came because there were men who never gave me up. I was won by men who believed that they had failed."

Again there was a lump in his throat — once more an exultation flooded all his being. For to the old man — tired, stiff, smitten though he had been, there came again that same uplift which long before had come to the boy. Was there not here an answer to "What's the use?" For he would leave America as he came to it — loving it, believing in it. What were the work and the failure of a lifetime when there was something in his heart which was his? Should he say that he had fought in vain when he had kept it for himself? It was as real, as wonderful — yes, as inevitable, as it had been forty years before. Realities had taken his land, his career, his hopes for the boy. But realities had not stripped him of his dream. The futility of the years could not harm the things which were in his heart. Even in America he had not lost His America.

"Perhaps it is then that it is like that," he murmured, his vision carrying him back to the days of his broken English. "Perhaps it is that every man's America is in the inside of his own heart. Perhaps it is that it will come when it has grown big — big and very strong — in the hearts."

XII

THE ANARCHIST: HIS DOG

STUBBY had a route, and that was how he happened to get a dog. For the benefit of those who have never carried papers it should be thrown in that having a route means getting up just when there is really some fun in sleeping, lining up at the *Leader* office — maybe having a scrap with the fellow who says you took his place in the line — getting your papers all damp from the press and starting for the outskirts of the city. Then you double up the paper in the way that will cause all possible difficulty in undoubling and hurl it with what force you have against the front door. It is good to have a route, for you at least earn your salt, so your father can't say *that* any more. If he does, you know it isn't so.

When you have a route, you whistle. All the fellows whistle. They may not feel like it, but it is the custom — as could be sworn to by many sleepy citizens. And as time goes on you succeed in acquiring the easy manner of a brigand.

Stubby was little and everything about him seemed sawed off just a second too soon,— his nose, his fingers, and most of all, his hair. His head was a faithful replica of a chestnut burr. His hair did not lie down and take things easy. It stood up — and out! — gentle ladies couldn't possibly have let their hands sink into it — as we are told they do — for the hands just wouldn't sink. They'd have to float.

And alas, gentle ladies didn't particularly want their hands to sink into it. There was not that about Stubby's short person to cause the hands of gentle ladies to move instinctively to his head. Stubby bristled. That is, he appeared to bristle. Inwardly, Stubby yearned, though he would have swung into his very best brigand manner on the spot were you to suggest so offensive a thing. Just to look at Stubby you'd never in a thousand years guess what a funny feeling he had sometimes when he got to the top of the hill where his route began and could see a long way down the river and the town curled in on the other side. Sometimes when the morning sun was shining through a mist — making things awful queer — some of the mist got into Stubby's squinty little eyes. After the mist behaved that way he always whistled so rakishly and threw his papers with such abandonment that people turned over in their beds and muttered things about having that little heathen of a paper boy shot.

All along the route are dogs. Indeed, routes are distinguished by their dogs. Mean routes are those that have terraces and mean dogs; good routes —

where the houses are close together and the dogs run out and wag their tails. Though Stubby's greater difficulty came through the wagging tails; he carried in a collie neighbourhood, and all collies seemed consumed with mighty ambitions to have routes. If you spoke to them — and how could you *help* speaking to a collie when he came bounding out to you that way? — you had an awful time chasing him back, and when he got lost — and it seemed collies spent most of their time getting lost — the woman would put her head out next morning and want to know if you had coaxed her dog away!

Some of the fellows had dogs that went with them on their routes. One day one of them asked Stubby why he didn't have a dog and he replied in surly fashion that he didn't have one 'cause he didn't want one. If he wanted one, he guessed he'd have one.

And there was no one within ear-shot old enough or wise enough — or tender enough? — to know from the meanness of Stubby's tone, and by his evil scowl, that his heart was just breaking to own a dog.

One day a new dog appeared along the route. He was yellow, and looked like a cheap edition of a bull-dog. He was that kind of dog most accurately described by saying it is hard to describe him, the kind you say is just dog — and everybody knows.

He tried to follow Stubby; not in the trusting, bounding manner of the collies — not happily, but hopingly. Stubby, true to the ethics of his profession, chased him back where he had come from. That there might be nothing whatever on his conscience, he even threw a stone after him. Stubby was an expert in throwing things at dogs. He could seem to just miss them and yet never hit them.

The next day it happened again; but just as he had a clod poised for throwing, a window went up and a woman called: "For pity *sake,* little boy, don't chase him back *here.*"

"Why — why, ain't he yours?" called Stubby.

"Mercy, *no.* We can't chase him away."

"Who's is he?" demanded Stubby.

"Why, he's nobody's! He just hangs around. I wish you'd coax him away."

Well, that was a *new* one! And then all in a heap it rushed over Stubby that this dog who was nobody's dog could, if he coaxed him away — and the woman *wanted* him coaxed away — be his dog.

And because that idea had such a strange effect on him he sang out, in off-hand fashion: "Oh, all right, I'll take him away and drown him for you!"

"Oh, little *boy,*" called the woman, "why, don't *drown* him!"

"Oh, all right, I'll shoot him then!" called obliging Stubby, whistling for the dog — while all morning long the woman grieved over having sent a helpless little dog away with that perfectly *brutal* paper boy!

Stubby's mother was washing. She looked up from her tubs on the back porch to say, "Wish you'd take that bucket —" then seeing what was slinking behind her son, straightway assumed the rôle of destiny with, "Git out o' here!"

Stubby snapped his fingers behind his back as much as to say, "Wait a minute."

"A woman gave him to me," he said to his mother.

"*Gave* him to you?" she scoffed. "I sh' think she would!"

Then something happened that had not happened many times in Stubby's short lifetime. He acknowledged his feelings.

"I'd like to keep him. I'd like to have a dog."

His mother shook her hands and the flying suds seemed expressing her scorn. "Huh! *That* ugly good-for-nothing thing?"

The dog had edged in between Stubby's feet and crouched there. "He could go with me on my route," said Stubby. "He'd kind of be company for me."

And when he had said that he knew all at once just how lonesome he had been sometimes on his route, how he had wanted something to "kind of be company" for him.

His face twitched as he stooped down to pat the dog. Mrs. Lynch looked at her son — youngest of her five. Not the hardness of her heart but the hardness of her life had made her unpractised in moments of tenderness. Something in the way Stubby was patting the dog suggested to her that Stubby was a "queer one." He *was* kind of little to be carrying papers all by himself.

Stubby looked up. "He could eat what's thrown away."

That was an error in diplomacy. The woman's face hardened. "Mighty little 'll be thrown away *this* winter," she muttered.

But just then Mrs. Johnson appeared on the other side of the fence and began hanging up her clothes and with that Mrs. Lynch saw her way to justify herself in indulging her son. Mrs. Johnson and Mrs. Lynch had "had words." "You just let him stay around, Stubby," she called, and you would have supposed from her tone it was Stubby who was on the other side of the fence, "maybe he'll keep the neighbour's chickens out! Them that ain't got chickens o' their own don't want to be bothered with the neighbours'!"

That was how it happened that he stayed; and no one but Stubby knew — and possibly Stubby didn't either — how it happened that he was named Hero. It would seem that Hero should be a noble St. Bernard, or a particularly mean-looking bulldog, not a stocky, shapeless, squint-eyed yellow dog with one ear bitten half off and one leg built on an entirely different plan from its fellow legs. Possibly Stubby's own spiritual experiences had suggested to him that you weren't necessarily the way you looked.

The chickens were pretty well kept out, though no one ever saw Hero doing any of it. Perhaps Hero had been too long associated with chasing to desire any part in it — even with rôles reversed. If Stubby could help it, no one really saw Stubby doing the chasing either; he became skilled in chasing when he did not appear to be chasing; then he would get Hero to barking and turn to his mother with, "Guess you don't see so many chickens round nowadays."

The fellows in the line jeered at Hero at first, but they soon tired of it when Stubby said he didn't want the cur but his mother made him stay around to keep the chickens out. He was a fine chicken dog, Stubby grudgingly admitted. He couldn't keep him from following, said Stubby, so he just let him come. Sometimes when they were waiting in line Stubby made ferocious threats at Hero. He was going to break his back and wring his head off and do other heartless things which for some reason he never started in right then and there to accomplish.

It was different when they were alone — and they were alone a good deal. Stubby's route wasn't nearly so long after he had Hero to go with him. When winter came and five o'clock was dark and cold for starting out it was pretty good to have Hero trotting at his heels. And Hero always wanted to go; it was never so rainy nor so cold that that yellow dog seemed to think he would rather stay home by the fire. Then Hero was always waiting for him when he came home from school. Stubby would sing out, " Hello, cur! " and the tone was such that Hero did not grasp that he was being insulted. Sometimes when there was nobody about, Stubby picked Hero up in his arms and squeezed him — Stubby had not had a large experience with squeezing. At those times Hero would lick Stubby's face and whimper a little love whimper and such were the workings of Stubby's heart and mind that that made him of quite as much account as if he really had chased the chickens. Stubby, who had seen the way dogs can look at you out of their eyes, was not one to say of a dog, " What good is he? "

But it seemed there were such people. There were even people who thought you oughtn't to have a dog to love and to love you if you weren't one of those rich people who could pay two dollars and a half a year for the luxury.

Stubby first heard of those people one night in June. The father of the Lynch family was sitting in the back yard reading the paper when Hero and Stubby came running in from the alley. It was one of those moments when Hero, forgetting the bleakness of his youth, abandoned himself to the joy of living. He was tearing round and round Stubby, barking, when Stubby's father called out: " Here!

— shut up there, you cur. You better lie low. You're going to be shot the first of August."

Stubby, and as regards the joy of living Hero had done as much for Stubby as Stubby for Hero, came to a halt. The fun and frolic just died right out of him and he stood there staring at his father, who had turned the page and was settling himself to a new horror. At last Stubby spoke. "Why's he going to be shot on the first of August?" he asked in a tight little voice.

His father looked up. "Why's he going to be shot? You got any two dollars and a half to pay for him?"

He laughed as though that were a joke. Well, it was something of a joke. Stubby got ten cents a week out of his paper money. The rest he "turned in."

Then he went back to his paper. There was another long pause before Stubby asked, in that tight queer little voice: "What'd I have to pay two dollars and a half for? Nobody owns him."

His parent stirred scornfully. "Suppose you never heard of a dog tax, did you? S'pose they don't learn you nothing like that at school?"

Yes, Stubby did know that dogs had to have checks, but he hadn't thought anything about that in connection with Hero. He ventured another question. "You have to have 'em for all dogs, even if you just picked 'em up on the street and took care of 'em when nobody else would?"

"You bet you do," his parent assured him genially. "You pay your dog tax or the policeman comes on the first of August and shoots your dog."

With that he dismissed it for good, burying himself in his paper. For a minute the boy stood there in silence. Then he walked slowly round the house and sat down where his father couldn't see him. Hero followed — it was a way Hero had. The dog sat down beside the boy and after a couple of minutes the boy's arm stole furtively around him and they sat there very still for a long time.

As nobody but Hero paid much attention to him, nobody save Hero noticed how quiet and queer Stubby was for the next three days. Hero must have noticed it, for he was quiet and queer too. He followed wherever Stubby would let him, and every time he got a chance he would nestle up to him and look into his face — that way even cur dogs have of doing when they fear something is wrong.

At the end of three days Stubby, his little freckled face set and grim, took his stand in front of his father and came right out with: "I want to keep one week's paper money to pay Hero's tax."

His father's chair had been tilted back against a tree. Now it came down with a thud. "Oh, you *do*, do you?"

"I can earn the other fifty cents at little jobs."

"You *can*, can you? Now ain't you smart!"

The tone brought the blood to Stubby's face. "I think I got a right to," he said, his voice low.

The man's face, which had been taunting, grew ugly. "Look a-here, young man, none o' your lip!"

The tears rushed to Stubby's eyes but he stumbled on: "I guess Hero's got a right to some of my paper money when he goes with me every day on my route."

At that his father stared for a minute and then burst into a loud laugh. Blinded with tears, the boy turned to the house.

After she had gone to bed that night Stubby's mother heard a sound from the alcove at the head of the stairs where her youngest child slept. As the sound kept on she got out of her bed and went to Stubby's cot.

"Look here," she said, awkwardly but not unkindly, "this won't do. We're poor folks, Freddie" (it was only once in a while she called him that), "all we can do to live these times — we can't pay no dog tax."

As Stubby did not speak she added: "I know you've taken to the dog, but just the same you ain't to feel hard to your pa. He can't help it — and neither can I. Things is as they is — and nobody can help it."

As, despite this bit of philosophy Stubby was still gulping back sobs, she added what she thought a master stroke in consolation. "Now you just go right to sleep, and if they come to take this dog away maybe you can pick up another one in the fall."

The sobs suddenly stopped and Stubby stared at her. And what he said after a long stare was: "I guess there ain't no use in you and me talking about it."

"That's right," said she, relieved; "now you go right off to sleep." And she left him, never dreaming why Stubby had seen there was no use talking about it.

Nor did he talk about it; but a change came over Stubby's funny little person in the next few days. The change was particularly concerned with his jaw, though there was something different, too, in the light in his eyes as he looked straight ahead, and something different in his voice when he said: "Come on, Hero."

He got so he could walk into a store and demand, in a hard little voice: "Want a boy to do anything for you?" and when they said, "Got more boys than we know what to do with, sonny," Stubby would say, "All right," and stalk sturdily out again. Sometimes they laughed and said: "What could *you* do?" and then Stubby would stalk out, but possibly a little less sturdily.

Vacation came the next week, and still he had found nothing. His father, however, had been more successful. He found a place where they wanted a boy to work in a yard a couple of hours in the morning. For that Stubby was to get a dollar and a half a week. But that was to be turned in for his "keep." There were lots of mouths to feed — as Stubby's mother was always calling to her neighbour across the alley.

But the yard gave Stubby an idea, and he earned some dimes and one quarter in the next week. Most folks thought he was too little — one kind lady told him he ought to be playing, not working — but there were people who would let him take a big shears and cut grass around flower beds, and things like that. This he had to do afternoons, when he was supposed to be off playing, and when he came home his mother sometimes said some folks had it easy — playing around all day.

It was now the first week in July and Stubby had a dollar and twenty cents. It was getting to the point where he would wake in the night and find himself sitting up in bed, hands clenched. He dreamed dreams about how folks would let him live if he had ninety-nine cents but how he only had ninety-seven and a half, so they were going to shoot him.

Then one day he found Mr. Stuart. He was passing the house after having asked three people if they wanted a boy, and they didn't, and seemed so surprised at the idea of their wanting him that Stubby's throat was all tight, when Mr. Stuart sang out: " Say, boy, want a little job? "

It seemed at first it must be a joke — or a dream — anybody asking him if he *wanted* one, but the man was beckoning to him, so he pulled himself together and ran up the steps.

" Now here's a little package "— he took something out of the mail box. " It doesn't belong here. It's to go to three-hundred-two Pleasant street. You take it for a dime? "

Stubby nodded.

As he was going down the steps the man called: " Say, boy, how'd you like a steady job? "

For the first minute it seemed pretty mean — making fun of a fellow that way!

" This will be here every day. Suppose you come each day, about this time, and take it over there — not mentioning it to anybody."

Stubby felt weak. " Why, all right," he managed to say.

" I'll give you fifty cents a week. That fair? "

" Yes, sir," said Stubby, doing some quick calculation.

" Then here goes for the first week "— and he handed him the other forty cents.

It was funny how fast the world could change! Stubby wanted to run — he hadn't been doing much running of late. He wanted to go home and get Hero to go with him to Pleasant street, but didn't.

No, *sir*, when you had a job you had to 'tend to things!

Well, a person could do things, if he had to, thought Stubby. No use saying you couldn't, you *could*, if you had to. He was back in tune with life. He whistled; he turned up his collar in the old rakish way; he threw a stick at a cat. Back home he jumped over the fence instead of going in the gate — lately he had actually been using the gate. And he cried, "Get out of my sight, you cur!" in tones which, as Hero understood things, meant anything but getting out of his sight.

He was a little boy again. He slept at night as little boys sleep. He played with Hero along the route — taught him some new tricks. His jaw relaxed from its grown-upishness.

It was funny about those Stuarts. Sometimes he saw Mr. Stuart, but never anybody else; the place seemed shut up. But each day the little package was there, and every day he took it to Pleasant street and left it at the door there — that place seemed shut up, too.

When it was well into the second week Stubby ventured to say something about the next fifty cents.

The man fumbled in his pockets. Something in his face was familiar to experienced Stubby. It suggested a having to have two dollars and a half by August first and only having a dollar and a quarter state of mind.

"I haven't got the change. Pay you at the end of next week for the whole business. That all right?"

Stubby considered. "I've got to have it before the first of August," he said.

At that the man laughed — funny kind of laugh, it was, and muttered something. But he told Stubby he would have it before the first.

It bothered Stubby. He wished the man had given it to him *then.* He would rather get it each week and keep it himself. A little of the grown-up look stole back.

After that he didn't see Mr. Stuart, and one day, a week or so later, the package was not in the box and a man who wore the kind of clothes Stubby's father wore came around the house and asked him what he was doing.

Stubby was wary. "Oh, I've got a little job I do for Mr. Stuart."

The man laughed. "I had a little job I did for Mr. Stuart, too. You paid in advance?"

Stubby pricked up his ears.

"'Cause if you ain't, I'd advise you to look out for a little job some'eres else."

Then it came out. Mr. Stuart was broke; more than that, he was "off his nut." Lots of people were doing little jobs for him — there was no sense in any of them, and now he had suddenly been called out of town!

There was a trembly feeling through Stubby's insides, but outwardly he was bristling just like his hair bristled as he demanded: "Where am I to get what's coming to me?"

"'Fraid you won't get it, sonny. We're all in the same boat." He looked Stubby up and down and then added: "Kind of little for that boat."

"I *got* to have it!" cried Stubby. "I tell you, I *got* to!"

The man shook his head. "*That* cuts no ice. Hard luck, sonny, but we've got to take our medicine in this world. 'Taint no medicine for kids, though," he muttered.

Stubby's face just then was too much for him. He put his hand in his pocket and drew out a dime, saying: "There now. You run along and get you a soda and forget your troubles. It ain't always like this. You'll have better luck next time."

But Stubby did not get the soda. He put the dime in his pocket and turned toward home. Something was the matter with his legs — they acted funny about carrying him. He tried to whistle, but something was the matter with his lips, too.

Counting this dime, he now had a dollar and eighty cents, and it was the twenty-eighth day of July. "Thirty days has September — April, June and November —" he was saying to himself. Then July was one of the long ones. Well, *that* was a good thing! Been a great deal worse if July was a short one. Again he tried to whistle, and that time did manage to pipe out a few shrill little notes.

When Hero came running up the hill to meet him he slapped him on the back and cried, "Hello, Hero!" in tones fairly swaggering with bravado.

That night he engaged his father in conversation — the phrase is well adapted to the way Stubby went about it. "How is it about — 'bout things like taxes"— Stubby crossed his knees and swung one foot to show his indifference — "if you have *almost* enough — do they sometimes let you off?" — the detachment was a shade less perfect on that last.

His father laughed scoffingly. "Well, I guess *not!*"

"I thought maybe," said Stubby, "if a person had *tried* awful hard — and had *most* enough —"

Something inside him was all shaky, so he didn't go on. His father said that *trying* didn't have anything to do with it.

It was hard for Stubby not to sob out that he thought trying *ought* to have something to do with it, but he only made a hissing noise between his teeth that took the place of the whistle that wouldn't come.

"Kind of seems," he resumed, "if a person would have had enough if they hadn't been beat out of it, maybe — if he done the best he could —"

His father snorted derisively and informed him

that doing the best you could made no difference to the government; hard luck stories didn't *go* when it came to the laws of the land.

Thereupon Stubby took a little walk out to the alley and spent a considerable time in contemplation of the neighbour's chicken-yard. When he came back he walked right up to his father and standing there, feet planted, shoulders squared, wanted to know, in a desperate little voice: "If some one else was to give — say a dollar and eighty cents for Hero, could I take the other seventy out of my paper money?"

The man turned upon him roughly. "Uh-*huh! That's* it, is it? *That's* why you're getting so smart all of a sudden about government! Look a-here. Just I'me tell you something. You're lucky if you git enough to *eat* this winter. Do you know there's talk of the factory shuttin' down? *Dog* tax! Why you're lucky if you git *shoes*."

Stubby had turned away and was standing with his back to his father, hands in his pockets.

"And I'me tell you some'en else, young man. If you got any dollar and eighty cents, you give it to your mother!"

As Stubby was turning the corner of the house he called after him: "How'd you like to have me get you an automobile?"

He went doggedly from house to house the next afternoon, but nobody had any jobs. When Hero came running out to him that night he patted him, but didn't speak.

That evening as they were sitting in the back yard — Stubby and Hero a little apart from the others — his father was discoursing with his brother about anarchists. They were getting commoner, his father thought. There were a good many of them at the shop. They didn't call themselves that, but that was what they were.

"Well, what is an anarchist, anyhow?" Stubby's mother wanted to know.

"Why, an anarchist," her lord informed her, "is one that's against the government. He don't believe in the law and order. The real bad anarchists shoot them that tries to enforce the laws of the land. Guess if you'd read the papers these days you'd know."

Stubby's brain had been going round and round and these words caught in it as it whirled. The government — the laws of the land — why, it was the government and the laws of the land that were going to shoot Hero! It was the government — the laws of the land — that didn't care how hard you had *tried* — didn't care whether you had been cheated — didn't care how you *felt* — didn't care about anything except getting the money! His brain got hotter. Well, *he* didn't believe in the government, either. He was one of those people — those anarchists — that were against the laws of the land.

He'd done the very best he could and now the government was going to take Hero away from him just because he couldn't get — *couldn't* get — that other seventy cents.

Stubby's mother didn't hear her son crying that night. That was because Stubby was successful in holding the pillow over his head.

The next morning he looked in one of the papers he was carrying to see what it said about anarchists. Sure enough, some place way off somewhere, the anarchists had shot somebody that was trying to enforce the laws of the land. The laws of the land — that didn't *care.*

That afternoon as Stubby tramped around looking for jobs he saw a good many boys playing with dogs. None of them seemed to be worrying about whether their dogs had checks. To Stubby's hot little brain and sore little heart came the thought that they didn't love their dogs any more than he loved Hero, either. But the government didn't care whether he loved Hero or not! Pooh! — what was that to the government? All it cared about was getting the money. He stood for a long time watching a boy giving his dog a bath. The dog was trying to get away and the boy and another boy were having lots of fun about it. All of a sudden Stubby turned and ran away — ran down an alley, ran through a number of alleys, just kept on running, blinded by the tears.

And that night, in the middle of the night, that something in his head going round and round, getting hotter and hotter, he decided that the only thing for him to do was to shoot the policeman who came to take Hero away on the morning of August first — that would be day after to-morrow.

All night long policemen with revolvers stood around his bed. When his mother called him at half-past four he was shaking so he could scarcely get into his clothes.

On his way home from his route Stubby had to pass a police-station. He went on the other side of the street and stood there looking across. One of the policemen was playing with a dog!

Suddenly he wanted to rush over and throw himself down at that policeman's feet — sob out the story — ask him to please, *please* wait till he could get that other seventy cents.

But just then the policeman got up and went in the station, and Stubby was afraid to go in the police-station.

That policeman complicated things for Stubby. Before that it had been quite simple. The policeman would come to enforce the law of the land; but he did not believe in the law of the land, so he would just kill the policeman. But it seemed a policeman wasn't just a person who enforced the laws of the land. He was also a person who played with a dog.

After a whole day of walking around thinking about it — his eyes burning, his heart pounding — he decided that the thing to do was to warn the policeman by writing a letter. He did not know whether real anarchists warned them or not, but Stubby couldn't get reconciled to the idea of killing a person without telling him you were going to do it. It seemed that even a policeman should be told — especially a policeman who played with a dog.

The following letter was pencilled by a shaking hand, late that afternoon. It was written upon a barrel in the Lynch wood-shed, on a piece of wrapping paper, a bristly little head bending over it:

To the Policeman who comes to take my dog 'cause I ain't got the two fifty —'cause I tried but could only get one eighty —'cause a man was off his nut and didn't pay me what I earned —

This is to tell you I am an anarchist and do not believe in the government or the law and the order and will shoot you when you come. I wouldn't a been an anarchist if I could a got the money and I tried to get it but I couldn't get it — not enough. I don't think the government had ought to take things you like like I like Hero so I am against the government.

Thought I would tell you first.

Yours truly,

F. Lynch.

I don't see how I can shoot you 'cause where would I get the revolver. So I will have to do it with the butcher knife. Folks are sometimes killed that way 'cause my father read it in the paper.

If you wanted to take the one eighty and leave Hero till I can get the seventy I will not do anything to you and would be very much obliged.

1113 Willow street.

The letter was properly addressed and sealed — not for nothing had Stubby's teacher given those instructions in the art of letter writing. The stamp he paid for out of the dime the man gave him to get a soda with — and forget his troubles.

Now Bill O'Brien was on the desk at the police-station and Miss Murphy of the *Herald* stood in with Bill. That was how it came about that the next morning a fat policeman, an eager-looking girl and a young fellow with a kodak descended into the hollow to 1113 Willow street.

A little boy peeped around the corner of the house — such a wild-looking little boy — hair all standing up and eyes glittering. A yellow dog ran out and barked. The boy darted out and grabbed the dog in his arms and in that moment the girl called to the man with the black box: "Right now! Quick! Get him!"

They were getting ready to shoot Hero! That box was the way the police did it! He must — oh, he *must* — *must* . . . Boy and dog sank to the ground — but just the same the boy was shielding the dog!

When Stubby had pulled himself together the policeman was holding Hero. He said that Hero was certainly a fine dog — he had a dog a good deal like him at home. And Miss Murphy — she was choking back sobs herself — knew how he could earn the seventy cents that afternoon.

In such wise do a good anarchist and a good story go down under the same blow. Some of those sobs Miss Murphy choked back got into what she wrote about Stubby and his yellow dog and the next day citizens with no sense of the dramatic sent money enough to check Hero through life.

At first Stubby's father said he had a good mind to lick him. But something in the quality of Miss Murphy's journalism left a hazy feeling of there being something remarkable about his son. He confided to his good wife that it wouldn't surprise him much if Stubby was some day President. Somebody had to be President, said he, and he had noticed it was generally those who in their youthful days did things that made lively reading in the newspapers.

XIII

AT TWILIGHT

A BREEZE from the May world without blew through the class-room, and as it lifted his papers he had a curious sense of freshness and mustiness meeting. He looked at the group of students before him, half smiling at the way the breath of spring was teasing the hair of the girls sitting by the window. Anna Lawrence was trying to pin hers back again, but May would have none of such decorum, and only waited long enough for her to finish her work before joyously undoing it. She caught the laughing, admiring eyes of a boy sitting across from her and sought to conceal her pleasure in her unmanageable wealth of hair by a wry little face, and then the eyes of both strayed out to the trees that had scented that breeze for them, looking with frank longing at the campus which stretched before them in all its May glory that sunny afternoon. He remembered having met this boy and girl strolling in the twilight the evening before, and as a buoyant breeze that instant swept his own face he had a sudden, irrelevant consciousness of being seventy-three years old.

Other eyes were straying to the trees and birds and lilacs of that world from which the class-room was for the hour shutting them out. He was used to it — that straying of young eyes in the spring. For more than forty years he had sat at that desk and talked to young men and women about philosophy, and in those forty years there had always been straying eyes in May. The children of some of those boys and girls had in time come to him, and now there were other children who, before many years went by, might be sitting upon those benches, listening to lectures upon what men had thought about life, while their eyes strayed out where life called. So it went on — May, perhaps, the philosopher triumphant.

As, with a considerable effort — for the languor of spring, or some other languor, was upon him too — he brought himself back to the papers they had handed in, he found himself thinking of those first boys and girls, now men and women, and parents of other boys and girls. He hoped that philosophy had, after all, done something more than shut them out from May. He had always tried, not so much to instruct them in what men had thought, as to teach them to think, and perhaps now, when May had become a time for them to watch the straying of other eyes, they were the less desolate because of the habits he had helped them to form. He wanted to think that he had done something more than hold them prisoners.

There was a sadness to-day in his sympathy. He

was tired. It was hard to go back to what he had been saying about the different things the world's philosophers had believed about the immortality of the soul. So, as often when his feeling for his thought dragged, he turned to Gretta Loring. She seldom failed to bring a revival of interest — a freshening. She was his favourite student. He did not believe that in all the years there had been any student who had not only pleased, but helped him as she did.

He had taught her father and mother. And now there was Gretta, clear-eyed and steady of gaze, asking more of life than either of them had asked; asking, not only May, but what May meant. For Gretta there need be no duality. She was one of those rare ones for whom the meaning of life opened new springs to the joy of life, for whom life intensified with the understanding of it. He never said a thing that gratified him as reaching toward the things not easy to say but that he would find Gretta's face illumined — and always that eager little leaning ahead for more.

She had that look of waiting now, but to-day it seemed less an expectant than a troubled look. She wanted him to go on with what he had been saying about the immortality of the soul. But it was not so much a demand upon him — he had come to rely upon those demands, as it was — he had an odd, altogether absurd sense of its being a fear for him.

She looked uncomfortable, fretted; and suddenly he was startled to see her searching eyes blurred by something that must be tears.

She turned away, and for just a minute it seemed to leave him alone and helpless. He rubbed his forehead with his hand. It felt hot. It got that way sometimes lately when he was tired. And the close of that hour often found him tired.

He believed he knew what she wanted. She would have him declare his own belief. In the youthful flush of her modernism she was impatient with that fumbling around with what other men had thought. Despising the muddled thinking of some of her classmates, she would have him put it right to them with "As for yourself —"

He tried to formulate what he would care to say. But, perhaps just because he was too tired to say it right, the life the robin in the nearest tree was that moment celebrating in song seemed more important than anything he had to say about his own feeling toward the things men had thought about the human soul.

It was ten minutes before closing time, but suddenly he turned to his class with: "Go out-of-doors and think about it. This is no day to sit within and talk of philosophy. What men have thought about life in the past is less important than what you feel about it to-day." He paused, then added, he could not have said why, "And don't let the shadow of either belief or unbelief fall across the days that are here for you now." Again he stopped, then surprised himself by ending, "Philosophy should quicken life, not deaden it."

They were not slow in going, their astonishment in his wanting them to go quickly engulfed in their pleasure in doing so. It was only Gretta who lingered a moment, seeming too held by his manner in sending her out into the sunshine to care about going there. He thought she was going to come to the desk and speak to him. He was sure she wanted to. But at the last she went hastily, and he thought, just before she turned her face away, that it was a tear he saw on her lashes.

Strange! Was she unhappy, she through whom life surged so richly? And yet was it not true that where it gave much it exacted much? Feeling much, and understanding what she felt, and feeling for what she understood — must she also suffer much? Must one always pay?

He sighed, and began gathering together his papers. Thoughts about life tired him to-day.

On the steps he paused, unreasonably enough a little saddened as he watched some of them beginning a tennis game. Certainly they were losing no time — eager to let go thoughts about life for its pleasures, very few of them awake to that rich life he had tried to make them ready for. He drooped still more wearily at the thought that perhaps the most real gift he had for them was that unexpected ten minutes.

Remembering a book he must have from the library, he turned back. He went to the alcove where the works on philosophy were to be found, and was reaching up for the volume he wanted, when a sentence from a lowly murmured conversation in the next aisle came to him across the stack of books.

"That's all very well; we know, of course, that he doesn't believe, but what will he do when it comes to *himself?*"

It arrested him, coming as it did from one of the girls who had just left his class-room. He stood there motionless, his hand still reaching up for the book.

"Do? Why, face it, of course. Face it as squarely as he's faced every other fact of life."

That was Gretta, and though, mindful of the library mandate for silence, her tone was low, it was vibrant with a fine scorn.

"Well," said the first speaker, "I guess he'll have to face it before very long."

That was not answered; there was a movement on the other side of the barricade of books — it might have been that Gretta had turned away. His hand dropped down from the high shelf. He was leaning against the books.

"Haven't you noticed, Gretta, how he's losing his grip?"

At that his head went up sharply; he stood altogether tense as he waited for Gretta to set the other girl right — Gretta, so sure-seeing, so much wiser and truer than the rest of them. Gretta would *laugh!*

But she did not laugh. And what his strained ear caught at last was — not her scornful denial, but a little gasp of breath suggesting a sob.

"*Noticed* it? Why it breaks my heart!"

He stared at the books through which her low, passionate voice had carried. Then he sank to the chair that fortunately was beside him. Power for standing had gone from him.

"Father says — father's on the board, you know" (it was the first girl who spoke) —"that they don't know what to do about it. It's not justice to the school to let him begin another year. These things are arranged with less embarrassment in the big schools, where a man begins emeritus at a certain time. Though of course they'll pension him — he's done a lot for the school."

He thanked Gretta for her little laugh of disdain. The memory of it was more comforting — more satisfying — than any attempt to put it into words could have been.

He heard them move away, their skirts brushing the book-stacks in passing. A little later he saw them out in the sunshine on the campus. Gretta joined one of the boys for a game of tennis. Motionless, he sat looking out at her. She looked so very young as she played.

For an hour he remained at the table in the alcove where he had overheard what his students had to say of him. And when the hour had gone by he took up the pen which was there upon the study table and wrote his resignation to the secretary of the board of trustees. It was very brief — simply that he felt the time had come when a younger man could do more for the school than he, and that he should like his resignation to take effect at the close of the present school year. He had an envelope, and sealed and stamped the letter — ready to drop in the box in front of the building as he left. He had always served the school as best he could; he lost no time now, once convinced, in rendering to it the last service he could offer it — that of making way for the younger man.

Looking things squarely in the face, and it was the habit of a lifetime to look things squarely in the face, he had not been long in seeing that they were right. Things tired him now as they had not once tired him. He had less zest at the beginning of the hour, more relief at the close of it. He seemed stupid in not having seen it for himself, but possibly many people were a little stupid in seeing that their own time was over. Of course he had thought, in a vague way, that his working time couldn't be much longer, but it seemed part of the way human beings managed with themselves that things in even the very near future kept the remoteness of future things.

Now he understood Gretta's troubled look and her tears. He knew how those fine nerves of hers must have suffered, how her own mind had wanted to leap to the aid of his, how her own strength must have tormented her in not being able to reach his flagging powers. It seemed part of the whole hardness of life that she who would care the most would be the one to see it most understandingly.

What he was trying to do was to see it all very simply, in matter-of-fact fashion, that there might be no bitterness and the least of tragedy. It was nothing unique in human history he was facing. One did one's work; then, when through, one stopped. He tried to feel that it was as simple as it sounded, but he wondered if back of many of those brief letters of resignation that came at quitting-time there was the hurt, the desolation, that there was no use denying to himself was back of his.

He hoped that most men had more to turn to. Most men of seventy-three had grandchildren. That would help, surrounding one with a feeling of the naturalness of it all. But that school had been his only child. And he had loved it with the tenderness one gives a child. That in him which would have gone to the child had gone to the school.

The woman whom he loved had not loved him; he

had never married. His life had been called lonely; but lonely though it undeniably had been, the life he won from books and work and thinking had kept the chill from his heart. He had the gift of drawing life from all contact with life. Working with youth, he kept that feeling for youth that does for the life within what sunshine and fresh air do for the room in which one dwells.

It was now that the loneliness that blights seemed waiting for him. . . . Life *used* one — and that in the ugly, not the noble sense of being used. Stripped of the fine fancies men wove around it, what was it beyond just a matter of being sucked dry and then thrown aside? Why not admit that, and then face it? And the abundance with which one might have given — the joy in the giving — had no bearing upon the fact that it came at last to that question of getting one out of the way. It was no one's unkindness; it was just that life was like that. Indeed, the bitterness festered around the thought that it *was* life itself — the way of life — not the brutality of any particular people. "They'll pension him — he's done a lot for the school." Even the grateful memory of Gretta's tremulous, scoffing little laugh for the way it fell short could not follow to the deep place that had been hurt.

Getting himself in hand again, and trying to face this as simply and honestly as he had sought to face the other, he knew that it was true he had done a great deal for the school. He did not believe it too much to say he had done more for it than any other man. Certainly more than any other man he had given it what place it had with men who thought. He had come to it in his early manhood, and at a time when the school was in its infancy — just a crude, struggling little Western college. Gretta Loring's grandfather had been one of its founders — founding it in revolt against the cramping sectarianism of another college. He had gloried in the spirit which gave it birth, and it was he who, through the encroachings of problems of administration and the ensnarements and entanglements of practicality, had fought to keep unattached and unfettered that spirit of freedom in the service of truth.

His own voice had been heard and recognised, and a number of times during the years calls had come from more important institutions, but he had not cared to go. For year by year there deepened that personal love for the little college to which he had given the youthful ardour of his own intellectual passion. All his life's habits were one with it. His days seemed beaten into the path that cut across the campus. The vines that season after season went a little higher on the wall out there indicated his strivings by their own, and the generation that had worn down even the stones of those front steps had furrowed his forehead and stooped his shoulders. He had grown old along with it! His days were twined around it. It was the place of his efforts and satisfactions (joys perhaps he should not call them), of his falterings and his hopes. He loved it because he had given himself to it; loved it because he had helped to bring it up. On the shelves all around him were books which it had been his pleasure — because during some of those hard years they were to be had in no other way — to order himself and pay for from his own almost ludicrously meagre salary. He remembered the excitement there always was in getting them fresh from the publisher and bringing them over there in his arms; the satisfaction in coming in next day and finding them on the shelves. Such had been his dissipations, his indulgences of self. Many things came back to him as he sat there going back over busy years, the works on philosophy looking down upon him, the shadows of that spring afternoon gathering around him. He looked like a very old man indeed as he at last reached out for the letter he had written to the trustees, relieving them of their embarrassment.

Twilight had come on. On the front steps he paused and looked around the campus. It was growing dark in that lingering way it has in the spring — daylight creeping away under protest, night coming gently, as if it knew that the world having been so pleasant, day would be loath to go. The boys and girls were going back and forth upon the campus and the streets. They could not bear to go within. For more than forty years it had been like that. It would be like that for many times forty years — indeed, until the end of the world, for it would be the end of the world when it was not like that. He was glad that they were out in the twilight, not indoors trying to gain from books something of the meaning of life. That course had its satisfactions along the way, but it was surely no port of peace to which it bore one at the last.

He shrunk from going home. There were so many readjustments he must make, once home. So, lingering, he saw that off among the trees a girl was sitting alone. She threw back her head in a certain way just then, and he knew by the gesture that it was Gretta Loring. He wondered what she was thinking about. What did one who thought think about — over there on the other side of life? Youth and age looked at life from opposite sides. Then they could not see it alike, for what one saw in life seemed to depend so entirely upon how the light was falling from where one stood.

He could not have said just what it was made him cross the campus toward her. Part of it was the desire for human sympathy — one thing, at least, which age did not deaden. But that was not the whole of it, nor the deepest thing in it. It was an urge of the spirit to find and keep for itself a place where the light was falling backward upon life.

She was quiet in her greeting, and gentle. Her cheeks were still flushed, her hair tumbled from her game, but her eyes were thoughtful and, he thought, sad. He felt that the sadness was because of him; of him and the things of which he made her think. He knew of her affection for him, the warmth there was in her admiration of the things for which he had fought. He had discovered that it hurt her now that others should be seeing and not he, pained her to watch so sorry a thing as his falling below himself, wounded both pride and heart that men whom she would doubtless say had never appreciated him were whispering among themselves about how to get rid of him. Why, the poor child might even be tormenting herself with the idea she ought to tell him!

That was why he told her. He pointed to the address on the envelope, saying: "That carries my resignation, Gretta."

Her start and the tears which rushed to her eyes told him he was right about her feeling. She did not seem able to say anything. Her chin was trembling.

"I see that the time has come," he said, "when a younger man can do more for the school than I can hope to do for it."

Still she said nothing at all, but her eyes were deepening and she had that very steadfast, almost inspired look that had so many times quickened him in the class-room.

She was not going to deny it! She was not going to pretend!

After the first feeling of not having got something needed he rose to her high ground — ground she had taken it for granted he would take.

"And will you believe it, Gretta," he said, rising to that ground and there asking, not for the sympathy that bends down, but for a hand in passing, "there comes a hard hour when first one feels the time has come to step aside and be replaced by that younger man?"

She nodded. "It must be," she said, simply; "it must be very much harder than any of us can know till we come to it."

She brought him a sense of his advantage in experience — his riches. To be sure, there was that.

And he was oddly comforted by the honesty in her which could not stoop to dishonest comforting. In what superficially might seem her failure there was a very real victory for them both. And there was nothing of coldness in her reserve! There was the fulness of understanding, and of valuing the moments too highly for anything there was to be said about it. There was a great spiritual dignity, a nobility, in the way she was looking at him. It called upon the whole of his own spiritual dignity. It was her old demand upon him, but this time the tears through which her eyes shone were tears of pride in fulfilment, not of sorrowing for failure.

Suddenly he felt that his life had not been spent in vain, that the lives of all those men of his day who had fought the good fight for intellectual honesty — spiritual dignity — had not been spent in vain if they were leaving upon the earth even a few who were like the girl beside them.

It turned him from himself to her. She was what counted — for she was what remained. And he remained in just the measure that he remained through her; counted in so far as he counted for her. It was as if he had been facing in the wrong direction and now a kindly hand had turned him around. It was not in looking back there he would find himself. He was not back there to be found. Only so much of him lived as had been able to wing itself ahead — on in the direction she was moving.

It did not particularly surprise him that when she at last spoke it was to voice a shade of that same feeling. "I was thinking," she began, "of that younger man. Of what he must mean to the man who gives way to him."

She was feeling her way as she went — groping among the many dim things that were there. He had always liked to watch her face when she was thinking her way step by step.

"I think you used a word wrongly a minute ago," she said, with a smile. "You spoke of being replaced. But that isn't it. A man like you isn't replaced; he's" — she got it after a minute and came forth with it triumphantly —"fulfilled!"

Her face was shining as she turned to him after that. "Don't you see? He's there waiting to take your place because you *got* him ready. Why, you *made* that younger man! Your whole life has been a getting ready for him. He can do his work because you first did yours. Of course he can go farther than you can! Wouldn't it be a sorry commentary on you if he couldn't?"

Her voice throbbed warmly upon that last, and during the pause the light it had brought still played upon her face. "We were talking in class about immortality," she went on, more slowly. "There's one form of immortality I like to think about. It's that all those who from the very first have given anything to the world are living in the world to-day." There was a rush of tears to her eyes and of affection to her voice as she finished, very low: "*You'll* never die. You've deepened the consciousness of life too much for that."

They sat there as twilight drew near to night, the old man and the young girl, silent. The laughter of boys and girls and the good-night calls of the birds were all around them. The fragrance of life was around them. It was one of those silences to which come impressions, faiths, longings, not yet born as thoughts.

Something in the quality of that silence brought the rescuing sense of its having been good to have lived and done one's part — that sense which, from places of desolation and over ways rough and steep and dark, can find its way to the meadows of serenity.

THE END

Trifles

Characters

GEORGE HENDERSON, County Attorney
HENRY PETERS, Sheriff
LEWIS HALE, A Neighboring Farmer
MRS. PETERS
MRS. HALE

SCENE

The kitchen in the now abandoned farmhouse of JOHN WRIGHT, *a gloomy kitchen, and left without having been put in order—unwashed pans under the sink, a loaf of bread outside the breadbox, a dish towel on the table—other signs of incompleted work. At the rear the outer door opens and the* SHERIFF *comes in followed by the* COUNTY ATTORNEY *and* HALE. *The* SHERIFF *and* HALE *are men in middle life, the* COUNTY ATTORNEY *is a young man; all are much bundled up and go at once to the stove. They are followed by two women—the* SHERIFF's *wife first; she is a slight wiry woman, a thin nervous face.* MRS. HALE *is larger and would ordinarily be called more comfortable looking, but she is disturbed now and looks fearfully about as she enters. The women have come in slowly, and stand close together near the door.*

COUNTY ATTORNEY. [*Rubbing his hands.*] This feels good. Come up to the fire, ladies.

MRS. PETERS. [*After taking a step forward.*] I'm not—cold.

SHERIFF. [*Unbuttoning his overcoat and stepping away from the stove as if to mark the beginning of official business.*] Now, Mr. Hale, before we move things about, you explain to Mr. Henderson just what you saw when you came here yesterday morning.

COUNTY ATTORNEY. By the way, has anything been moved? Are things just as you left them yesterday?

SHERIFF. [*Looking about.*] It's just the same. When it dropped below zero last night I thought I'd better send Frank out this morning to make a fire for us—no use getting pneumonia with a big case on, but I told him not to touch anything except the stove—and you know Frank.

COUNTY ATTORNEY. Somebody should have been left here yesterday.

SHERIFF. Oh—yesterday. When I had to send Frank to Morris Center for that man who went crazy—I want you to know I had my hands full yesterday, I knew you could get back from Omaha by today and as long as I went over everything here myself—

COUNTY ATTORNEY. Well, Mr. Hale, tell just what happened when you came here yesterday morning.

HALE. Harry and I had started to town with a load of potatoes. We came along the road from my place and as I got here I said, "I'm going to see if I can't get John Wright to go in with me on a party telephone." I spoke to Wright about it once before and he put me off, saying folks talked too much anyway, and all he asked was peace and quiet—I guess you know about how much he talked himself; but I thought maybe if I went to the house and talked about it before his wife, though I said to Harry that I didn't know as what his wife wanted made much difference to John—

COUNTY ATTORNEY. Let's talk about that later, Mr. Hale. I do want to talk about that, but tell now just what happened when you got to the house.

HALE. I didn't hear or see anything; I knocked at the door, and still it was all quiet inside. I knew they must be up, it was past eight o'clock. So I knocked again, and I thought I heard somebody say, "Come in." I wasn't sure, I'm not sure yet, but I opened the door—this door [*Indicating the door by which the two women are still standing.*] and there in that rocker—[*Pointing to it.*] sat Mrs. Wright.

[*They all look at the rocker.*]

COUNTY ATTORNEY. What—was she doing?

HALE. She was rockin' back and forth. She had her apron in her hand and was kind of—pleating it.

COUNTY ATTORNEY. And how did she—look?

HALE. Well, she looked queer.

COUNTY ATTORNEY. How do you mean—queer?

HALE. Well, as if she didn't know what she was going to do next. And kind of done up.

COUNTY ATTORNEY. How did she seem to feel about your coming?

HALE. Why, I don't think she minded—one way or other. She didn't pay much attention. I said, "How do, Mrs. Wright, it's cold, ain't it?" And she said, "Is it?"—and went on kind of pleating at her apron. Well, I was surprised; she didn't ask me to come up to the stove, or to set down, but just sat there, not even looking at me, so I said, "I want to see John." And then she—laughed. I guess you would call it a laugh. I thought of Harry and the team outside, so I said a little sharp: "Can't I see

John?" "No," she says, kind o' dull like. "Ain't he home?" says I. "Yes," says she, "he's home." "Then why can't I see him?" I asked her, out of patience. "'Cause he's dead," says she. "*Dead?*" says I. She just nodded her head, not getting a bit excited, but rockin' back and forth. "Why—where is he?" says I, not knowing what to say. She just pointed upstairs—like that [*Himself pointing to the room above.*] I got up, with the idea of going up there. I walked from there to here—then I says, "Why, what did he died of?" "He died of a rope round his neck," says she, and just went on pleatin' at her apron. Well, I went out and called Harry. I thought I might—need help. We went upstairs and there he was lyin'—

COUNTY ATTORNEY. I think I'd rather have you go into that upstairs, where you can point it all out. Just go on now with the rest of the story.

HALE. Well, my first thought was to get that rope off. It looked . . . [*Stops, his face twitches.*] . . . but Harry, he went up to him, and he said, "No, he's dead all right, and we'd better not touch anything." So we went back down stairs. She was still sitting that same way. "Has anybody been notified?" I asked. "No," says she, unconcerned. "Who did this, Mrs. Wright?" said Harry. He said it businesslike—and she stopped pleatin' of her apron. "I don't know," she says. "You don't *know?*" says Harry. "No," says she. "Weren't you sleepin' in the bed with him?" says Harry. "Yes," says she, "but I was on the inside." "Somebody slipped a rope round his neck and strangled him and you didn't wake up?" says Harry. "I didn't wake up," she said after him. We must 'a looked as if we didn't see how that could be, for after a minute she said, "I sleep sound." Harry was going to ask her more questions but I said maybe we ought to let her tell her story first to the coroner, or the sheriff, so Harry went fast as he could to Rivers' place, where there's a telephone.

COUNTY ATTORNEY. And what did Mrs. Wright do when she knew that you had gone for the coroner?

HALE. She moved from that chair to this one over here [*Pointing to a small chair in the corner.*] and just sat there with her hands held together and looking down. I got a feeling that I ought to make some conversation, so I said I had come in to see if John wanted to put in a telephone, and at that she started to laugh, and then she stopped and looked at me—scared. [*The* COUNTY ATTORNEY, *who has had his notebook out, makes a note.*] I dunno, maybe it wasn't scared. I wouldn't like to say it was. Soon Harry got back, and then Dr. Lloyd came, and you, Mr. Peters, and so I guess that's all I know that you don't.

COUNTY ATTORNEY. [*Looking around.*] I guess we'll go upstairs first—and then out to the barn and around there. [*To the* SHERIFF.] You're convinced that there was nothing important here—nothing that would point to any motive.

SHERIFF. Nothing here but kitchen things.

[*The* COUNTY ATTORNEY, *after again looking around the kitchen, opens the door of a cupboard closet. He gets up on a chair and looks on a shelf. Pulls his hand away, sticky.*]

COUNTY ATTORNEY. Here's a nice mess.

[*The women draw nearer.*]

MRS. PETERS. [*To the other woman.*] Oh, her fruit; it did

freeze. [*To the* COUNTY ATTORNEY.] She worried about that when it turned so cold. She said the fire'd go out and her jars would break.

SHERIFF. Well, can you beat the women! Held for murder and worryin' about her preserves.

COUNTY ATTORNEY. I guess before we're through she may have something more serious than preserves to worry about.

HALE. Well, women are used to worrying over trifles.

[*The two women move a little closer together.*]

COUNTY ATTORNEY. [*With the gallantry of a young politician.*] And yet, for all their worries, what would we do without the ladies? [*The women do not unbend. He goes to the sink, takes a dipperful of water from the pail and pouring it into a basin, washes his hands. Starts to wipe them on the roller towel, turns it for a cleaner place.*] Dirty towels! [*Kicks his foot against the pans under the sink.*] Not much of a housekeeper, would you say, ladies?

MRS. HALE. [*Stiffly.*] There's a great deal of work to be done on a farm.

COUNTY ATTORNEY. To be sure. And yet [*With a little bow to her.*] I know there are some Dickson County farmhouses which do not have such roller towels.

[*He gives it a pull to expose its full length again.*]

MRS. HALE. Those towels get dirty awful quick. Men's hands aren't always as clean as they might be.

COUNTY ATTORNEY. Ah, loyal to your sex, I see. But you and Mrs. Wright were neighbors. I suppose you were friends, too.

MRS. HALE. [*Shaking her head.*] I've not seen much of her

of late years. I've not been in this house—it's more than a year.

COUNTY ATTORNEY. And why was that? You didn't like her?

MRS. HALE. I liked her all well enough. Farmers' wives have their hands full, Mr. Henderson. And then—

COUNTY ATTORNEY. Yes—?

MRS. HALE. [*Looking about.*] It never seemed a very cheerful place.

COUNTY ATTORNEY. No—it's not cheerful. I shouldn't say she had the homemaking instinct.

MRS. HALE. Well, I don't know as Wright had, either.

COUNTY ATTORNEY. You mean that they didn't get on very well?

MRS. HALE. No, I don't mean anything. But I don't think a place'd be any cheerfuler for John Wright's being in it.

COUNTY ATTORNEY. I'd like to talk more of that a little later. I want to get the lay of things upstairs now.

[*He goes to the left, where three steps lead to a stair door.*]

SHERIFF. I suppose anything Mrs. Peter does'll be all right. She was to take in some clothes for her, you know, and a few little things. We left in such a hurry yesterday.

COUNTY ATTORNEY. Yes, but I would like to see what you take, Mrs. Peters, and keep an eye out for anything that might be of use to us.

MRS. PETERS. Yes, Mr. Henderson.

[*The women listen to the men's steps on the stairs, then look about the kitchen.*]

MRS. HALE. I'd hate to have men coming into my kitchen, snooping around and criticizing.

[*She arranges the pans under sink which the* COUNTY ATTORNEY *had shoved out of place.*]

MRS. PETERS. Of course it's no more than their duty.

MRS. HALE. Duty's all right, but I guess that deputy sheriff that came out to make the fire might have got a little of this on. [*Gives the roller towel a pull.*] Wish I'd thought of that sooner. Seems mean to talk about her for not having things slicked up when she had to come away in such a hurry.

MRS. PETERS. [*Who has gone to a small table in the left rear corner of the room, and lifted one end of a towel that covers a pan.*] She had bread set.

[*Stands still.*]

MRS. HALE. [*Eyes fixed on a loaf of bread beside the breadbox, which is on a low shelf at the other side of the room. Moves slowly toward it.*] She was going to put this in there. [*Picks up loaf, then abruptly drops it. In a manner of returning to familiar things.*] It's a shame about her fruit. I wonder if it's all gone. [*Gets up on the chair and looks.*] I think there's some here that's all right, Mrs. Peters. Yes—here; [*Holding it toward the window.*] this is cherries, too. [*Looking again.*] I declare I believe that's the only one. [*Gets down, bottle in her hand. Goes to the sink and wipes if off on the outside.*] She'll feel awful bad after all her hard work in the hot weather. I remember the afternoon I put up my cherries last summer.

[*She puts the bottle on the big kitchen table, center of the room. With a sigh, is about to sit down in the rocking-chair. Before she is seated realizes what chair it is; with a slow look at it, steps back. The chair which she has touched rocks back and forth.*]

MRS. PETERS. Well, I must get those things from the front room closet. [*She goes to the door at the right, but after looking into the other room, steps back.*] You coming with me, Mrs. Hale? You could help me carry them.

[*They go in the other room; reappear,* MRS. PETERS *carrying a dress and skirt,* MRS. HALE *following with a pair of shoes.*]

MRS. PETERS. My, it's cold in there.

[*She puts the clothes on the big table, and hurries to the stove.*]

MRS. HALE. [*Examining her skirt.*] Wright was close. I think maybe that's why she kept so much to herself. She didn't even belong to the Ladies Aid. I suppose she felt she couldn't do her part, and then you don't enjoy things when you feel shabby. She used to wear pretty clothes and be lively, when she was Minnie Foster, one of the town girls singing in the choir. But that—oh, that was thirty years ago. This all you was to take in?

MRS. PETERS. She said she wanted an apron. Funny thing to want, for there isn't much to get you dirty in jail, goodness knows. But I suppose just to make her feel more natural. She said they was in the top drawer in this cupboard. Yes, here. And then her little shawl that always hung behind the door. [*Opens stair door and looks.*] Yes, here it is.

[*Quickly shuts door leading upstairs.*]

MRS. HALE. [*Abruptly moving toward her.*] Mrs. Peters?

MRS. PETERS. Yes, Mrs. Hale?

MRS. HALE. Do you think she did it?

MRS. PETERS. [*In a frightened voice.*] Oh, I don't know.

MRS. HALE. Well, I don't think she did. Asking for an

apron and her little shawl. Worrying about her fruit.

MRS. PETERS. [*Starts to speak, glances up, where foot-steps are heard in the room above. In a low voice.*] Mr. Peters says it looks bad for her. Mr. Henderson is awful sarcastic in a speech and he'll make fun of her sayin' she didn't wake up.

MRS. HALE. Well, I guess John Wright didn't wake when they was slipping that rope under his neck.

MRS. PETERS. No, it's strange. It must have been done awful crafty and still. They say it was such a—funny way to kill a man, rigging it all up like that.

MRS. HALE. That's just what Mr. Hale said. There was a gun in the house. He says that's what he can't under-stand.

MRS. PETERS. Mr. Henderson said coming out that what was needed for the case was a motive; something to show anger, or—sudden feeling.

MRS. HALE. [*Who is standing by the table.*] Well, I don't see any signs of anger around here. [*She puts her hand on the dish towel which lies on the table, stands looking down at table, one half of which is clean, the other half messy.*] It's wiped to here. [*Makes a move as if to finish work, then turns and looks at loaf of bread outside the breadbox. Drops towel. In that voice of coming back to familiar things.*] Wonder how they are finding things upstairs. I hope she had it a little more red-up up there. You know, it seems kind of *sneaking*. Locking her up in town and then coming out here and trying to get her own house to turn against her!

MRS. PETERS. But Mrs. Hale, the law is the law.

MRS. HALE. I s'pose 'tis. [*Unbuttoning her coat.*] Better loosen up your things, Mrs. Peters. You won't feel them when you go out.

[MRS. PETERS *takes off her fur tippet, goes to hang it on hook at back of room, stands looking at the under part of the small corner table.*]

MRS. PETERS. She was piecing a quilt.

[*She brings the large sewing basket and they look at the bright pieces.*]

MRS. HALE. It's log cabin pattern. Pretty, isn't it? I wonder if she was goin' to quilt it or just knot it?

[*Footsteps have been heard coming down the stairs. The* SHERIFF *enters followed by* HALE *and the* COUNTY ATTORNEY.]

SHERIFF. They wonder if she was going to quilt it or just knot it!

[*The men laugh; the women look abashed.*]

COUNTY ATTORNEY. [*Rubbing his hands over the stove.*] Frank's fire didn't do much up there, did it? Well, let's go out to the barn and get that cleared up.

[*The men go outside.*]

MRS. HALE. [*Resentfully.*] I don't know as there's anything so strange, our takin' up our time with little things while we're waiting for them to get the evidence. [*She sits down at the big table smoothing out a block with decision.*] I don't see as it's anything to laugh about.

MRS. PETERS. [*Apologetically.*] Of course they've got awful important things on their minds.

[*Pulls up a chair and joins* MRS. HALE *at the table.*]

MRS. HALE. [*Examining another block.*] Mrs. Peters, look at this one. Here, this is the one she was working on, and look at the sewing! All the rest of it has been so nice and even. And look at this! It's all over the place! Why, it looks as if she didn't know what she was about! [*After she has said this they look at each other, then start to glance back at the door. After an instant* MRS. HALE *has pulled at a knot and ripped the sewing.*]

MRS. PETERS. Oh, what are you doing, Mrs. Hale?

MRS. HALE. [*Mildly.*] Just pulling out a stitch or two that's not sewed very good. [*Threading a needle.*] Bad sewing always made me fidgety.

MRS. PETERS. [*Nervously.*] I don't think we ought to touch things.

MRS. HALE. I'll just finish up this end. [*Suddenly stopping and leaning forward.*] Mrs. Peters?

MRS. PETERS. Yes, Mrs. Hale?

MRS. HALE. What do you suppose she was so nervous about?

MRS. PETERS. Oh—I don't know. I don't know as she was nervous. I sometimes sew awful queer when I'm just tired. [MRS. HALE *starts to say something, looks at* MRS. PETERS, *then goes on sewing.*] Well, I must get these things wrapped up. They may be through sooner than we think. [*Putting apron and other things together.*] I wonder where I can find a piece of paper, and string.

MRS. HALE. In that cupboard, maybe.

MRS. PETERS. [*Looking in cupboard.*] Why, here's a birdcage. [*Holds it up.*] Did she have a bird, Mrs. Hale?

MRS. HALE. Why, I don't know whether she did or not—I've not been here for so long. There was a man around last year selling canaries cheap, but I don't know as she took one; maybe she did. She used to sing real pretty herself.

MRS. PETERS. [*Glancing around.*] Seems funny to think

of a bird here. But she must have had one, or why would she have a cage? I wonder what happened to it.

MRS. HALE. I s'pose maybe the cat got it.

MRS. PETERS. No, she didn't have a cat. She's got that feeling some people have about cats—being afraid of them. My cat got in her room and she was real upset and asked me to take it out.

MRS. HALE. My sister Bessie was like that. Queer, ain't it?

MRS. PETERS. [*Examining the cage.*] Why, look at this door. It's broke. One hinge is pulled apart.

MRS. HALE. [*Looking too.*] Looks as if someone must have been rough with it.

MRS. PETERS. Why, yes.

[*She brings the cage forward and puts it on the table.*]

MRS. HALE. I wish if they're going to find any evidence they'd be about it. I don't like this place.

MRS. PETERS. But I'm awful glad you came with me, Mrs. Hale. It would be lonesome for me sitting here alone.

MRS. HALE. It would, wouldn't it? [*Dropping her sewing.*] But I tell you what I do wish, Mrs. Peters. I wish I had come over sometimes when *she* was here. I—[*Looking around the room.*]—wish I had.

MRS. PETERS. But of course you were awful busy, Mrs. Hale—your house and your children.

MRS. HALE. I could've come. I stayed away because it weren't cheerful—and that's why I ought to have come. I—I've never liked this place. Maybe because it's down in a hollow and you don't see the road. I dunno what it is but it's a lonesome place and always was. I wish I had come over to see Minnie Foster sometimes. I can see now—

[*Shakes her head.*]

MRS. PETERS. Well, you mustn't reproach yourself, Mrs. Hale. Somehow we just don't see how it is with other folks until—something comes up.

MRS. HALE. Not having children makes less work—but it makes a quiet house, and Wright out to work all day, and no company when he did come in. Did you know John Wright, Mrs. Peters?

MRS. PETERS. Not to know him; I've seen him in town. They say he was a good man.

MRS. HALE. Yes—good; he didn't drink, and kept his word as well as most, I guess, and paid his debts. But he was a hard man, Mrs. Peters. Just to pass the time of day with him—[*Shivers.*] Like a raw wind that gets to the bone. [*Pauses, her eye falling on the cage.*] I should think she would 'a wanted a bird. But what do you suppose went with it?

MRS. PETERS. I don't know, unless it got sick and died.

[*She reaches over and swings the broken door, swings it again. Both women watch it.*]

MRS. HALE. You weren't raised round here, were you? [MRS. PETERS *shakes her head.*] You didn't know—her?

MRS. PETERS. Not till they brought her yesterday.

MRS. HALE. She—come to think of it, she was kind of like a bird herself—real sweet and pretty, but kind of timid and—fluttery. How—she—did—change. [*Silence; then as if struck by a happy thought and relieved to get back to everyday things.*] Tell you what, Mrs. Peters, why don't you take the quilt in with you? It might take up her mind.

MRS. PETERS. Why, I think that's a real nice idea, Mrs. Hale. There couldn't possibly be any objection to it, could there? Now, just what would I take? I wonder if her patches are in here—and her things. [*They look in the sewing basket.*]

MRS. HALE. Here's some red. I expect this has got sewing things in it. [*Brings out a fancy box.*] What a pretty box. Looks like something somebody would give you. Maybe her scissors are in here. [*Opens box. Suddenly puts her hand to her nose.*] Why—[MRS. PETERS *bends nearer, then turns her face away.*] There's something wrapped up in this piece of silk.

MRS. PETERS. Why, this isn't her scissors.

MRS. HALE. [*Lifting the silk.*] Oh, Mrs. Peters—it's—

[MRS. PETERS *bends closer.*]

MRS. PETERS. It's the bird.

MRS. HALE. [*Jumping up.*] But, Mrs. Peters—look at it! Its neck! Look at its neck! It's all—other side *to.*

MRS. PETERS. Somebody—wrung—its—neck.

[*Their eyes meet. A look of growing comprehension, of horror. Steps are heard outside.* MRS. HALE *slips box under quilt pieces, and sinks into her chair. Enter* SHERIFF *and* COUNTY ATTORNEY. MRS. PETERS *rises.*]

COUNTY ATTORNEY. [*As one turning from serious things to little pleasantries.*] Well, ladies, have you decided whether she was going to quilt it or knot it?

MRS. PETERS. We think she was going to—knot it.

COUNTY ATTORNEY. Well, that's interesting, I'm sure. [*Seeing the birdcage.*] Has the bird flown?

MRS. HALE. [*Putting more quilt pieces over the box.*] We think the—cat got it.

COUNTY ATTORNEY. [*Preoccupied.*] Is there a cat?

[MRS. HALE *glances in a quick covert way at* MRS. PETERS.]

MRS. PETERS. Well, not *now*. They're superstitious, you know. They leave.

COUNTY ATTORNEY. [*To* SHERIFF PETERS, *continuing an interrupted conversation.*] No sign at all of anyone having come from the outside. Their own rope. Now let's go up again and go over it piece by piece. [*They start upstairs.*] It would have to have been someone who knew just the—

[MRS. PETERS *sits down. The two women sit there not looking at one another, but as if peering into something and at the same time holding back. When they talk now it is in the manner of feeling their way over strange ground, as if afraid of what they are saying, but as if they cannot help saying it.*]

MRS. HALE. She liked the bird. She was going to bury it in that pretty box.

MRS. PETERS. [*In a whisper.*] When I was a girl—my kitten—there was a boy took a hatchet, and before my eyes—and before I could get there—[*Covers her face an instant.*] If they hadn't held me back I would have—[*Catches herself, looks upstairs where steps are heard, falters weakly.*]—hurt him.

MRS. HALE. [*With a slow look around her.*] I wonder how it would seem never to have had any children around. [*Pause.*] No, Wright wouldn't like the bird—a thing that sang. She used to sing. He killed that, too.

MRS. PETERS. [*Moving uneasily.*] We don't know who killed the bird.

MRS. HALE. I knew John Wright.

MRS. PETERS. It was an awful thing was done in this house that night, Mrs. Hale. Killing a man while he slept, slipping a rope around his neck that choked the life out of him.

MRS. HALE. His neck. Choked the life out of him.

[*Her hand goes out and rests on the birdcage.*]

MRS. PETERS. [*With rising voice.*] We don't know who killed him. We don't *know*.

MRS. HALE. [*Her own feeling not interrupted.*] If there'd been years and years of nothing, then a bird to sing to, it would be awful—still, after the bird was still.

MRS. PETERS. [*Something within her speaking.*] I know what stillness is. When we homesteaded in Dakota, and my first baby died—after he was two years old, and me with no other then—

MRS. HALE. [*Moving.*] How soon do you suppose they'll be through, looking for the evidence?

MRS. PETERS. I know what stillness is. [*Pulling herself back.*] The law has got to punish crime, Mrs. Hale.

MRS. HALE. [*Not as if answering that.*] I wish you'd seen Minnie Foster when she wore a white dress with blue ribbons and stood up there in the choir and sang. [*A look around the room.*] Oh, I *wish* I'd come over here once in a while! That was a crime! That was a crime! Who's going to punish that?

MRS. PETERS. [*Looking upstairs.*] We mustn't—take on.

MRS. HALE. I might have known she needed help! I know how things can be—for women. I tell you, it's queer, Mrs. Peters. We live close together and we live far apart. We all go through the same things—it's all just a different kind of the same thing. [*Brushes her eyes; noticing the bottle of fruit, reaches out for it.*] If I was you I wouldn't tell her her fruit was gone. Tell her it *ain't.* Tell her it's all right. Take this in to prove it to her. She—she may never know whether it was broke or not.

MRS. PETERS. [*Takes the bottle, looks about for something to wrap it in; takes petticoat from the clothes brought from the other room, very nervously begins winding this around the bottle. In a false voice.*] My, it's a good thing the men couldn't hear us. Wouldn't they just laugh! Getting all stirred up over a little thing like a—dead canary. As if that could have anything to do with—with—wouldn't they *laugh!*

[*The men are heard coming down stairs.*]

MRS. HALE. [*Under her breath.*] Maybe they would—maybe they wouldn't.

COUNTY ATTORNEY. No, Peters, it's all perfectly clear except a reason for doing it. But you know juries when it comes to women. If there was some definite thing. Something to show—something to make a story about—a thing that would connect up with this strange way of doing it—

[*The women's eyes meet for an instant. Enter* HALE *from outer door.*]

HALE. Well, I've got the team around. Pretty cold out there.

COUNTY ATTORNEY. I'm going to stay here a while by myself. [*To the* SHERIFF.] You can send Frank out for me, can't you? I want to go over everything. I'm not satisfied that we can't do better.

SHERIFF. Do you want to see what Mrs. Peters is going to take in?

[*The* COUNTY ATTORNEY *goes to the table, picks up the apron, laughs.*]

COUNTY ATTORNEY. Oh, I guess they're not very dangerous things the ladies have picked out. [*Moves a few things about, disturbing the quilt pieces that cover the box. Steps back.*] No, Mrs. Peters doesn't need supervising. For that matter, a sheriff's wife is married to the law. Ever think of it that way, Mrs. Peters?

MRS. PETERS. Not—just that way.

SHERIFF. [*Chuckling.*] Married to the law. [*Moves toward the other room.*] I just want you to come in here a minute, George. We ought to take a look at these windows.

COUNTY ATTORNEY. [*Scoffingly.*] Oh, windows!

SHERIFF. We'll be right out, Mr. Hale.

[HALE *goes outside. The* SHERIFF *follows the* COUNTY ATTORNEY *into the other room. Then* MRS. HALE *rises, hands tight together, looking intensely at* MRS. PETERS, *whose eyes make a slow turn, finally meeting* MRS. HALE'*s. A moment* MRS. HALE *holds her, then her own eyes point the way to where the box is concealed. Suddenly* MRS. PETERS *throws back quilt pieces and tries to put the box in the bag she is wearing. It is too big. She opens box, starts to take bird out, cannot touch it, goes to pieces, stands there helpless. Sound of a knob turning in the other room.* MRS. HALE *snatches the box and puts it in the pocket of her big coat. Enter* COUNTY ATTORNEY *and* SHERIFF.]

COUNTY ATTORNEY. [*Facetiously.*] Well, Henry, at least we found out that she was not going to quilt it. She was going to—what is it you call it, ladies?

MRS. HALE. [*Her hand against her pocket.*] We call it—knot it, Mr. Henderson.

CURTAIN

A Jury of Her Peers

When Martha Hale opened the storm door and got a cut of the north wind, she ran back for her big woolen scarf. As she hurriedly wound that round her head her eye made a scandalized sweep of her kitchen. It was no ordinary thing that called her away—it was probably farther from ordinary than anything that had ever happened in Dickson County. But what her eye took in was that her kitchen was in no shape for leaving: her bread all ready for mixing, half the flour sifted and half unsifted.

She hated to see things half done; but she had been at that when the team from town stopped to get Mr. Hale, and then the sheriff came running in to say his wife wished Mrs. Hale would come too—adding, with a grin, that he guessed she was getting scary and wanted another woman along. So she had dropped everything right where it was.

"Martha!" now came her husband's impatient voice. "Don't keep folks waiting out here in the cold."

She again opened the storm door, and this time joined the three men and the one woman waiting for her in the big two-seated buggy.

After she had the robes tucked around her she took another look at the woman who sat beside her on the back seat. She had met Mrs. Peters the year before at the county fair, and the thing she remembered about her was that she didn't seem like a sheriff's wife. She was small and thin and didn't have a strong voice. Mrs. Gorman, sheriff's wife before Gorman went out and Peters came in, had a voice that somehow seemed to be backing up the law with every word. But if Mrs. Peters didn't look like a sheriff's wife, Peters made it up in looking like a sheriff. He was to a dot the kind of man who could get himself elected sheriff—a heavy man with a big voice, who was particularly genial with the law-abiding, as if to make it plain that he knew the difference between criminals and noncriminals. And right there it came into Mrs. Hale's mind, with a stab, that this man who was so pleasant and lively with all of them was going to the Wrights' now as a sheriff.

"The country's not very pleasant this time of year," Mrs. Peters at last ventured, as if she felt they ought to be talking as well as the men.

Mrs. Hale scarcely finished her reply, for they had gone up a little hill and could see the Wright place now, and seeing it did not make her feel like talking. It looked very lonesome this cold March morning. It had always been a lonesome-looking place. It was down in a hollow, and the poplar trees around it were lonesome-looking trees. The men were looking at it and talking about what had happened. The county attorney was bending to one side of the buggy, and kept looking steadily at the place as they drew up to it.

"I'm glad you came with me," Mrs. Peters said nervously, as the two women were about to follow the men in through the kitchen door.

Even after she had her foot on the doorstep, her hand on the knob, Martha Hale had a moment of feeling she could not cross that threshold. And the reason it seemed she couldn't cross it now was simply because she hadn't crossed it before. Time and time again it had been in her mind. "I ought to go over and see Minnie Foster"—she still thought of her as Minnie Foster, though for twenty years she had been Mrs. Wright. And then there was always something to do and Minnie Foster would go from her mind. But *now* she could come.

The men went over to the stove. The women stood close together by the door. Young Henderson, the county attorney, turned around and said, "Come up to the fire, ladies."

Mrs. Peters took a step forward, then stopped. "I'm not—cold," she said.

And so the two women stood by the door, at first not even so much as looking around the kitchen.

The men talked for a minute about what a good thing it was the sheriff had sent his deputy out that morning to make a fire for them, and then Sheriff Peters stepped back from the stove, unbuttoned his outer coat, and leaned his hands on the kitchen table in a way that seemed to mark the beginning of official business. "Now, Mr. Hale," he said in a sort of semi-official voice, "before we move things about, you tell Mr. Henderson just what it was you saw when you came here yesterday morning."

The county attorney was looking around the kitchen.

"By the way," he said, "has anything been moved?" He turned to the sheriff. "Are things just as you left them yesterday?"

Peters looked from cupboard to sink; from that to a small worn rocker a little to one side of the kitchen table.

"It's just the same."

"Somebody should have been left here yesterday," said the county attorney.

"Oh—yesterday," returned the sheriff, with a little gesture as of yesterday having been more than he could bear to think of. "When I had to send Frank to Morris Center for that man who went crazy—let me tell you, I had my hands full *yesterday.* I knew you could get back from Omaha by today, George, and as long as I went over everything here myself—"

"Well, Mr. Hale," said the county attorney, in a way of letting what was past and gone go, "tell just what happened when you came here yesterday morning."

Mrs. Hale, still leaning against the door, had that sinking feeling of the mother whose child is about to speak a piece. Lewis often wandered along and got things mixed up in a story. She hoped he would tell this straight and plain, and not say unnecessary things that would just make things harder for Minnie Foster. He didn't begin at once, and she noticed that he looked queer—as if standing in that kitchen and having to tell what he had seen there yesterday morning made him almost sick.

"Yes, Mr. Hale?" the county attorney reminded.

"Harry and I had started to town with a load of potatoes," Mrs. Hale's husband began.

Harry was Mrs. Hale's oldest boy. He wasn't with them now, for the very good reason that those potatoes never got to town yesterday and he was taking them this morning, so he hadn't been home when the sheriff stopped to say he wanted Mr. Hale to come over to the Wright place and tell the county attorney his story there, where he could point it all out. With all Mrs. Hale's other emotions came the fear that maybe Harry wasn't dressed warm enough—they hadn't any of them realized how that north wind did bite.

"We come along this road," Hale was going on, with a motion of his hand to the road over which they had just come, "and as we got in sight of the house I says to Harry, 'I'm goin' to see if I can't get John Wright to take a telephone.' You see," he explained to Henderson, "unless I can get somebody to go in with me they won't come out this branch road except for a price *I* can't pay. I'd spoke to Wright about it once before; but he put me off, saying folks talked too much anyway, and all he asked was peace and quiet—guess you know about how much he talked himself. But I thought maybe if I went to the house and talked about it before his wife, and said all the womenfolks liked the telephones, and that in this lonesome stretch of road it would be a good thing—well, I said to Harry that that was what I was going to say—though I said at the same time that I didn't know as what his wife wanted made much difference to John—"

Now, there he was!—saying things he didn't need to say. Mrs. Hale tried to catch her husband's eye, but fortunately the county attorney interrupted with:

"Let's talk about that a little later, Mr. Hale. I do want to talk about that, but I'm anxious now to get along to just what happened when you got here."

When he began this time, it was very deliberately and carefully:

"I didn't see or hear anything. I knocked at the door. And still it was all quiet inside. I knew they must be up—it was past eight o'clock. So I knocked again, louder, and I thought I heard somebody say 'Come in.' I wasn't sure—I'm not sure yet. But I opened the door—this door," jerking a hand toward the door by which the two women stood, "and there, in that rocker"—pointing to it—"sat Mrs. Wright."

Everyone in the kitchen looked at the rocker. It came into Mrs. Hale's mind that the rocker didn't look in the least like Minnie Foster—the Minnie Foster of twenty years before. It was a dingy red, with wooden rungs up the back, and the middle rung was gone, and the chair sagged to one side.

"How did she—look?" the county attorney was inquiring.

"Well," said Hale, "she looked—queer."

"How do you mean—queer?"

As he asked it he took out a notebook and pencil. Mrs. Hale did not like the sight of that pencil. She kept her eye fixed on her husband, as if to keep him from saying unnecessary things that would go into that notebook and make trouble.

Hale did speak guardedly, as if the pencil had affected him too.

"Well, as if she didn't know what she was going to do next. And kind of—done up."

"How did she seem to feel about your coming?"

"Why, I don't think she minded—one way or other. She didn't pay much attention. I said, 'Ho' do, Mrs. Wright? It's cold, ain't it!' And she said, 'Is it?'—and went on pleatin' at her apron.

"Well, I was surprised. She didn't ask me to come up to the stove, or to sit down, but just set there, not even lookin' at me. And so I said: 'I want to see John.'

"And then she—laughed. I guess you would call it a laugh.

"I thought of Harry and the team outside, so I said, a little sharp, 'Can I see John?' 'No,' says she—kind of dull like. 'Ain't he home?' says I. Then she looked at me. 'Yes,' says she, 'he's home.' 'Then why can't I see him?' I asked her, out of patience with her now. 'Cause he's dead,' says she, just as quiet and dull—and fell to pleatin' her apron. 'Dead?' says I, like you do when you can't take in what you've heard.

"She just nodded her head, not getting a bit excited, but rockin' back and forth.

"'Why—where is he?' says I, not knowing *what* to say.

"She just pointed upstairs—like this"—pointing to the room above.

"I got up, with the idea of going up there myself. By this time I—didn't know what to do. I walked from there to here; then I says: 'Why, what did he die of?'

"'He died of a rope around his neck,' says she; and just went on pleatin' at her apron."

Hale stopped speaking, and stood staring at the rocker, as if he were still seeing the woman who had sat there the morning before. Nobody spoke; it was as if everyone were seeing the woman who had sat there the morning before.

"And what did you do then?" the county attorney at last broke the silence.

"I went out and called Harry. I thought I might—need help. I got Harry in, and we went upstairs." His voice fell almost to a whisper. "There he was—lying over the—"

"I think I'd rather have you go into that upstairs," the county attorney interrupted, "where you can point it all out. Just go on now with the rest of the story."

"Well, my first thought was to get that rope off. It looked—"

He stopped, his face twitching.

"But Harry, he went up to him, and he said, 'No, he's dead all right, and we'd better not touch anything.' So we went downstairs.

"She was still sitting the same way. 'Has anybody been notified?' I asked. 'No,' says she, unconcerned.

"'Who did this, Mrs. Wright?' said Harry. He said it business-like, and she stopped pleatin' at her apron. 'I don't know,' she says. 'You don't *know?*' says Harry. 'Weren't you sleepin' in the bed with him?' 'Yes,' says she, 'but I was on the inside.' 'Somebody slipped a rope round his neck and strangled him, and you didn't wake up?' says Harry. 'I didn't wake up,' she said after him.

"We may have looked as if we didn't see how that could be, for after a minute she said, 'I sleep sound.'

"Harry was going to ask her more questions, but I said maybe that weren't our business; maybe we ought to let her tell her story first to the coroner or the sheriff. So Harry went fast as he could over to High Road—the Rivers' place, where there's a telephone."

"And what did she do when she knew you had gone for the coroner?" The attorney got his pencil in his hand all ready for writing.

"She moved from that chair to this one over here"—Hale pointed to a small chair in the corner—"and just sat there with her hands held together and looking down. I got a feeling that I ought to make some conversation, so I said I had come in to see if John wanted to put in a telephone; and at that she started to laugh, and then she stopped and looked at me—scared."

At the sound of a moving pencil the man who was telling the story looked up.

"I dunno—maybe it wasn't scared," he hastened; "I wouldn't like to say it was. Soon Harry got back, and then Dr. Lloyd came, and you, Mr. Peters, and so I guess that's all I know that you don't."

He said that last with relief, and moved a little, as if relaxing. Everyone moved a little. The county attorney walked toward the stair door.

"I guess we'll go upstairs first—then out to the barn and around there."

He paused and looked around the kitchen.

"You're convinced there was nothing important here?"

he asked the sheriff. "Nothing that would—point to any motive?"

The sheriff too looked all around, as if to reconvince himself.

"Nothing here but kitchen things," he said, with a little laugh for the insignificance of kitchen things.

The county attorney was looking at the cupboard—a peculiar, ungainly structure, half closet and half cupboard, the upper part of it being built in the wall, and the lower part just the old-fashioned kitchen cupboard. As if its queerness attracted him, he got a chair and opened the upper part and looked in. After a moment he drew his hand away sticky.

"Here's a nice mess," he said resentfully.

The two women had drawn nearer, and now the sheriff's wife spoke.

"Oh—her fruit," she said, looking to Mrs. Hale for sympathetic understanding. She turned back to the county attorney and explained: "She worried about that when it turned so cold last night. She said the fire would go out and her jars might burst."

Mrs. Peters' husband broke into a laugh.

"Well, can you beat the women! Held for murder, and worrying about her preserves!"

The young attorney set his lips.

"I guess before we're through with her she may have something more serious than preserves to worry about."

"Oh, well," said Mrs. Hale's husband, with good-natured superiority, "women are used to worrying over trifles."

The two women moved a little closer together. Neither of them spoke. The county attorney seemed suddenly to remember his manners—and think of his future.

"And yet," said he, with the gallantry of a young politician, "for all their worries, what would we do without the ladies?"

The women did not speak, did not unbend. He went to the sink and began washing his hands. He turned to wipe them on the roller towel—whirled it for a cleaner place.

"Dirty towels! Not much of a housekeeper, would you say, ladies?"

He kicked his foot against some dirty pans under the sink.

"There's a great deal of work to be done on a farm," said Mrs. Hale stiffly.

"To be sure. And yet"—with a little bow to her—"I know there are some Dickson County farmhouses that do not have such roller towels." He gave it a pull to expose its full length again.

"Those towels get dirty awful quick. Men's hands aren't always as clean as they might be."

"Ah, loyal to your sex, I see," he laughed. He stopped and gave her a keen look. "But you and Mrs. Wright were neighbors. I suppose you were friends, too."

Martha Hale shook her head.

"I've seen little enough of her of late years. I've not been in this house—it's more than a year."

"And why was that? You didn't like her?"

"I liked her well enough," she replied with spirit. "Farmers' wives have their hands full, Mr. Henderson. And then"—She looked around the kitchen.

"Yes?" he encouraged.

"It never seemed a very cheerful place," said she, more to herself than to him.

"No," he agreed; "I don't think anyone would call it cheerful. I shouldn't say she had the homemaking instinct."

"Well, I don't know as Wright had, either," she muttered.

"You mean they didn't get on very well?" he was quick to ask.

"No; I don't mean anything," she answered, with decision. As she turned a little away from him, she added: "But I don't think a place would be any the cheerfuler for John Wright's bein' in it."

"I'd like to talk to you about that a little later, Mrs. Hale," he said. "I'm anxious to get the lay of things upstairs now."

He moved toward the stair door, followed by the two men.

"I suppose anything Mrs. Peters does'll be all right?" the sheriff inquired. "She was to take in some clothes for her, you know—and a few little things. We left in such a hurry yesterday."

The county attorney looked at the two women whom they were leaving alone there among the kitchen things.

"Yes—Mrs. Peters," he said, his glance resting on the woman who was not Mrs. Peters, the big farmer woman who stood behind the sheriff's wife. "Of course Mrs. Peters is one of us," he said, in a manner of entrusting responsibility. "And keep your eye out, Mrs. Peters, for anything that might be of use. No telling; you women might come upon a clue to the motive—and that's the thing we need."

Mr. Hale rubbed his face after the fashion of a showman getting ready for a pleasantry.

"But would the women know a clue if they did come upon it?" he said; and, having delivered himself of this, he followed the others through the stair door.

The women stood motionless and silent, listening to the footsteps, first upon the stairs, then in the room above them.

Then, as if releasing herself from something strange, Mrs. Hale began to arrange the dirty pans under the sink, which the county attorney's disdainful push of the foot had deranged.

"I'd hate to have men comin' into my kitchen," she said testily—"snoopin' round and criticizin'."

"Of course it's no more than their duty," said the sheriff's wife, in her manner of timid acquiescence.

"Duty's all right," replied Mrs. Hale bluffly; "but I guess that deputy sheriff that come out to make the fire might have got a little of this on." She gave the roller towel a pull. "Wish I'd thought of that sooner! Seems mean to talk about her for not having things slicked up, when she had to come away in such a hurry."

She looked around the kitchen. Certainly it was not "slicked up." Her eye was held by a bucket of sugar on a low shelf. The cover was off the wooden bucket, and beside it was a paper bag—half full.

Mrs. Hale moved toward it.

"She was putting this in there," she said to herself—slowly.

She thought of the flour in her kitchen at home—half sifted, half not sifted. She had been interrupted and had left things half done. What had interrupted Minnie Foster? Why had that work been left half done? She made a move as if to finish it,—unfinished things always bothered her,—and then she glanced around and saw that Mrs. Peters was watching her—and she didn't want Mrs. Peters to get that feeling she had got of work begun and then—for some reason—not finished.

"It's a shame about her fruit," she said, and walked toward the cupboard that the county attorney had opened, and got on the chair, murmuring: "I wonder if it's all gone."

It was a sorry enough looking sight, but "Here's one that's all right," she said at last. She held it toward the light. "This is cherries, too." She looked again. "I declare I believe that's the only one."

With a sigh, she got down from the chair, went to the sink, and wiped off the bottle.

"She'll feel awful bad, after all her hard work in the hot weather. I remember the afternoon I put up my cherries last summer."

She set the bottle on the table, and, with another sigh, started to sit down in the rocker. But she did not sit down. Something kept her from sitting down in that chair. She straightened—stepped back, and, half turned away, stood looking at it, seeing the woman who sat there "pleatin' at her apron."

The thin voice of the sheriff's wife broke in upon her: "I must be getting those things from the front room closet." She opened the door into the other room, started in, stepped back. "You coming with me, Mrs. Hale?" she asked nervously. "You—you could help me get them."

They were soon back—the stark coldness of that shut-up room was not a thing to linger in.

"My!" said Mrs. Peters, dropping the things on the table and hurrying to the stove.

Mrs. Hale stood examining the clothes the woman who was being detained in town had said she wanted.

"Wright was close!" she exclaimed, holding up a shabby black skirt that bore the marks of much making over. "I think maybe that's why she kept so much to herself. I s'pose she felt she couldn't do her part; and then, you don't enjoy things when you feel shabby. She used to wear pretty clothes and be lively—when she was Minnie Foster, one of the town girls, singing in the choir. But that—oh, that was twenty years ago."

With a carefulness in which there was something tender, she folded the shabby clothes and piled them at one corner of the table. She looked at Mrs. Peters, and there was something in the other woman's look that irritated her.

"She don't care," she said to herself. "Much difference it makes to her whether Minnie Foster had pretty clothes when she was a girl."

Then she looked again, and she wasn't so sure; in fact, she hadn't at any time been perfectly sure about Mrs. Peters. She had that shrinking manner, and yet her eyes looked as if they could see a long way into things.

"This all you was to take in?" asked Mrs. Hale.

"No," said the sheriff's wife; "she said she wanted an apron. Funny thing to want," she ventured in her nervous little way, "for there's not much to get you dirty in jail, goodness knows. But I suppose just to make her feel more natural. If you're used to wearing an apron—. She said they were in the bottom drawer of this cupboard. Yes—here they are. And then her little shawl that always hung on the stair door."

She took the small gray shawl from behind the door leading upstairs, and stood a minute looking at it.

Suddenly Mrs. Hale took a quick step toward the other woman.

"Mrs. Peters!"

"Yes, Mrs. Hale?"

"Do you think she—did it?"

A frightened look blurred the other things in Mrs. Peters' eyes.

"Oh, I don't know," she said, in a voice that seemed to shrink away from the subject.

"Well, I don't think she did," affirmed Mrs. Hale stoutly. "Asking for an apron, and her little shawl. Worryin' about her fruit."

"Mr. Peters says—" Footsteps were heard in the room above; she stopped, looked up, then went on in a lowered voice: "Mr. Peters says—it looks bad for her. Mr. Henderson is awful sarcastic in a speech, and he's going to make fun of her saying she didn't—wake up."

For a moment Mrs. Hale had no answer. Then, "Well, I guess John Wright didn't wake up—when they was slippin' that rope under his neck," she muttered.

"No, it's *strange,*" breathed Mrs. Peters. "They think it was such a—funny way to kill a man."

She began to laugh; at sound of the laugh, abruptly stopped.

"That's just what Mr. Hale said," said Mrs. Hale, in a resolutely natural voice. "There was a gun in the house. He says that's what he can't understand."

"Mr. Henderson said, coming out, that what was needed for the case was a motive. Something to show anger—or sudden feeling."

"Well, I don't see any signs of anger around here," said Mrs. Hale. "I don't—"

She stopped. It was as if her mind tripped on something. Her eye was caught by a dish towel in the middle of the kitchen table. Slowly she moved toward the table. One half of it was wiped clean, the other half messy. Her eyes made a slow, almost unwilling turn to the bucket of sugar and the half empty bag beside it. Things begun—and not finished.

After a moment she stepped back, and said, in that manner of releasing herself:

"Wonder how they're finding things upstairs? I hope she had it a little more red-up up there. You know,"—she paused, and feeling gathered,—"it seems kind of *sneaking;* locking her up in town and coming out here to get her own house to turn against her!"

"But, Mrs. Hale," said the sheriff's wife, "the law is the law."

"I s'pose 'tis," answered Mrs. Hale shortly.

She turned to the stove, saying something about that fire not being much to brag of. She worked with it a minute, and when she straightened up she said aggressively:

"The law is the law—and a bad stove is a bad stove. How'd you like to cook on this?"—pointing with the poker to the broken lining. She opened the oven door and started to express her opinion of the oven; but she was swept into her own thoughts, thinking of what it would mean, year after year, to have that stove to wrestle with. The thought of Minnie Foster trying to bake in that oven—and the thought of her never going over to see Minnie Foster—.

She was startled by hearing Mrs. Peters say: "A person gets discouraged—and loses heart."

The sheriff's wife had looked from the stove to the sink—to the pail of water which had been carried in from outside. The two women stood there silent, above them the footsteps of the men who were looking for evidence against the woman who had worked in that kitchen. That look of seeing into things, of seeing through a thing to something else, was in the eyes of the sheriff's wife now. When Mrs. Hale next spoke to her, it was gently:

"Better loosen up your things, Mrs. Peters. We'll not feel them when we go out."

Mrs. Peters went to the back of the room to hang up the fur tippet she was wearing. A moment later she exclaimed, "Why, she was piecing a quilt," and held up a large sewing basket piled high with quilt pieces.

Mrs. Hale spread some of the blocks on the table.

"It's log-cabin pattern," she said, putting several of them together. "Pretty, isn't it?"

They were so engaged with the quilt that they did not

hear the footsteps on the stairs. Just as the stair door opened Mrs. Hale was saying:

"Do you suppose she was going to quilt it or just knot it?"

The sheriff threw up his hands.

"They wonder whether she was going to quilt it or just knot it!"

There was a laugh for the ways of women, a warming of hands over the stove, and then the county attorney said briskly:

"Well, let's go right out to the barn and get that cleared up."

"I don't see as there's anything so strange," Mrs. Hale said resentfully, after the outside door had closed on the three men—"our taking up our time with little things while we're waiting for them to get the evidence. I don't see as it's anything to laugh about."

"Of course they've got awful important things on their minds," said the sheriff's wife apologetically.

They returned to an inspection of the blocks for the quilt. Mrs. Hale was looking at the fine, even sewing, and preoccupied with thoughts of the woman who had done that sewing, when she heard the sheriff's wife say, in a queer tone:

"Why, look at this one."

She turned to take the block held out to her.

"The sewing," said Mrs. Peters, in a troubled way. "All the rest of them have been so nice and even—but—this one. Why, it looks as if she didn't know what she was about!"

Their eyes met—something flashed to life, passed between them; then, as if with an effort, they seemed to pull away from each other. A moment Mrs. Hale sat there, her hands folded over that sewing which was so unlike all the rest of the sewing. Then she had pulled a knot and drawn the threads.

"Oh, what are you doing, Mrs. Hale?" asked the sheriff's wife, startled.

"Just pulling out a stitch or two that's not sewed very good," said Mrs. Hale mildly.

"I don't think we ought to touch things," Mrs. Peters said, a little helplessly.

"I'd just finish up this end," answered Mrs. Hale, still in that mild, matter-of-fact fashion.

She threaded a needle and started to replace bad sewing with good. For a little while she sewed in silence. Then, in that thin, timid voice, she heard:

"Mrs. Hale!"

"Yes, Mrs. Peters?"

"What do you suppose she was so—nervous about?"

"Oh, *I* don't know," said Mrs. Hale, as if dismissing a thing not important enough to spend much time on. "I don't know as she was—nervous. I sew awful queer sometimes when I'm just tired."

She cut a thread, and out of the corner of her eye looked up at Mrs. Peters. The small, lean face of the sheriff's wife seemed to have tightened up. Her eyes had that look of peering into something. But the next moment she moved, and said in her thin, indecisive way:

"Well, I must get those clothes wrapped. They may be through sooner than we think. I wonder where I could find a piece of paper—and string."

"In that cupboard, maybe," suggested Mrs. Hale, after a glance around.

One piece of the crazy sewing remained unripped. Mrs. Peters' back turned, Martha Hale now scrutinized that piece, compared it with the dainty, accurate sewing of the other blocks. The difference was startling. Holding this block made her feel queer, as if the distracted thoughts of the woman who had perhaps turned to it to try and quiet herself were communicating themselves to her.

Mrs. Peters' voice roused her.

"Here's a birdcage," she said. "Did she have a bird, Mrs. Hale?"

"Why, I don't know whether she did or not." She turned to look at the cage Mrs. Peters was holding up. "I've not been here in so long." She sighed. "There was a man round last year selling canaries cheap—but I don't know as she took one. Maybe she did. She used to sing real pretty herself."

Mrs. Peters looked around the kitchen.

"Seems kind of funny to think of a bird here." She half laughed—an attempt to put up a barrier. "But she must have had one—or why would she have a cage? I wonder what happened to it."

"I suppose maybe the cat got it," suggested Mrs. Hale, resuming her sewing.

"No; she didn't have a cat. She's got that feeling some people have about cats—being afraid of them. When they brought her to our house yesterday, my cat got in the room, and she was real upset and asked me to take it out."

"My sister Bessie was like that," laughed Mrs. Hale.

The sheriff's wife did not reply. The silence made Mrs. Hale turn round. Mrs. Peters was examining the birdcage.

"Look at this door," she said slowly. "It's broke. One hinge has been pulled apart."

Mrs. Hale came nearer.

"Looks as if someone must have been—rough with it."

Again their eyes met—startled, questioning, apprehensive. For a moment neither spoke nor stirred. Then Mrs. Hale, turning away, said brusquely:

"If they're going to find any evidence, I wish they'd be about it. I don't like this place."

"But I'm awful glad you came with me, Mrs. Hale." Mrs. Peters put the birdcage on the table and sat down. "It would be lonesome for me—sitting here alone."

"Yes, it would, wouldn't it?" agreed Mrs. Hale, a certain determined naturalness in her voice. She picked up the sewing, but now it dropped in her lap, and she murmured in a different voice: "But I tell you what I *do* wish, Mrs. Peters. I wish I had come over sometimes when she was here. I wish—I had."

"But of course you were awful busy, Mrs. Hale. Your house—and your children."

"I could've come," retorted Mrs. Hale shortly. "I stayed away because it weren't cheerful—and that's why I ought to have come. I"—she looked around—"I've never liked this place. Maybe because it's down in a hollow and you don't see the road. I don't know what it is, but it's a lonesome place, and always was. I wish I had come over to see Minnie Foster sometimes. I can see now—" She did not put it into words.

"Well, you mustn't reproach yourself," counseled Mrs. Peters. "Somehow, we just don't see how it is with other folks till—something comes up."

"Not having children makes less work," mused Mrs. Hale, after a silence, "but it makes a quiet house—and Wright out to work all day—and no company when he did come in. Did you know John Wright, Mrs. Peters?"

"Not to know him. I've seen him in town. They say he was a good man."

"Yes—good," conceded John Wright's neighbor grimly.

"He didn't drink, and kept his word as well as most, I guess, and paid his debts. But he was a hard man, Mrs. Peters. Just to pass the time of day with him—." She stopped, shivered a little. "Like a raw wind that gets to the bone." Her eye fell upon the cage on the table before her, and she added, almost bitterly: "I should think she would've wanted a bird!"

Suddenly she leaned forward, looking intently at the cage. "But what do you s'pose went wrong with it?"

"I don't know," returned Mrs. Peters; "unless it got sick and died."

But after she said it she reached over and swung the broken door. Both women watched it as if somehow held by it.

"You didn't know—her?" Mrs. Hale asked, a gentler note in her voice.

"Not till they brought her yesterday," said the sheriff's wife.

"She—come to think of it, she was kind of like a bird herself. Real sweet and pretty, but kind of timid and—fluttery. How—she—did—change."

That held her for a long time. Finally, as if struck with a happy thought and relieved to get back to everyday things, she exclaimed:

"Tell you what, Mrs. Peters, why don't you take the quilt in with you? It might take up her mind."

"Why, I think that's a real nice idea, Mrs. Hale," agreed the sheriff's wife, as if she too were glad to come into the atmosphere of a simple kindness. "There couldn't possibly be any objection to that, could there? Now, just what will I take? I wonder if her patches are in here—and her things."

They turned to the sewing basket.

"Here's some red," said Mrs. Hale, bringing out a roll of

cloth. Underneath that was a box. "Here, maybe her scissors are in here—and her things." She held it up. "What a pretty box! I'll warrant that was something she had a long time ago—when she was a girl."

She held it in her hand a moment; then, with a little sigh, opened it.

Instantly her hand went to her nose.

"Why—!"

Mrs. Peters drew nearer—then turned away.

"There's something wrapped up in this piece of silk," faltered Mrs. Hale.

"This isn't her scissors," said Mrs. Peters in a shrinking voice.

Her hand not steady, Mrs. Hale raised the piece of silk. "Oh, Mrs. Peters!" she cried. "It's—"

Mrs. Peters bent closer.

"It's the bird," she whispered.

"But, Mrs. Peters!" cried Mrs. Hale. "*Look* at it! Its neck—look at its neck! It's all—other side *to.*"

She held the box away from her.

The sheriff's wife again bent closer.

"Somebody wrung its neck," said she, in a voice that was slow and deep.

And then again the eyes of the two women met—this time clung together in a look of dawning comprehension, of growing horror. Mrs. Peters looked from the dead bird to the broken door of the cage. Again their eyes met. And just then there was a sound at the outside door.

Mrs. Hale slipped the box under the quilt pieces in the basket, and sank into the chair before it. Mrs. Peters stood holding to the table. The county attorney and the sheriff came in from outside.

"Well, ladies," said the county attorney, as one turning

from serious things to little pleasantries, "have you decided whether she was going to quilt it or knot it?"

"We think," began the sheriff's wife in a flurried voice, "that she was going to—knot it."

He was too preoccupied to notice the change that came in her voice on that last.

"Well, that's very interesting, I'm sure," he said tolerantly. He caught sight of the birdcage. "Has the bird flown?"

"We think the cat got it," said Mrs. Hale in a voice curiously even.

He was walking up and down, as if thinking something out.

"Is there a cat?" he asked absently.

Mrs. Hale shot a look up at the sheriff's wife.

"Well, not *now,*" said Mrs. Peters. "They're superstitious, you know; they leave."

She sank into her chair.

The county attorney did not heed her. "No sign at all of anyone having come in from the outside," he said to Peters, in the manner of continuing an interrupted conversation. "Their own rope. Now let's go upstairs again and go over it, piece by piece. It would have to have been someone who knew just the—"

The stair door closed behind them and their voices were lost.

The two women sat motionless, not looking at each other, but as if peering into something and at the same time holding back. When they spoke now it was as if they were afraid of what they were saying, but as if they could not help saying it.

"She liked the bird," said Martha Hale, low and slowly. "She was going to bury it in that pretty box."

"When I was a girl," said Mrs. Peters, under her breath,

"my kitten—there was a boy took a hatchet, and before my eyes—before I could get there—" She covered her face an instant. "If they hadn't held me back I would have"—she caught herself, looked upstairs where footsteps were heard, and finished weakly—"hurt him."

Then they sat without speaking or moving.

"I wonder how it would seem," Mrs. Hale at last began, as if feeling her way over strange ground—"never to have had any children around?" Her eyes made a slow sweep of the kitchen, as if seeing what that kitchen had meant through all the years. "No, Wright wouldn't like the bird," she said after that—"a thing that sang. She used to sing. He killed that too." Her voice tightened.

Mrs. Peters moved uneasily.

"Of course we don't know who killed the bird."

"I knew John Wright," was Mrs. Hale's answer.

"It was an awful thing was done in this house that night, Mrs. Hale," said the sheriff's wife. "Killing a man while he slept—slipping a thing round his neck that choked the life out of him."

Mrs. Hale's hand went out to the birdcage.

"His neck. Choked the life out of him."

"We don't *know* who killed him," whispered Mrs. Peters wildly. "We don't *know.*"

Mrs. Hale had not moved. "If there had been years and years of—nothing, then a bird to sing to you, it would be awful—still—after the bird was still."

It was as if something within her not herself had spoken, and it found in Mrs. Peters something she did not know as herself.

"I know what stillness is," she said, in a queer, monotonous voice. "When we homesteaded in Dakota, and my first baby died—after he was two years old—and me with no other then—"

Mrs. Hale stirred.

"How soon do you suppose they'll be through looking for evidence?"

"I know what stillness is," repeated Mrs. Peters, in just that same way. Then she too pulled back. "The law has got to punish crime, Mrs. Hale," she said in her tight little way.

"I wish you'd seen Minnie Foster," was the answer, "when she wore a white dress with blue ribbons, and stood up there in the choir and sang."

The picture of that girl, the fact that she had lived neighbor to that girl for twenty years, and had let her die for lack of life, was suddenly more than she could bear.

"Oh, I *wish* I'd come over here once in a while!" she cried. "That was a crime! That was a crime! Who's going to punish that?"

"We mustn't take on," said Mrs. Peters, with a frightened look toward the stairs.

"I might 'a' *known* she needed help! I tell you, it's *queer,* Mrs. Peters. We live close together, and we live far apart. We all go through the same things—it's all just a different kind of the same thing! If it weren't—why do you and I *understand?* Why do we *know*—what we know this minute?"

She dashed her hand across her eyes. Then, seeing the jar of fruit on the table, she reached for it and choked out:

"If I was you I wouldn't *tell* her her fruit was gone! Tell her it *ain't.* Tell her it's all right—all of it. Here—take this in to prove it to her! She—she may never know whether it was broke or not."

She turned away.

Mrs. Peters reached out for the bottle of fruit as if she were glad to take it—as if touching a familiar thing, having something to do, could keep her from something else. She got up, looked about for something to wrap the fruit in, took a petticoat from the pile of clothes she had brought from the front room, and nervously started winding that round the bottle.

"My!" she began, in a high, false voice, "it's a good thing the men couldn't hear us! Getting all stirred up over a little thing like a—dead canary." She hurried over that. "As if that could have anything to do with—with—My, wouldn't they *laugh?*"

Footsteps were heard on the stairs.

"Maybe they would," muttered Mrs. Hale—"maybe they wouldn't."

"No, Peters," said the county attorney incisively; "it's all perfectly clear, except the reason for doing it. But you know juries when it comes to women. If there was some definite thing—something to show. Something to make a story about. A thing that would connect up with this clumsy way of doing it."

In a covert way Mrs. Hale looked at Mrs. Peters. Mrs. Peters was looking at her. Quickly they looked away from each other. The outer door opened and Mr. Hale came in.

"I've got the team round now," he said. "Pretty cold out there."

"I'm going to stay here awhile by myself," the county attorney suddenly announced. "You can send Frank out for me, can't you?" he asked the sheriff. "I want to go over everything. I'm not satisfied we can't do better."

Again, for one brief moment, the two women's eyes found one another.

The sheriff came up to the table.

"Did you want to see what Mrs. Peters was going to take in?"

The county attorney picked up the apron. He laughed.

"Oh, I guess they're not very dangerous things the ladies have picked out."

Mrs. Hale's hand was on the sewing basket in which the box was concealed. She felt that she ought to take her hand off the basket. She did not seem able to. He picked up one of the quilt blocks which she had piled on to cover the box. Her eyes felt like fire. She had a feeling that if he took up the basket she would snatch it from him.

But he did not take it up. With another little laugh, he turned away, saying:

"No; Mrs. Peters doesn't need supervising. For that matter, a sheriff's wife is married to the law. Ever think of it that way, Mrs. Peters?"

Mrs. Peters was standing beside the table. Mrs. Hale shot a look up at her; but she could not see her face. Mrs. Peters had turned away. When she spoke, her voice was muffled.

"Not—just that way," she said.

"Married to the law!" chuckled Mrs. Peters' husband. He moved toward the door into the front room, and said to the county attorney:

"I just want you to come in here a minute, George. We ought to take a look at these windows.

"Oh—windows," said the county attorney scoffingly.

"We'll be right out, Mr. Hale," said the sheriff to the farmer, who was still waiting by the door.

Hale went to look after the horses. The sheriff followed the county attorney into the other room. Again—for one moment—the two women were alone in that kitchen.

Martha Hale sprang up, her hands tight together, looking at that other woman, with whom it rested. At first she could not see her eyes, for the sheriff's wife had not turned back, since she turned away at that suggestion of being married to the law. But now Mrs. Hale made her turn back. Her eyes made her turn back. Slowly, unwillingly, Mrs. Peters turned her head until her eyes met the eyes of the other woman. There was a moment when they held each other in a steady, burning look in which there was no evasion nor flinching. Then Martha Hale's eyes pointed the way to the basket in which was hidden the thing that would make certain the conviction of the other woman—that woman who was not there and yet who had been there with them all through the hour.

For a moment Mrs. Peters did not move. And then she did it. With a rush forward, she threw back the quilt pieces, got the box, tried to put it in her handbag. It was too big. Desperately she opened it, started to take the bird out. But there she broke—she could not touch the bird. She stood helpless, foolish.

There was the sound of a knob turning in the inner door. Martha Hale snatched the box from the sheriff's wife, and got it in the pocket of her big coat just as the sheriff and the county attorney came back into the kitchen.

"Well, Henry," said the county attorney facetiously, "at least we found out that she was not going to quilt it. She was going to—what is it you call it, ladies?"

Mrs. Hale's hand was against the pocket of her coat.

"We call it—knot it, Mr. Henderson."

"Finality" in Freeport

It never would have happened at all if Mr. William Wilkes, president of the Freeport Ice Company, had not stopped to look in a window at some puppies. This was very wrong of Mr. Wilkes, for as it was he had barely time to get to the library to meet his wife at four o'clock, and four o'clock, as she had impressed upon him at noon, was as late as one dared be in setting forth to look at rugs—did not daylight wane and stores close? But the puppies were tumbling over one another altogether irresistibly and so Mr. Wilkes was lured from the path of duty, and thus was the history of a town changed.

And, just as one evil always leads to another, so, as President Wilkes was about to tear himself from the puppies, along came J. E. Carsons and asked him when he was going to join the Elks. And thus passed another ten minutes in which Mrs. Wilkes sat in the reading room and looked from *Current Ideas* to the clock over the door and thought how hard are the ways of women and bitterly considered the unworthiness of man.

When, at ten minutes after four, Mr. Wilkes had not arrived, Mrs. Wilkes stepped to the desk and acidly inquired whether the library possessed a copy of *The Finality of Christianity.* Mrs. Wilkes, in waiting for her loitering spouse, had been reading the book reviews. She was a woman who prided herself on "keeping up." What she particularly liked was keeping up with books her acquaintances had not yet come in sight of.

Now Mrs. Wilkes inquired whether the library possessed the book in the manner of supposing of course the library didn't. In fact she asked for the work, not so much because she wanted to see it, as because she had to be as disagreeable to someone else as Mr. Wilkes was being to her.

The girl at the desk replied that they did not have the book. Mrs. Wilkes wanted to know why. The girl didn't know why. Mrs. Wilkes said she would like to speak to the librarian.

And as she was speaking to the librarian along came Rabbi Lewisohn. Mrs. Wilkes was a member of the Woman's Club, before which the brilliant young rabbi had spoken just the week before on "Religious Feeling in Modern Fiction." In fact Rabbi Lewisohn was the intellectual idol of Freeport.

Rabbi Lewisohn said he considered the book important. Yes, it was a book which the library should have. Miss Archer looked a little worried and said she would put it on her list. This was the first call for it, and of course one could not buy all the books.

"But one should buy the most important ones," said Mrs. Wilkes impressively, looking to the rabbi for his nod of approbation. And at this moment there arrived a perspiring and guilty-looking Mr. Wilkes.

Mrs. Wilkes became immersed in house furnishings and, to tell the truth, did not think of *The Finality of Christianity* again until she saw Rabbi Lewisohn at the annual reception given by the Woman's Club. And then, in the presence of women who looked upon themselves as intellectually far in advance of Mrs. Wilkes, the brilliant young rabbi exclaimed: "Oh, Mrs. Wilkes, did you know the library board refuses to buy our book?"

"Refuses?" cried Mrs. Wilkes, in a tone of tremendous

incredulity, and thrilling to the inmost recesses of her brain at the "our book."

"Deacon Judson maintains that the shelves are already too crowded with advanced theology," laughed the rabbi.

Mrs. Wilkes set down her teacup in the manner of not having strength to hold it, and "How outrageous!" breathed she.

The other ladies crowded around for enlightenment. It was apparent that there were a few who cherished a secret sympathy with Deacon Judson. These few melted away into less advanced groups leaving a pure circle of the indignant at heart, and then and there the campaign was planned. It was said in excusing the censorship that there had been only two inquiries for this book. Very well then—there should be two hundred! If necessary, let there be two thousand!

At the next monthly meeting of the library board Miss Archer tremblingly announced that there had been two hundred and forty-three inquiries for Dr. Mosher's book, *The Finality of Christianity.*

The back of Deacon Judson stiffened. There were only nine members of the board present that day and four of these, led to believe that all they had long held dear was in danger of being at once swept away by this menacing body of godless fellow citizens, voted with Deacon Judson. The library board went on record as refusing to purchase a book for which two hundred and forty-three citizens clamored.

The telephone operators of Freeport were very busy that night. The next evening the Freeport *Clarion,* under the particularly black heading "What is Liberty?" printed a letter from Rabbi Lewisohn. "What do the citizens intend to do about this?" the young rabbi inquired with fervor.

It was immediately apparent that the first thing they intended to do was to write letters to the *Clarion.* That organ printed a page of letters next afternoon, apologizing for being able to print so few. The library board was attacked and defended from a dizzying variety of angles. Citizens who had not known there was such a book spoke with withering scorn of a library which did not possess it.

Three days later an enterprising bookseller announced in a sign which swung the entire length of his store, "*The Finality of Christianity* Is On Sale Here." The streetcars then presented the unusual spectacle of men coming from their daily toil with heads bent menacingly over a grave-looking volume. Freeport's leading barber practically abandoned work that he might sit in his window scowling over the learned pages, ever and anon raising his head and looking vengeance out into the street. When he did take a hand at the chairs, he would discourse to the helpless about the superiority of the work he was reading, and, emphasizing his feeling with passionate gestures along the neck of the victim, he would want to know whether we lived in a civilized country or whether we did not?

The newspaper controversy grew a little blurred. Deacon Judson, perhaps feeling he could not make out the most convincing case against a work which he said he had not read, and had gone on record as declaring principle would not permit him to read, here shifted the issue to George Sand. In a Chicago paper he read of a few kind words Professor Mosher had, in a lecture, spoken about that lady. Were the townspeople acquainted with the morals of this George Sand? Deacon Judson inquired. For fear they were not, he cited the facts of her life as given by the library's foremost encyclopedia of biography. He gave names and dates. This to Deacon Judson's mind appeared to prove Professor Mosher guilty and to settle for all time the question of who should select the books the people of Freeport were to read.

The Constitution of the United States also played a lively part. One of the city's rising young attorneys discussed with heat, light, and many quotations whether the Supreme Court of the United States had ever proclaimed Christianity the official religion. Answer—It had not. This brought a volley of replies from the clergy. Then J. Herman Ketchem, the "radical" member of the library board and the town's leading infidel, contributed a eulogy of Tom Paine, apparently under the impression that it could not fail to advance the cause of freedom in the present specific instance. And there was Socialism, which made its bow as an issue because one of the men who held that the people should have the books the people wanted chanced to be a Socialist. This brought the hot retort that Socialism was a fallacy—and that anyhow it was on the wane.

Meanwhile a steady procession of taxpayers moved up the library steps and approached the desk with the inquiry for the latest book by Dr. Mosher. Perhaps never before in the whole history of learning has a critical work been demanded by so widely varied an audience. Plumber, milliner, baker, and banker portentously demanded *The Finality of Christianity.*

The cause of intellectual freedom became rather hopelessly intertwined with the street-cleaning department. But then the cause of intellectual freedom has had many strange companions in its time. Lovers of liberty and seekers after justice seem bound to be joined by those who fight, either for the joy of the fighting, or because they have something against the people who are being fought. Doubtless Brutus and Martin Luther too had adherents who lined up with them because the opposing party harbored men who threw things over the back fence, or who had a dog that had killed a cat—or a cat that ate the canary. We know that human relationships have a way of balling up the purity of intellectual issues. So it was in Freeport, until there were nights when the most assiduous perusal of the *Clarion* could not have made it plain whether it was intellectual freedom or Pat McGuire's record as an alderman that was making all the trouble. There were a few men and women who tried to keep the purity of the flame, but the poor little torch was almost hidden by the bizarre dance that raged around it. It was a beautiful open arena for suppressed grudges and for fighting powers ennuied by long peace.

So great was the pressure brought upon the library board that one timid soul resigned, saying he did not feel he could assume the responsibility of deciding whether or not the library should place upon its shelves a copy of *The Finality of Christianity.* But as this member had been absent from the first meeting the situation was not changed by his modest feeling of unworthiness for great tasks.

However, two nights before the next regular meeting of the board the *Clarion* electrified the town with the tremendous heading, "JOHNSON FLOPS." Mr. Johnson, it appeared, had undergone nothing short of a conversion. He had seen the light. The people must have the books the people wanted. Perhaps it is small-spirited to mention here that Mr. Johnson ran a dry-goods store, and that many of the people were finding what they wanted at a rival emporium. Mr. Johnson announced his conversion and a great bargain sale in one and the same issue. With that it was assumed that victory was at hand, but when the board gathered and the vote was taken whether two thousand people of Freeport should have a book which they wanted, it transpired that the head of Johnson Brothers was not alone in his flopping.

Mrs. Martin McFarland had also flopped—and flopped the other way! In the beginning Mrs. McFarland had stood for enlightenment. But the degree of enlightenment had been too much for her. Appalled, she ran for cover, and the library board stood precisely where it had stood before an exercised town had pressed upon it.

The passion engendered by this deadlock formed itself into what was called The Ethical Society. The personnel of this organization was unusual. Interspersed with men and women who on principle objected to being told they were not to read what Deacon Judson did not approve of their reading was a body of men who saw in The Ethical Society a possible fighting machine for the "petition of consent" which Freeport saloon-keepers would have to circulate the following year. At the first meeting of the society, spinsters who wished to appear intellectual shared benches with men who "wanted to throw it into the mayor."

With stern enthusiasm it was voted to invite Professor Mosher to come to Freeport and address the first open meeting of the society. A somewhat bewildered letter was received saying the professor would come, and there then opened a campaign of publicity such as has perhaps never before been laid at the feet of any savant. In magnitude and quality it was unique.

A slight, stooped man of mild and gentle mien stepped from the five o'clock train on the afternoon of the great Mosher lecture in Freeport. He was one of those men who bear the marks of having walked the quiet ways of the student's life, a man who, when out in the great world, has the manner of being somewhere else. He had devoted his life to a study of comparative religion. He looked it. With a diffident though pleasant look through his spectacles he assured Rabbi Lewisohn that he was indeed Dr. Mosher. He was introduced to Mrs. Wilkes and, apparently to his surprise, was presented to a small but impressive body of citizens who stood solemnly apart and received him in a manner of being willing to fight till the last ditch, which seemed to leave the professor rather at sea.

But being at sea was, for the time, to become Professor Mosher's state. He was borne away in Mrs. Wilkes' automobile to the lady's house, where he was to be entertained at dinner. As they rounded the corner from the station the man from the halls of learning saw flung from a barber shop a huge pennant inscribed, "Mosher and Freedom!"

"Why—why—" he gasped.

They passed through a decorated town. There were tremendous banners bearing the single word, "MOSHER!" There were exhortations to crush the tyrants, there were unflattering words about a benighted administration. "Do You Believe in Liberty? Hear Mosher at the Armory Tonight!" The bookstore had flung wide its sign, "*The Finality of Christianity* Is On Sale Here." From Socialist headquarters waved the red-lettered suggestion, "Why Not Let Socialism Settle the Mosher Question?" Flags flew; a band played.

In the house of President Wilkes of the Freeport Ice Company, his feet upon the very rug Mrs. Wilkes was setting forth to purchase on the day she put the momentous inquiry for a book called *The Finality of Christianity,* Rabbi Lewisohn told the dazed professor something of what he had done to Freeport. The author of sober, critical books which had never permeated far beyond the small group of people who were studying his subject learned now that two thousand seven hundred and thirty-two citizens of that town were demanding that his latest book be installed in the public library. He learned that old friendships were being broken because of him, that on account of *The Finality of Christianity* old political parties were being reshaped on new lines.

Ere he could gather himself together, a reporter from the *Clarion* arrived to interview him. No, he murmured weakly, he had not known of the Freeport "scrap." He—indeed he was quite surprised to hear of it. In fact, he—couldn't understand it. He had not thought of his book as—revolutionary. He admitted, upon demand, that it did take for granted the standpoint of the so-called higher criticism. But had not all that been fought out? the professor inquired anxiously. Not in all circles, the reporter assured him briskly. He was asked to define "finality" which he did in a stricken sort of way. Finality meant authority. No, he did not have in mind the demise of Christianity—indeed, not at all. But was it true he did not believe in the miracles? The professor replied that he believed in faith. The miracles? pressed the reporter. Not literally, replied the professor. At which the reporter took heart to inquire whether Professor Mosher did not perhaps feel it would be a better thing if Christianity were now abolished. "No!" cried the professor in distress. "Not at all!"

Rabbi Lewisohn's amused view of the dilemma slightly rallied the lecturer, but he inquired whether it would not be possible to cancel the engagement for the evening. He thought he might do this on the ground of not having understood the situation, and of the lecture he was prepared to give being unsuitable. He confessed that he had never in his life addressed a large audience. He was accustomed to talking to students and to societies studying his subject. He had several times spoken before ethical culture societies, and he had thought, reading the letter, as he now saw, carelessly, that it was an ethical culture society which was inviting him to Freeport. It had surprised him to be called to a place so far away, but he had been pleased by the indication of interest in his subject. He had expected to speak in someone's house, or perhaps in the Unitarian church—something of the sort. He had never dreamed, he said with a visible shudder, of speaking in a large public hall such as the Armory appeared to be. And of course he had not anticipated the—the feeling which seemed to prevail. He was accustomed to speaking to people who received him quietly. He was prepared to speak on Greek culture. Did the rabbi not agree with him that Greek culture was most unsuited to the occasion?

But the rabbi said that perhaps Greek culture would do Freeport good, and that certainly the preparations of the lecture had been on too magnificent a scale to permit the people to be disappointed. Professor Mosher would have to conquer his personal feeling and give the lecture.

It is perhaps not too much to say that in the whole history of the world such a theme and such a setting never got together before. I leave it to the most sophisticated reader of this chronicle whether it is usual to receive a speaker on Greek culture with a brass band. Is it customary for flags to fly throughout a hall in which men have gathered to hear a critical appreciation of the beauties of an ancient civilization? For that matter, is it customary for two thousand people to get together in any way to hear about something that happened two thousand years before?

Dr. Mosher was introduced by the new candidate for mayor, who, after having been received with vociferous cheers, spoke fearlessly and with passion of liberty. Men had died for it in the past. Men would die for it again! *(Cheers.)* This magnificent audience had assembled to do honor to one who stood for liberty—prolonged cheering from the magnificent audience and uneasy shuffling on the part of the one who stood for liberty. The speaker then hastened to make plain that he, too, was one who stood for liberty. He called attention to his record to back up this assertion. He called attention to the record of a certain other person in order to demonstrate that there were men who did not stand for liberty. *(Hisses.)* He closed with a few eloquent words about the enlightened element of the community being seated before him and told them they were now to be addressed by one in whose hands the banner of freedom would never falter.

The professor then rose falteringly to his feet, looking as if the banner of freedom was something he hadn't bargained with. There were cries of "Mosher! Mosher!" and the great audience had risen and was giving the student of comparative religion the Chautauqua salute. When the frenzy had finally abated, the professor, in timorous voice, began to speak of the beauties of ancient Greece.

The enlightened element of the community listened with passionate respect. The professor unfortunately pitched his voice in the ethical culture society rather than ethical society key so that only a small proportion of the enlightened element could hear what he said. But this did not greatly matter; they listened with a high defiant fervor and aggressively pronounced it an uplifting address.

Professor Mosher, looking a good deal wilted for one in whose hands the banner of freedom would never falter, escaped on the eleven o'clock train, attended to the station by a brass band. Next day the library board met and there were several interesting modifications as a result of the lecture. First, Mrs. Martin McFarland flopped back, assuaged by Greek culture. But J. Herman Ketchem, the most savagely radical person in town, Freeport's incarnation of unbelief, flopped to the anti-Mosher camp! He gave as his reason that the lecture had been far less radical than he had been led to believe it would be. He had been deceived; this Mosher did not stand for free thought at all. J. Herman Ketchem said he could not lend his sympathy to halfway measures and that he took the stand he now did as a protest against pseudoradicalism.

Again a deadlock, and it seemed that the library board had entered upon a long and futile career of floppings annulled by crossfloppings when Miss Amy Parsons, who taught English in the high school, timidly announced that in the interests of peace she would change her vote and favor the purchase of the book. Miss Parsons hoped no one would misunderstand her. Her vote represented, not her personal conviction, but her desire to live once more in a happy and harmonious town. She ventured to say that she did not believe any harm the book could do would exceed the harm wrought by this dissension. But she did earnestly hope that she would not be misunderstood.

With that the petition of three thousand Freeport residents to place upon the library shelves a work called *The Finality of Christianity* was granted over the head of Deacon Judson and that gentleman straightway retired to private life. The following month the mayor also retired to private life—though not voluntarily. The new mayor lost not a week in appointing Rabbi Lewisohn to the library board. The street-cleaning department was greatly improved. The circulation of the *Clarion* had increased materially. Mrs. William Wilkes was elected president of the Woman's Club and Pat McGuire was retired from office. There appeared upon the shelves of the Public Library a sober-looking volume entitled *The Finality of Christianity.* The three thousand citizens who had been ready to fight and die for the book managed to restrain their impatience and, doubtless on the theory that they could not all read it at once, politely waited their turn—so politely that there were many days when the book rested peacefully upon the shelves.

Professor Mosher received a singularly respectful letter from his publishers inquiring when his next book would be ready. They said that the sale on this one had encouraged them to do more with his work in the future. The mild little man continued to teach his classes in the Study of Comparative Religion, but something new was remarked in him. They said he was more "on to himself." And doubtless a man is bound to be a little more on to himself after a brass band has played for him and two thousand people have risen to their feet to hail him as Liberator.

And then, two years after Freeport had fought for, and failed to read, *The Finality of Christianity,* it happened that certain churches combined and had an expert in Bible Schools come there to instruct the teachers—among them Deacon Judson. J. Herman Ketchem was standing at the library desk one day when the deacon came in to return some books. The title of one of them caught the astonished eye of Mr. Ketchem. It was *The Finality of Christianity.*

"You haven't been *reading* that?" he demanded incredulously.

"Why shouldn't I?" inquired the deacon belligerently.

"I thought you couldn't read it without violating your conscience!"

"It is included in the recommended reading of our Bible School," replied Deacon Judson with dignity.

"Well," said Mr. Ketchem, "I hope you enjoyed it more than I did."

"I naturally would," replied the deacon.

Ann Arbor Paperbacks

Waddell, *The Desert Fathers*
Erasmus, *The Praise of Folly*
Donne, *Devotions*
Malthus, *Population: The First Essay*
Berdyaev, *The Origin of Russian Communism*
Einhard, *The Life of Charlemagne*
Edwards, *The Nature of True Virtue*
Gilson, *Héloïse and Abélard*
Aristotle, *Metaphysics*
Kant, *Education*
Boulding, *The Image*
Duckett, *The Gateway to the Middle Ages* (3 vols.): *Italy; France and Britain; Monasticism*
Bowditch and Ramsland, *Voices of the Industrial Revolution*
Luxemburg, *The Russian Revolution* and *Leninism or Marxism?*
Rexroth, *Poems from the Greek Anthology*
Zoshchenko, *Scenes from the Bathhouse*
Thrupp, *The Merchant Class of Medieval London*
Procopius, *Secret History*
Adcock, *Roman Political Ideas and Practice*
Swanson, *The Birth of the Gods*
Xenophon, *The March Up Country*
Trotsky, *The New Course*
Buchanan and Tullock, *The Calculus of Consent*
Hobson, *Imperialism*
Pobedonostsev, *Reflections of a Russian Statesman*
Kinietz, *The Indians of the Western Great Lakes 1615–1760*
Bromage, *Writing for Business*
Lurie, *Mountain Wolf Woman, Sister of Crashing Thunder*
Leonard, *Baroque Times in Old Mexico*
Meier, *Negro Thought in America, 1880–1915*
Burke, *The Philosophy of Edmund Burke*
Michelet, *Joan of Arc*
Conze, *Buddhist Thought in India*
Arberry, *Aspects of Islamic Civilization*
Chesnutt, *The Wife of His Youth and Other Stories*
Gross, *Sound and Form in Modern Poetry*
Zola, *The Masterpiece*
Chesnutt, *The Marrow of Tradition*
Aristophanes, *Four Comedies*
Aristophanes, *Three Comedies*
Chesnutt, *The Conjure Woman*
Duckett, *Carolingian Portraits*
Rapoport and Chammah, *Prisoner's Dilemma*
Aristotle, *Poetics*
Peattie, *The View from the Barrio*
Duckett, *Death and Life in the Tenth Century*
Langford, *Galileo, Science and the Church*
McNaughton, *The Taoist Vision*
Anderson, *Matthew Arnold and the Classical Tradition*
Milio, *9226 Kercheval*
Weisheipl, *The Development of Physical Theory in the Middle Ages*
Breton, *Manifestoes of Surrealism*
Gershman, *The Surrealist Revolution in France*
Burt, *Mammals of the Great Lakes Region*
Scholz, *Carolingian Chronicles*
Wik, *Henry Ford and Grass-roots America*
Sahlins and Service, *Evolution and Culture*
Wickham, *Early Medieval Italy*
Waddell, *The Wandering Scholars*
Rosenberg, *Bolshevik Visions* (2 parts in 2 vols.)
Mannoni, *Prospero and Caliban*
Aron, *Democracy and Totalitarianism*
Shy, *A People Numerous and Armed*
Taylor, *Roman Voting Assemblies*
Hesiod, *The Works and Days; Theogony; The Shield of Herakles*
Raverat, *Period Piece*
Lamming, *In the Castle of My Skin*
Fisher, *The Conjure-Man Dies*
Strayer, *The Albigensian Crusades*
Lamming, *The Pleasures of Exile*
Lamming, *Natives of My Person*
Glaspell, Lifted Masks *and Other Works*
Grand, *The Heavenly Twins*
Cornford, *The Origin of Attic Comedy*
Allen, *Wolves of Minong*
Brathwaite, *Roots*
Fisher, *The Walls of Jericho*
Lamming, *The Emigrants*
Loudon, *The Mummy!*
Kemble and Butler Leigh, *Principles and Privilege*
Thomas, *Out of Time*
Flanagan, *You Alone Are Dancing*
Kotre and Hall, *Seasons of Life*
Shen, *Almost a Revolution*
Meckel, *Save the Babies*
Laver and Schofield, *Multiparty Government*
Rutt, *The Bamboo Grove*
Endelman, *The Jews of Georgian England, 1714–1830*
Lamming, *Season of Adventure*
Radin, *Crashing Thunder*
Mirel, *The Rise and Fall of an Urban School System*
Brainard, *When the Rainbow Goddess Wept*
Brook, *Documents on the Rape of Nanking*
Mendel, *Vision and Violence*
Hymes, *Reinventing Anthropology*
Mulroy, *Early Greek Lyric Poetry*